Growing Herbs

A Beginners Guide to Growing, Using, Harvesting and Storing Herbs

Jason Johns

Visit me at www.OwningAnAllotment.com for gardening tips and advice or follow me at www.YouTube.com/OwningAnAllotment for my video diary and tips. Join me on Facebook at www.Facebook.com/OwningAnAllotment.

Follow me on Instagram and Twitter as @allotmentowner for regular updates, tips and to ask your gardening questions.

If you have enjoyed this book, please leave a review on Amazon. I read each review personally and the feedback helps me to continually improve my books.

The information in this book is not a substitute for medical advice. Do not use any herbs in this book for medical purposes without consulting a medical professional. If you are pregnant or nursing, or taking any prescription medication, consult a medical professional before taking any herbs medicinally.

As someone who has bought this book on Amazon you are entitled to a free download of the Kindle version. This will enable you to get the full color book in electronic format. Unfortunately I have to publish these books in black and white in order to make them affordable due to the high cost of color printing. Please download this from Amazon; you can read it on a Kindle or any tablet, cell phone or computer with the free Kindle Reader installed from your app store.

TABLE OF CONTENTS

WHY GROW YOUR OWN HERBS?

One of my favorite type of plants to grow are herbs. Herbs are very versatile plants that can add exquisite flavor to your cooking, can be used in a multitude of beauty products, but also have healing properties to help your wellbeing. They are incredibly useful, but easy to grow, with many able to grow all year round in many areas.

Whether you create a herb garden, have a few herbs on your windowsill or have some pots by your kitchen door, you can grow herbs at home no matter where you live. There are so many different types of herb, and all of them have different properties, tastes and textures. I love cooking with herbs and a handful thrown strategically into a dish can give it that extra flavor to make it special. I also use herbs to make teas which help strengthen the immune system, fight off colds and generally improve my health.

This book will help you understand the many different types of herbs that you can grow, how to grow them in your area and how to use them for cooking, health and beauty. You will learn how to grow herbs both indoors and outside so that no matter what space you have available to you or where you live, you can enjoy the benefits of fresh herbs.

The great thing about most herbs is that they are generally low maintenance plants once you have them in the right type of soil. Herbs are not only useful plants, but many are very attractive. The large, purple flowers of chives are gorgeous and loved by bees; the four or five feet tall cilantro (coriander) plant stands out in a crowd, and the purple flowers of marjoram are covered with butterflies, bees and other pollinating insects.

Herbs have been used for thousands of years, since humans started cooking food and have been cultivated for almost as long. Before the advent of modern medicine, herbs were the sole way of treating illness or disease with some prized and valued for their taste and healing properties. Many of the tablets and medicines we have today are derived from this traditional, herbal knowledge and pharmaceutical companies are spending vast amounts of moneys exploring how the plant kingdom can provide new and innovative medicines.

Growing herbs at home is very easy to do, as you are about to find out. Most herbs can be grown in containers, and many will happily grow indoors. The wonderful thing about a herb garden is you can make it as simple or as complex as you want. They can be a design feature of your garden or purely utilitarian. A great way to make a pretty herb garden is to lay a wagon wheel on the soil and grow herbs in each of the spokes.

Although herbs can provide some great medicinal and health benefits, you should always check with your medical practitioner before you start taking them as sometimes they can work against modern medicines. If you are taking birth control tablets or anti-depressants, you should avoid St. John's Wort, a common mood lifting drug, as it stops both medicines from working. It you take any prescription medication or have any long term health issues, it is vital you consult your doctor before prescribing yourself herbs.

Dried herbs can be used as potpourri for a natural air freshener. Dried lavender flowers can be sown into cotton bags and placed in drawers to freshen clothing. Basil is vital for any Italian dish and an egg mayo sandwich is not the same without some chives! Mint is a must for boiled new potatoes, and parsley and cilantro are used as a garnish on virtually any meal!

Starting my first herb garden with bay, chives, marjoram and more

The words spices and herbs are used interchangeably, but in fact refer to different parts of a plant. Herbs always come from the leafy part of a plant whereas a spice is any other part of the plant that is dried and used for cooking. Spices can come from seeds such as cumin, coriander, mustard and so on or bark (cinnamon) or fruit such as vanilla or peppercorns, flower buds (cloves) or even roots such as horseradish.

In this book you will learn about both spices and herbs, though we refer to the process as growing herbs, you are actually going to be growing spices too. All of these plants have numerous health and culinary benefits and can be used for anything from flavoring a meal to improving your skin.

Herbs are incredibly useful at home and are something you can easily grow yourself. You will learn everything you need to know about growing herbs as you read this book and can enjoy the many benefits of herbal medicine and the taste of herbs in your cooking!

How to Grow Herbs at Home

Anyone can grow herbs at home and you will be surprised just how many you can grow. Whether you have a garden, a balcony or can only use your kitchen windowsill, you will be able to grow at least a few herbs. How much you can grow will depend on the space available to you, but many of the popular culinary herbs can be grown indoors in small containers. Supermarkets now sell some of the more common herbs such as parsley, basil, and cilantro in pots that you can grow at home. These are a very good way to quickly start growing herbs and do not take up a lot of room.

This chapter will explain everything you need to know about how to grow herbs, no matter how you are going to grow them. It's a complete guide to herb gardening before you find out more about the various herbs and their specific needs and uses.

Annual, Biennial and Perennial Explained

Plants fall into one of three categories, depending on how long they live, when they flower and when they seed. These are:

1. Annual
2. Biennial
3. Perennial

Annual plants will live for a year, meaning they complete an entire growing cycle, i.e. flower and seed, in a single year. Many hot climate plants such as basil and chilies are grown as annuals in temperate zones because they cannot survive the cold winters.

Commonly grown annual herbs include dill, cilantro and summer savory. Parsley, although a biennial, is usually grown as an annual as the flavor decreases in the second year. You can cut and use annual herbs throughout the growing season, but before they die off for winter, harvest the entire plant. Some annual plants such as dill, will self-seed if you let it flower.

Biennial plants, such as parsley, stevia and sage, live for two years. They will usually grow lots of leaves in the first year and then flower and seed in the second before dying off.

Perennial plants such as fennel, feverfew, ginger and chives, live year after year, flowering and seeding each year. Many perennial herbs will die back to ground level and remain dormant over winter, until spring comes and they grow back. Winter hardiness of perennial herbs does vary, so you need to check whether the herbs you want to grow will survive the winter where you live. If they will not, then either grow them in containers and move them to a protected location in winter, or grow them as annual plants and re-sow every spring.

Understanding which category each herb falls in helps you to plan your herb garden and know which plants you have to buy or grow again every year. When you read the herb directory, each section will tell you which of these categories each herb falls into. Some may be in more than one, as they are grown as annuals in colder areas as well as their proper category when grown in their native environment.

Growing Herbs Indoors

Many herbs such as parsley, cilantro, oregano, rosemary, basil, chives and more can be grown indoors. When growing indoors, you are not constrained by the weather, which means you can have fresh herbs all year round. You can grow your herbs from seed or buy live plants from the supermarket, which is much quicker, though you are limited to the varieties they sell. Because the plants are in a relatively small pot, they will not grow to full size, though many of these herbs will be used up before they grow too big.

When growing indoors in containers, make sure there is a saucer or something under each pot to catch run-off water. When you water the herbs, some of it will run through the pot and come out of the bottom. You do not want this to leak all over your kitchen, so having something underneath the pots catches the excess water and stops it making a mess. A little while after watering your plants, empty the saucer of water so the pots are not standing in water, which many herbs do not like.

Make sure you position your herbs somewhere that they like. A good sunny windowsill is usually good for most herbs, though some will be happier in a slightly shady position. In the colder months, watch out for draughts from the window which can cool the herbs so they struggle to grow. Move them a little way from the window in winter so their leaves do not touch the glass as the temperature differential on the glass can damage the plant. Most herbs grow slower in winter and require less water, so be more careful harvesting and watering them.

Kitchen grown herbs are very easy to harvest, you can pull leaves off by hand or use scissors to snip some off whenever you need to use it. A quick wash and the herbs are ready to use! Fresh herbs have a much stronger flavor than those that have been dried and stored. Generally, the more you harvest a herb plant, the more it will grow, but you will need to give it time to grow back as it is not instant. If you regularly use a specific herb, it may be worth having multiple plants so you have a plentiful supply.

In the winter months, your herbs may struggle from a lack of light, particularly if they are located on a north facing windowsill that does not get a lot of light. Plants that are struggling with too little light will often wilt, the leaves turn brown and start to fall off. Some plants will adjust to this and others will end up dying from lack of light. Mediterranean herbs such as basil love a lot of light and will struggle if it does not get enough. In this case, either find a brighter location for your herbs or invest in a cheap grow light solution such as LED lights or fluorescent lighting which will give the plants the right spectrum of light they need to thrive.

Plants bought from supermarkets are generally happy in low light levels as they are used to it, having known no different. They will often last for several weeks, though if planted outdoors will mature into full size plants.

Some herbs are not so keen on being grown indoors. Rosemary and dill are not good to grow indoors due to the low light levels and lack of room to grow in a pot. You can try to acclimatize rosemary to being indoors if you have grown it yourself by gradually moving it to a shadier and shadier location until you see new growth still appearing while it is in the shade. Then you know it has adjusted to being out of bright light and will be safe to bring indoors.

Your indoor plants are completely dependent on you for food and water, but be careful not to overwater your plants as that is just as bad for them as under watering them. Follow the instructions for each herb with respect to watering and make sure that they get enough, but not too much, water.

Herbs will need fertilizing too as the nutrients in the soil will only be sufficient to support them for a couple of weeks at most. While they are actively growing, i.e. in spring and summer, feed them once a week with a liquid tomato feed or other high nitrogen liquid feed. Follow the instructions on the feed and use it once a week when you water them. Nitrogen encourages plants to grow plenty of leaves, which is what you want on your herb plants. There is no need to use pelleted or solid fertilizers, as your plants will grow fine with this weekly liquid feed.

Indoor herbs are less susceptible to diseases and pests, but can occasionally succumb. Pests can make their way in through an open window and take up residence on your herb plants. The most common pest you will find will be aphids and whiteflies, which are just annoying when in your kitchen. Either pick the bugs off by hand, or take your herbs outside and treat them. In smaller infestations, you can use a water spray to spray off the bugs, but in more serious infestations you may find an organic spray the only solution. If you do spray a plant, leave it outside for an hour or two after spraying so it can dry and then bring it back inside. Depending on the pest and the level of infestation, multiple treatments may be required. Checking your plants regularly will help catch any pests before they can get established and when they are much easier to remove. Be careful when using store brought pest or disease treatments and ensure that anything you use is food safe. The residue from these chemical treatments will remain on your herbs for a while, so do not use the herbs for a few days after treatment.

Most of the herbs that are commonly used for cooking can be grown indoors on your windowsill or kitchen counters. Some of these can even be grown hydroponically, which we will talk about in more depth shortly. This is a great way for you to have quick access to the herbs you need, when you need it. Although it is great to have a lovely herb garden outdoors, you do not want to have to run outside in the rain, high winds or snow to pick some herbs for the meal you are preparing. Many people will have a selection of commonly used herbs indoors and even more outdoors. It works well if you have multiple pots of each herb so you can move herbs you have harvested outdoors to recover while bringing fresh herbs indoors to use.

If you are growing from seed, try planting a fresh pot of herbs every two or three weeks throughout the growing season. This gives you an almost constant supply of fresh herbs through the year and then, if the plant is annual, you can harvest the whole plant before winter to dry and store the herbs.

Growing indoors is a great way for you to have fresh herbs at home that are easy to access. Whether you just grow herbs for cooking or herbs for tea and beauty products is entirely up to you, but being able to grab a handful of fresh herbs when you need them is wonderful. Many of the popular herbs grow very well indoors in small pots that sit nicely on your kitchen window sill. What herbs do you cook with and which can you grow on your window sill?

Growing Herbs Outdoors

Growing herbs outdoors allows you to grow on a much larger scale, with many more plants, all of which can reach their full size when grown in the ground. Your eight-inch cilantro plant on your windowsill may give you just enough herb for your cooking, but wait until you see a five-foot-tall plant with all the cilantro you could ever want and more!

Outdoor growing is more challenging as there are potentially more problems from pests, diseases, and the environment such as late frosts, early snow, high wind and heavy rainfall or not enough rain. However, it is very rewarding whether you grow in the ground or in containers. Your herb garden can be very practical, can be an eye catching feature of your garden or it could be squeezed in around existing flowers or vegetables.

When growing outdoors, understanding whether your herbs are annual or perennial will help you plan your herb garden. Annual and biennial herbs need to be sown at intervals during the year so that you have a continual supply of fresh herbs. Perennial herbs such as mint, thyme and rosemary, once established, can grow to quite a large size and will usually provide enough herbs for the year. Make sure that perennial herbs are placed somewhere that is not going to require them to be moved, so they can establish themselves and grow to their full size.

Perennial herbs also require pruning every year. Rosemary, sage and lavender will all grow to a substantial size and need pruning back every year to prevent them becoming leggy and unproductive. Pruning also helps to maintain the shape of the plant and, of course, the parts pruned off can be used as herbs!

Each herb will have its own preferred growing conditions and it is up to you to determine the best place in your garden for each plant. If you have a heavy clay soil, then you will need to dig in organic matter to improve the drainage as most herbs prefer a well-drained soil. If your garden is shaded by trees, you may need to get the pruning saw out to let in some light so your herbs can thrive. The majority of herbs will grow well in a sunny, sheltered location with well-drained soil. There are a few that prefer other conditions, but they can easily be grown in containers so you can give them the ideal growing conditions. The growing conditions for each herb is detailed in the herb directory later on.

Most herbs prefer neutral or alkaline soil, though some will tolerate a slightly acidic soil, though not grow as strong as those in less acidic soil. If your herbs are struggling in the ground, check the quality of your soil to make sure it drains well enough and test its pH level too. If it is too acidic, a lot of herbs will struggle, so add lime to it (follow the instructions on the packet) to make it more alkaline.

Herbs such as lemon balm, mint, chives, chervil and parsley grow very well in shady spots with a damper soil. These are ideal to grow in locations where other herbs will not grow. Remember to plant your mint or lemon balm in containers rather than the ground as they both spread like wildfire and can take over a patch of ground very quickly. In fact, a surprising number of these herbs are actually classified as invasive plants with some banned in certain States because of how quickly they can spread!

If you are concerned about your soil quality or do not want to mess around amending the soil, then grow your herbs in raised beds. Herbs grow very well in raised beds and it allows you to create the ideal growing environment for the herbs. Read my book, Raised Bed Gardening, available on Amazon as a paperback and e-book, for more information on building and maintaining raised beds.

You may have space for a dedicated herb garden, or you may end up planting herbs in borders with flowers, in between vegetables and wherever you can in your garden. This can work very well, but in an established garden you may struggle for space and need a dedicated area or some containers. Many herbs will produce great flowers such as chives or Echinacea, which would not be out of place in a flower bed.

Seeds can be sown directly into the ground where you want the plant to grow, or they can be started off in pots and then transplanted out when they are larger. The downside of sowing directly is that you may not be able to tell the difference between weeds and the seedlings of your herb plants. When plants are that young, it is very hard to tell them apart and far too easy to pull up seedlings thinking they are weeds. Most herbs should not be planted outside until the risk of frost has passed otherwise they will be damaged by cold weather. Should there be a surprise frost, then use some horticultural fleece to cover your seedlings to keep them warm and protect them.

You can be very inventive with fitting herbs into your garden and as imaginative as you want. Remember to make sure it is easy to get to the herbs you use regularly, but some that are in the ground for the whole growing season could be placed at the back of beds where they slightly harder to reach.

A combination of indoor and outdoor herbs works very well for most people and you can grow a larger quantity of herbs outdoors. All of the leaves, particularly on annual herbs and those that die back, can be harvested before the first frost and stored for winter use. Herbs are a great addition to any garden and many will attract beneficial insects into your garden too.

You will need to be aware of the first and last frost dates in your area as many of these plants are frost tender or need the soil to have warmed before planting seeds. Check your frost dates at a website such as http://www.almanac.com/gardening/frostdates which will give you the average first and last frost dates where you live. Remember that these are just guidelines and there can still be late or early frosts. Keep some horticultural fleece at hand to cover your plants if they need it or be prepared to move them indoors if they are in containers. Keep an eye on the weather and on the forecast and take action to protect your tender plants should you feel there is the risk of frost.

Growing Herbs in Containers

Herbs will grow very well in containers outdoors and mean you can grow them in an each to reach location, such as by the kitchen door, or they can be brought indoors or put in a greenhouse to protect them during cold or inclement weather. Containers could stand on the floor, or there could be hanging baskets or planters attached to walls or fences, to keep herbs away from the prying hands of children and the curious household pets.

Although the initial cost is much higher than growing in the soil, long term maintenance tends to be lower as you are not battling weeds growing through the soil. Containers are a great way to make a herb garden whether you have limited space, a balcony, or even a full garden. Some of us are banned by our significant others from growing herbs in the flower beds and must use strategically placed containers!

It is possible to grow different types of herb in a single container, though you need to make sure that they have similar soil and sun needs. There is no point growing a herb that likes a moist soil with one that likes a dry soil as one or the other will suffer. It is best to use annual herbs when putting multiple plants in a single container as perennial herbs will grow too big and crowd out the smaller herbs. However, if you have rosemary or lavender in a container, you can always grow a trailing herb such as creeping thyme which will hang over the edge of the container and not compete for space with the larger plant.

Seeds can be planted directly into containers or you can plant seedlings or store bought plants, depending on the size of the container. A good way of extending your growing season is to start your herb seeds off indoors and then transplant them outdoors to containers when they have grown to a reasonable size and the risk of frost has passed.

There are many different types of container on the market made from anything from stone to plastic to resin or metal. What you buy will depend on your budget, the size container you want and the style container you like in your garden. Porous materials such as clay dry out much faster than those made of plastic or resin due to evaporation, which will influence the amount of watering you need to do.

All containers need drainage holes so that excess water can seep out of the container. If there are not sufficient drainage holes, then you need to create some. Most herbs will die back if their containers get waterlogged. Self-watering containers are a good idea if you are growing in a greenhouse, but when used outside, they fill up with rain water and drown your plants.

The key to making your herbs happy in containers is to use a good quality soil mix. Adjust the soil mix based on what the herb you are growing requires, but generally a mixture of a third each of vermiculite or pearlite, good quality compost and peat moss provides an excellent growing medium. Fill the container with soil and then push it down gently without compacting it as it is easier for the herb to grow in looser soil. Do not use soil from your garden as this will contain pests, weed seeds and potentially diseases too.

Containers are completely reliant on you for water and food. Once the herbs are established, their leaves will act as an umbrella and direct rain water away from the container, so you still need to water them when it rains. Water when required directly onto the soil rather than onto the leaves to prevent run-off and mold forming if the leaves get too damp.

Your herbs will need fertilizing regularly too, typically starting two weeks after planting mature plants and four weeks after planting seedlings or after seeds have germinated. After this time, the plants will have depleted the nutrients in the soil and they will need replenishing. Use a liquid feed such as a tomato feed or a general purpose vegetable feed. This will have plenty of nitrogen in it that your plants need to grow healthy leaves. Seaweed based feeds are ideal for containers because they are packed with micro-nutrients and plants love these fertilizers. Avoid any fertilizers that are higher in potassium (K) or phosphorus (P) as these will encourage the herbs to form flowers at which point the taste of the leaves can often diminish. Feed once a week during the growing season and no more than once a month during the dormant season.

To encourage leafy growth, cut or pinch off any flower heads that form. This forces the plant to direct its energy on producing more growth so it can produce more flowers. Many herbs produce attractive flowers which will look great as well as attract beneficial insects to your garden.

Feel free to put some flowers in the containers with your herbs for some extra color and interest. Nasturtiums, marigolds and pansies all look great in containers plus have edible parts. These can brighten up a container of otherwise drab green herbs.

Containers are a great way for you to start a herb garden. In a larger container you can easily grow several different types of herb, giving you a nice variety to use in your home. You can plant containers in amogst growing herbs in the garden or you can plant multiple containers and place them around your garden so the herbs get their ideal growing conditions.

Vertical Herb Gardens

A great way to make the best use of space for growing herbs is to grow them vertically, which means fixing containers on to a wall or fence and planting them up with herbs. This is a fascinating technique for growing a lot of plants in a small area of space.

For example, you have a sunny fence opposite your kitchen door, but no soil in which to grow herbs. You attach some containers to the wall, fill them with soil and then grow herbs in a great location that is handy for when you are cooking!

Vertical gardening works well for shorter, more compact herbs. Herbs that grow extremely tall or have large root systems are not well suited for vertical gardening because they are either susceptible to wind damage or need large containers which cannot be safely fixed to a wall or fence. You can plant each container with a single herb or multiple herbs, depending on your specific requirements.

Special wall mounted planters or window boxes can be used or you can buy special vertical garden planters, which are much more expensive. Alternatively, you can easily make your own planters out of old soda bottles! Lay the bottle on its side and cut a slot out of the upright side big enough to get a plant in. You can make one long slot or two smaller slots. Screw the cap onto the bottle firmly, then punch a small hole through the cap and the bottom of the bottle. Insert a piece of wire through this which will be used to hang the planter. Then fill it with soil, plant your herbs and put it up on your wall. This is a good opportunity to be creative as there are many different ways to re-use plastic containers as vertical garden planters.

Treat these planters as you would a normal container with respect to feeding and watering. Be aware that your plants may dry out quicker if they are exposed to wind or the sun and so need watering more. Remember that you have to reach the herbs easily if you are going to use them, so try not to position them too high where you will struggle to get to them as it will discourage you from using them.

Growing your herbs vertically is a good idea for anyone that has children or pets that use their garden. Cats are notorious for sitting on or chewing plants and leaving smelly little presents in them, while some dogs love to dig up your freshly planted herbs. Rabbits will enjoy eating most greenery and children can be curious and end up pulling up or walking on your herbs. Growing them in containers fixed to a wall keeps them away from these pests and allows you to enjoy the benefit of a herb garden.

This is a very clever way of growing herbs and can help you make the most of the limited space available to you. It's quite an in-depth subject and you can learn more in my book on Vertical Garden, available from Amazon. I would recommend doing this if it is difficult for you to grow herbs on the ground.

Hydroponic Herb Gardens

Hydroponics is a very exciting technology that involves growing plants without soil. Plants are grown in either a nutrient solution, a growing medium such as coconut coir or clay pebbles, or with their roots in the air being misted with nutrient solution. It is a very impressive technology that fascinates children and adults alike that is being investigated by NASA for use in long distance space travel. When I first started growing hydroponically, my children were fascinated by the idea and kept wanting to check there was no soil. They would tell everyone about it because they thought it was such a clever idea.

It can be very expensive to set up a hydroponic garden and it generally is not worth doing it for herbs because it is much cheaper in most cases to just buy the herbs.

However, in recent years, table top hydroponic systems have become available which are portable and use LED lighting to make them very affordable. Even Ikea now sell their own hydroponic kit which is perfect for growing herbs in your kitchen.

Most herbs can be grown hydroponically, though those that grow from bulbs or roots like ginger would struggle in most hydroponic systems. Unfortunately, the fact that the bulb or root is constantly getting damp causes it to rot before it can grow. Tall herbs are not suited for hydroponic growing environments, nor are herbs that have large or deep root systems. Small herbs such as basil, parsley, oregano and so on are ideally suited for this environment. One big advantage of hydroponically grown herbs is that they are ready to harvest several weeks before those grown in the soil as the environment speeds up the growth of the plant. They also generally have more taste because they have been grown in a soil free environment.

This subject, initially, may appear quite complex, but is surprisingly easy when you get into it. If you use a table top system, then you are not stuck measuring pH and cF levels and adjusting nutrient solutions. The Ikea system is very simple, you fill it with water and then add some nutrient solution, topping it up regularly as the water is used by your herbs.

There is more cost involved with a hydroponic solution than growing in pots or the ground, though the table top systems are much cheaper now and more practical than a traditional growing environment which will cost you several hundred dollars for a small one. If you are living in a cold environment where it is difficult to grow outside, love your herbs or have no outdoor space, this is the perfect way for you to grow herbs indoors that can be very conveniently placed in your kitchen.

Due to my kitchen windowsill receiving little sunlight in the winter, I use my table top hydroponic solution to grow herbs during these darker months and then in summer grow in containers outside as well as on the windowsill.

It is certainly worth looking into a small hydroponic system at home for growing herbs if you use a lot of them. Many top chefs swear that the taste of hydroponically grown herbs is superior to those grown in soil, but my palate is not developed enough to know the difference. You can learn all about hydroponic gardening in my book, Hydroponic Gardening for Beginners, available on Amazon.

Growing Herbs in a Greenhouse

You can grow herbs in a greenhouse, but most gardeners consider greenhouse space to be a premium so few waste it on herbs, unless they are exotic or difficult to grow in your area. A greenhouse is very useful for starting off herb seeds and for storing containers of herbs during winter to protect them from frost. When the growing seasons starts, most people evict the herbs from their greenhouse to make room for tomatoes, chilies, cucumbers and peppers.

However, it can be beneficial growing some herbs in a greenhouse because basil does very well when grown under glass. If you grow tomato plants, then planting three or four basil plants in the soil around each tomato plant helps to protect them from disease and improves the flavor of the tomatoes themselves. Of course, with the addition of some mozzarella cheese, you can enjoy tomato, mozzarella and basil! Basil is very commonly served with tomatoes, so growing them together makes a lot of sense plus they are great companion plants for each other!

A greenhouse is great to extend the growing season and to shelter plants in winter so you can continue to enjoy fresh herbs. Tarragon, mint and chives naturally die back over winter, meaning no fresh herbs, but you can force them to keep growing by keeping them in a greenhouse where it is slightly warmer. Herbs such as parsley, cilantro and chervil can be planted in early fall in your greenhouse and they will grow over winter. Your summer herb seeds can be started off much earlier in the year in a greenhouse and then planted out as soon as the ground is ready, giving you fresh herbs much earlier than if you waited to plant them outside.

Half-hardy herbs such as lemon verbena, aniseed and cumin can all be stored in your greenhouse over winter. When the foliage has died back, wrap the pot in bubble wrap and store it in your greenhouse. In spring, the herbs will come back to life again and start growing. Just harden them off for a few days before leaving them outside full time.

As a greenhouse is usually much warmer than outside, it is an ideal place to try growing more exotic herbs that would otherwise not grow in your garden. What about trying to grow ginger or cinnamon in your greenhouse?

Greenhouse grown plants tend to dry out much faster than those that are grown outside due to the heat levels under glass. They will need watering more often and basil in particular has a habit of wilting quickly if it does not receive enough water. You can install an irrigation system, or make your own out of soda bottles. Fill the bottle with water, put the cap on and pierce some holes in the cap. The number and size of the holes will determine how quickly or slowly the water drips out of the bottle onto your plant. Then turn the full bottle upside down and push the cap end into the soil by the roots of the plant being careful not to cause any damage. The water will then drip out of the bottle into the plant, watering it for you throughout the day.

A greenhouse is an excellent resource for any gardener and if you have not got the space for a full size greenhouse, look at a smaller, plastic walk-in greenhouse or even just a cold frame where you can start off herbs earlier and protect tender plants from the cold of winter. There is a lot more you can do in a greenhouse as you can find out in my book, Greenhouse Gardening, available on Amazon.

Looking After Your Herb Garden

Once they have established themselves, most herbs are not particularly demanding of attention. Apart from watering and feeding, they will mostly look after themselves, though they do benefit from you checking them for pests and diseases regularly.

Check the ground around your herbs for weeds and remove any that you do find. It is easy to remove them when they are little rather than leaving them to grow to a size where removing them causes damage to or disturbs the herb root system. Herbs grown in containers will have fewer weeds than those grown in the soil.

Annual and biennial herbs have no need to be pruned as you will be removing fresh growth regularly to use. Perennial herbs need pruning every year. Lavender needs the flowers and part of the new growth cutting back and rosemary needs trimming and shaping. Both of these will grow leggy and become unproductive if left to grow unchecked. Upright varieties of thyme benefit from a prune in late summer, though do remember that it will not shoot from old wood so should not be cut back too far. Sage likes to be pruned as it starts to flower to keep the leaves healthy and flavorsome.

Do not worry if you accidentally cut off some healthy growth. This can be planted in pots and used to create new plants.

Watering and feeding your plants is very important, particularly if they are grown in containers. Make sure you do this as we have discussed already in this book to keep them healthy. In the cooler months, the plants require watering a lot more infrequently and you should check how wet the soil is before providing watering again. Many plants get waterlogged in the winter or in heavy summer rains and end up dying. Some herbs such as dill, fennel and cilantro will bolt and flower if they get too dry, so pay special attention to these herbs and give them the water they need.

Herbs are relatively low maintenance plants to grow and are ideal for anyone who is busy or does not have much time to tend a garden. They do not require a great deal of time and most will thrive with nothing more than the occasional water and feed!

Starting Herbs from Seeds

One way to start your herb plants is from seeds. The advantage of growing from seeds that it is incredibly cheap, you can get hundreds of seeds for less than the cost of a single plant from the supermarket. The downside of growing from seeds is that it takes much longer for you to get a harvest from your plants. I like to grow some herbs from seed and buy others as ready grown plants simply so I do not have to wait weeks for my plants to mature so I can pick some leaves.

The other advantage of growing from seeds is that you have access to many more varieties of herb than you can find in the stores. You might be forgiven for thinking that basil is basil, but you can get classic basil which we are all familiar with and also basil Aristotle, purple ruffled basil, purple annual basil, Greek basil, bush basil, and more. There are lots of varieties of herbs that you will never see in a shop that either look fantastic or taste great!

Imagine planting a large container with several different types of basil to give an eye-catching display of color.

Starting herbs from seeds is quite easy to do and you do not need any special skills. You will need seed trays or pots to start your seeds in and a good quality potting compost, ideally mixed with vermiculite for drainage and moisture retention.

Push the soil down lightly so it is firm but not compact, then rough up the top layer of soil. Scatter the herb seeds over the soil and then cover them with a thin layer of compost or vermiculite. Water them so they are damp and put them somewhere warm to germinate. Seeds do not need light in order to germinate because they are under the soil in the dark anyway, but they need somewhere warm. Once the seeds have germinated, then they must be moved somewhere light to prevent the seeds from becoming weak and leggy.

A heated propagator is a great way to start seeds off if you have one, otherwise seed trays with plastic lids to keep the heat in are fantastic. These work very well and provide the heat and moisture a seed needs to germinate. Once the seeds have reached a size where you can transplant them, you can easily remove the lid.

Growing herbs from seed is not very difficult, just make sure you check the back of the packet to see if there are any specific instructions on germination temperature. Some seeds require temperatures above a certain level in order to germinate and some will not germinate if the temperature becomes too high. As a general rule of thumb, the warmer the original place the seeds come from, the warmer the seeds need to be in order to germinate.

Seeds vs Ready Grown Plants

Some purist gardeners will tell you that you should always grow from seed as it is the natural way of doing things. While that comment is technically correct, you have to take into account our modern day lives. We are all busy and may not have time to start seeds off. We may start seeds off and they fail to germinate or the germination rate was very low. An accident may befall our seedlings before we have chance to plant them out.

In these cases, often it is too late to plant the seeds again in order to get a harvest, so turn to ready grown plants, whether young or mature. This allows you to still grow some herbs even though you have had some problems with your seeds.

I always sow herb seeds every year, but I still buy fresh herb plants to grow so I have instant access to herbs rather than having to wait for the seeds to come up.

The advantage of growing from seed is that it is much cheaper and you have access to a wider variety of cultivars. The disadvantage of buying ready grown plants is you are limited to what the store stocks, which is usually just the most popular herbs. However, if you go to larger garden centers, you can sometimes find some of the more unusual herb varieties such as purple basil, apple mint, pineapple mint and more.

Buying ready grown plants is not a bad thing and is a very good way to get your herb garden established or to have fresh herbs quickly. You can also grow from seeds, but if your life is very busy or your space limited, this may not be possible for you.

Herb Pests and Problems

Herbs, like any plant, suffers from pests and problems. When you learn about the individual herbs you will also learn about the specific pests and problems that affect those plants. This section focuses on generic problems and pests that you may encounter. Generally, herbs are pretty much trouble free, though occasionally you will encounter some problems. Most herb problems tend to be environmental, but sometimes they will be pest related. Be aware that the pests and diseases you encounter depends on where in the world you live, so some of these you will never see if you live in the right area!

If you are planning on using any chemical sprays to treat problems on your herbs, make sure that it is food safe. Chemical residue in herbs you are eating or using topically can be harmful to you. It is possible to make your own organic sprays to treat many insect infestations, but in serious infestations you will need to resort to store bought sprays.

- **Wrong Soil -** A common problem with herbs is that they die because they are not in the right type of soil. Each herb has a specific type of soil it likes and if a herb that likes a free draining soil is in soil that retains moisture, it is going to struggle. Herbs in the wrong soil often grow into weak plants, may wilt a lot, the leaves could brown and they never look particularly healthy. Before you pot up or plant out your herbs, check the herb directory later in this book for their ideal soil conditions and give them the right type of soil!
- **Overwatering -** This can be a problem for many herbs as most plants do not like to stand in water. When the roots get too moist, they cannot

take up oxygen from the air because they are surrounded by water. This effectively causes the plant to drown. Overwatered plants exhibit many of the symptoms of plants that have not got enough water in that they start to wilt. Of course, most people see this and water their plants some more thinking they are thirsty and exacerbate the situation. If you are unsure whether your plant needs watering, either use a moisture meter to check the water level or do it the old fashioned way. Stick your finger in the soil down to the second knuckle. If the soil at the tip of your finger feels damp, do not water, but if it feels dry, then give your plant a good drink.

- **Under Watering -** Another common problem, indicated by the plant wilting, so check the moisture level in the soil. Plants in containers will need watering a lot more than plants in the ground, particularly in hot weather. Also remember that the plant leaves in crowded containers act like an umbrella during rain and directs water away from the soil, so you even have to water them in the rain. In the hotter months you may need to water your plants two or three times a day.
- **Aphids -** Aphids can be a problem on many herbs as they are attracted to new growth. They suck the sap out of the plant, causing the leaves to curl and the plant growth to be stunted. Aphids are not normally fatal to a plant, but they are more of an inconvenience than anything else. You do not want to grab a handful of herbs to throw in your spaghetti Bolognese only to realize they are covered in little green bugs! Ants often farm aphids for the nectar and help protect the population by killing predators such as lady bugs and hoverflies. In small infestations, aphids can be picked off by hand. In more serious infestations, you will need a spray. You can sometimes spray them off with jets of water, but this can damage the plant so you may have to resort to a food safe organic spray to remove these pests.

- **Slugs and Snails -** Slugs and snails will be a problem for your herb seedlings. They love the taste of young plants and will devour an entire sowing overnight given half a chance. Although you can use slug pellets, these can be harmful to other wildlife, particularly those beneficial predators such as frogs and toads that eat slugs. The best way to get rid of slugs is to use beer traps or to go out and dawn or dusk with a torch to pick them off by hand and dispose of them.

- **Too Much or Too Little Light -** Every herb has its own requirements for light and you need to take this into consideration when you plant them. A herb that likes a shady location will struggle or even die in full sun whereas a herb that likes full sun will struggle to grow properly in a shady location. Check the light requirements of your herbs and locate them somewhere that gets the amount of light they need. If you are growing your herbs indoors, then look at investing in artificial lighting if you do not have a bright enough place for your herbs.
- **Leggy/Weak Seedlings -** This is because they are not in a location with enough light and are having to stretch towards the light. The result is weak seedlings that use their energy reaching for the light rather than growing into strong plants. Invest in some artificial lighting or move your seedlings into a much brighter location.

These are just the most commonly encountered pests and problems found when growing herbs at home. In general, your herb garden is going to be absolutely fine, especially if you water and feed your plants regularly. Remember, it is better to spot and tackle a problem early rather than allow it to get established and damage your plants. A healthy plant will resist diseases and pests better than an unhealthy plant, just like we humans are more susceptible to illness when we are run down than we are when we are healthy.

Harvesting Herbs

Herbs can be harvested as and when you need them, or you can harvest the entire plant before the end of the season or before it flowers. Either pinch off the leaves you need by hand or use a pair of sharp scissors to cut the herbs. If you are harvesting the whole plant, then you will need to dry and store it, as detailed in the next section, so that the herbs will last over winter.

When harvesting herbs, look for undamaged leaves and fresh growth. That is always going to have the most flavor. Watch out for pests and any chewed leaves, though these can be discarded. You will sometimes find aphids or other insects hiding on the fresh growth which can be picked off and removed before washing and using the herbs.

Put the cut herbs in a clean bowl as you are harvesting them, using separate bowls if required to stop the flavors from mixing. When harvesting the entire plant, leave the bowl outside for a couple of hours which will allow any insects caught on the plant to leave. As you harvest the entire plant, put any damaged leaves to one side as these are not good to store for any length of time, but can be used in the next few days with the damaged parts removed.

Drying & Storing Your Herbs

At the end of the growing season, you are likely to end up with a glut of herbs, particularly from your annual herbs which die off over winter. Annual herbs are harvested completely and dug up/removed before the end of the growing season. Perennial herbs usually have a good percentage of their leaves harvested in fall, though if the plant drops its leaves over winter then you may as well harvest them all before this happens.

Using this quantity of herbs is going to be very difficult unless you are canning and preserving lots of other fresh produce at the same time. Most people will dry and store their excess herbs for use over the winter months when there is little growing in the garden.

There are a number of ways of preserving your herbs, though the easiest are either by drying or freezing your herbs. Some people say you can use a microwave, but I do not feel this is the best idea. It is hard to dry the herbs in a microwave without cooking them, and, personally, I am not sure about exposing the fresh, healthy herbs I am going to eat to microwave radiation.

When harvesting herbs for preserving, try to pick them on a dry day. If you cannot, then the drying process will take longer. It is better to pick the herbs wet than leave them outside, waiting for a dry day, and they get destroyed by frost. Herbs for drying are best picked in the morning when the oils are strongest so they have the best flavor.

Before preserving, check the herbs for pests and remove any damaged leaves which can either be discarded or used immediately. Try to ensure the herbs are all cut to roughly the same size when drying so that they dry evenly and in about the same amount of time. You do not want to be picking through trays of herbs trying to remove those that are dry and putting others back in to dry some more. If you store herbs that are not fully dry, then there is the risk that the herbs will become moldy and rot.

Once your herbs are dry and cooled, you can store them whole in a glass jar, which retains the most flavor or you can grind them up using a mortar and pestle and store them in a spice jar, which does reduce their flavor. Alternatively, you can combine them into your own spice mixes before storing in glass jars.

Oven Drying

Oven drying is an easy way to preserve your herbs, though if you are drying a big harvest it may be worth investing in a dehydrator as this keeps your oven in use for some time.

1. Pre-heat your oven to a low setting, 175F/80C is good. It must be below 200F/93C otherwise the herbs will bake rather than dry
2. Place your washed herbs in a single layer on a cookie sheet
3. Put the cookie sheets in the middle of the oven and leave the door cracked open so the air can circulate, allowing the herbs to dry rather than bake
4. Check the herbs every 10-15 minutes to see if they are dry. The amount of time this take will depend on the size of the herbs, how damp they are and their moisture content
5. Once the herbs crumble in your hand, they are dried and can be removed from the oven. Any that are not fully dry can be put back into your oven to dry further
6. Leave to cool and then store

Air Drying

Another method to dry your herbs is air drying. Herbs can be dried outdoors in the sun, but obviously this is not so practical in cooler climates, or indoors in an airing cupboard, near a cooker or over a heating boiler.

The important thing is to maintain a warm temperature, without over-heating the herbs, and ensuring there is sufficient air circulation to prevent mold forming. Herbs can be hung in the kitchen in bundles, though these are best hung near your stove where it is going to be warm.

Cover your herbs with a loose weaved, light fabric such as cheesecloth while drying. This keeps dust and any other debris off of them.

Air drying can take anything from a few hours to a couple of weeks, depending on the herb and the drying conditions. When the leaves are brittle and the stems of the herbs crack rather than bend, you know the herbs are fully dried.

Microwave Drying

A quick way to dry herbs is to use a microwave oven. This is not for everyone as many people feel microwaving damages the plant, but it is a way to dry your herbs.

Place two sheets of kitchen paper in the microwave, then put down a layer of herbs and cover it with another layer of kitchen paper. Microwave for 60 seconds and then in 20-30 second bursts, checking and moving the herbs around. Allow 5-10 seconds between bursts so you do not over-heat and burn the herbs.

Once they are dry, leave them to cool before storing them.

Using a Dehydrator

A dehydrator is a great way to dry many herbs, including basil, mints, lemon balm, tarragon and oregano, amongst others.

Rinse the herbs and carefully shake them to remove excess moisture; do not rub them dry as this will damage the leaves. Remove the leaves from the stems and discard any damaged or diseased leaves.

Place the leaves in a single layer on the dehydrator tray. Depending on the type of dehydrator you are using, you may need to cover the herbs with a fine screen to prevent them from falling off the tray.

The best flavor is obtained by drying on the lowest possible setting. Herbs will take anything up to four to six hours to dry, depending on the size of the herbs. Once completely dry, leave to cool and then store. Check the manufacturer's instructions for precise instructions on how to use your dehydrator correctly.

Freezing

Freezing is a popular way to dry herbs. It works for many herbs including basil, borage, chives (chop first), lemongrass (chop first), all mints, oregano, sage, summer and winter savory, sorrel, tarragon and thyme.

Wash the herbs well, then pat them dry. Remove the individual leaves from the main stems. Spread the herbs on a cookie tray in a single layer, then place the tray in the freezer.

Once frozen, put the herbs into sealed containers or bags, and return them to the freezer. If you can, vacuum seal them, but otherwise remove as much air as you can. Try using a straw to suck as much air as you can out of a plastic bag before sealing it. Remember to label the containers so you know exactly what is in each one.

If you are using plastic bags to store your frozen herbs in, make sure you use ones that are designed for use in a freezer. These are thicker than normal plastic bags and will protect your herbs while frozen.

Another popular way to freeze herbs is to mix them with oil or water and freeze them in ice cube trays with half or a whole teaspoon of herb in each cube. Once frozen, these can be transferred to plastic bags for long term storage in your freezer. These are very easy to use, just put an ice cube containing the herbs into whatever you are cooking! I mix together commonly used combinations of herbs in the ice cubes, so it saves even more time!

Storing Dried Herbs

Dried herbs can be hung in bundles in your kitchen, but these can gather dust, look untidy and generally get in the way. Strip the leaves and crush them, either with a rolling pin or a pestle and mortar, discarding the stalks and then store them. If you want a fine powder, push the crushed herbs through a sieve.

Once the herbs are thoroughly dry, store them in small, airtight containers. I use old herb jars or small lidded, Kilner jars. Herbs should be stored out of the light or in dark glass jars. Properly dried and stored, your herbs should last a year or two.

How to Root Cuttings

One way or propagating your herbs is through cuttings. This works for many woody type herbs and for those that do not grow well from seeds. In general, with herbs, cuttings are taken from above ground and then either rooted in water or in a growing medium. Be aware that roots produced in water are not as strong as those produced in soil and can often break off when the cutting is put into soil. However, there will usually be a period, sometimes a few weeks, where the plant does not appear to grow, which is when it is establishing a root system to support itself. After this, the plant will start to grow as normal once the new roots are formed.

Rooting hormone powder will help cuttings produce roots, but these are not usually organic so some people do not use them. For tricky to propagate plants, this can make life a lot easier for you and is worth using.

Always use healthy cuttings, ideally from newer growth as it is far more vigorous. Use a clean, sharp knife and cut off a piece of new growth ranging from 2 to 8 inches long. Ensure there is a growth node about an inch from the bottom of the cutting as this needs to be placed under the soil. Trim off the bottom leaves so they will not be touching the soil when the cutting is planted.

If using root hormone powder, dampen the bottom inch of the cutting and roll it in the powder. Then make a small hole in the soil and put the cutting in place; note that if you do not use rooting powder you can just push the cutting into the soil as the hole is made to stop the rooting powder rubbing off the cutting.

Press the soil down around the cutting so it is supported and then place in a bright position but not full sun. Cuttings thrive on heat and humidity, and prefer a location where they get dappled light or about 50% shade.

When the cutting starts to produce new growth, you know it is establishing itself. Leave it for a little while to produce a healthy root system and then transfer it to a new pot with new soil. Be careful not to overwater your cutting as too much water will cause it to rot.

Most leafy and woody herbs can be propagated from cuttings, e.g. rosemary. If the cuttings are refusing to root, try using a heated plant mat which should encourage the cuttings to grow new roots.

Making Herbal Mixtures

These are simple techniques for how to use the herbs medicinally and for beauty purposes. These the basic ways of using the herbs detailed in the next section, though each herb may be used in multiple ways. All of these can be made with a single herb or, if you want to combine effects from herbs, multiple herbs can be used.

Decoction

A decoction is similar to a herbal tea, made by boiling herbs in water. Decoctions have a very long history but have fallen out of favor somewhat today, mainly because it requires more work to make than a tea.

A basic decoction is made like this:

1. Use 1 teaspoon or tablespoon (depending on the strength required) of herbs per cup of water
2. Add the herbs and water to a saucepan
3. Bring to a gentle boil
4. Cover, a simmer lightly for between 20 and 40 minutes
5. Remove from the heat and allow to cool to drinking temperature
6. Strain the herbs, sweeten if required and enjoy

Any leftover liquid can be refrigerated and used in the next day or two. Usually, you can use the same herbs a couple of times for this, providing the decoction is still strong enough. Once you have finished with the herbs, they can be composted.

It is always best to start with cold water, rather than putting the herbs directly into boiling water. When herbs are placed in hot water, the albumen in the plant cells bind, which makes it very hard to get the beneficial constituents of the herb into the water.

Fresh or dried herbs can be used to make a decoction. You can grow these yourself, buy them from a supermarket or other supplier. Supermarket bought dried herbs will work for a decoction. As fresh herbs have a high water content, always use double the amount of fresh herbs compared to dried herbs.

Some people prefer to grind or crush the herbs before boiling them. This increases the surface area of the herb and so makes it easier to get the beneficial constituents out of the plant. If you have time, then this is something you can do.

Covering the pan while simmering is very important as many of the beneficial oils in a herb will evaporate off in the heat. The lid keeps these constituents in the pan and helps to concentrate them. If the herb is high in volatile oils, boil the woody parts of the herb and then add the leaves when you remove the pan from the heat. Keep the pan covered and this will prevent the volatile oils escaping and being lost. Herbs high in volatile oils include fennel, peppermint and valerian.

Infusion or Tea

A herbal infusion is very simply a herbal tea, it is nothing more complex! Infusions are usually made with leaves and flowers, but roots and seeds are used when boiling would lose volatile oils. Seeds and roots are best slightly crushed before infusing so that the water can get to the constituents inside.

Both fresh and dried herbs can be used, though adjust quantities as required for the strength infusion you prefer. Infusions can be drank or used as a hair rinse or skin toner, depending on the herbs.

Use one to two teaspoons of the dried herb per cup of water, or three teaspoons of fresh herb. Put the herbs into a cup, ideally using a strainer or tea ball, though you can put them in loose. I use a coffee cafetiere for my herbal infusions as it is simple to use and saves straining the herbs out later on.

Once the infusion has steeped for 10 to 20 minutes, depending on how strong you want it, then strain off the herbs and drink. Cover the infusion while it is steeping to prevent volatile oils escaping.

Infusions are best drank immediately or turned into an iced tea. They will keep for a day or two in your refrigerator.

Infused Oil

Infused oils can be used for beauty or culinary purposes and can be made from any light oil. Most people use extra-virgin olive oil, but any other oil will work such as rapeseed oil or sunflower oil.

It is best to use fresh herbs for an infused oil. Leave them to wilt for 12-24 hours by arranging them in a single layer on kitchen paper before infusing them. This removes some of the water content from the herb and prevents the oil from going moldy or spoiling. You can dry the herb fully first if you prefer and have time.

Quarter fill a heat proof jar with the herbs, crumbling them a little as you do. Slowly fill the jar with your choice of oil until the jar is mostly full; best to leave some headroom. Stir the contents of the jar well, seal and leave somewhere cool and dark for between 4-6 weeks. You can then strain the herbs from the oil and store the infused oil in a dark glass container in a cool, dark place.

Infused oils can be made more quickly by heating the jar in a double boiler for a few hours, though you need to be careful not to burn or overheat the herbs.

Poultice

Poultices have been used for thousands of years and are a very good way to use herbs on your skin. They allow you to enjoy the benefits of herbs without the concentration of a tincture or essential oil.

A poultice is a paste made from herbs mixed with anything from salts to clays to activated charcoal or a whole host of other, beneficial substances. However, you can just mix the herbs with water and use this, it has been effective for thousands of years! This is then wrapped in cloth and placed on your skin. This can then be covered with a waterproof covering and left on your skin for several hours. The poultice is changed regularly throughout the day.

A poultice can be made with fresh or dried herbs, depending on what you have available. The important thing is that the herbs are in contact with the skin. Poultices are used for anything from boils to burns to splinters and more.

A poultice should not be a substitute for medical treatment, but can be used to assist medical treatment. Make sure you tell your doctor that you are going to use a herbal poultice in case there is any interaction between the herbs and any prescription drugs you may be taking.

A poultice is made with water. Hot water is used when a poultice is trying to draw something out from a person, while cold water is used for inflammation. Traditionally, a mortar and pestle is used to crush herbs for a poultice, but these days' people are just as likely to use a food processor or blender. Ground dried herbs, such as those bought from a supermarket, can be used.

Adding a little bit of hot water to any poultice, directly to the herbs, can help the healing process as it will help to extract the beneficial constituents of the herbs. Then use hot/cold water to get a temperature that is comfortable for your skin and apply it.

You are aiming to create a thick paste that can be directly applied to the skin or wrapped in a clean cloth and applied. Cheesecloth works very well for this, though you can use any cloth that does not absorb a lot of liquid or is too thick for the herbs to come into contact with the skin.

A simple poultice is made for two or three tablespoons of herbs ground down and mixed with hot or cold water to form a paste. Healing clays or activated charcoal can be added, depending on what you are treating. This is then cooled to room temperature (if hot) before applying, or applying directly if cold water was used. Depending on the herbs used, you can wrap the poultice in cheesecloth and then use a waterproof covering such as kitchen plastic wrap, to keep the poultice in place.

Leave it on the skin for anywhere from 20 minutes to up to three hours, repeating as needed.

Poultices can be made out of almost any herb, though with some you need to be careful not to apply the herb directly to the skin. A poultice made out of plantain, which grows freely as a weed virtually everywhere is excellent to heal insect bites and bee stings. Cabbage leaf poultices are good for treating mastitis and a fresh garlic poultice is said to cure warts!

Tincture

Tinctures are herbal infusions made with alcohol. They store well, usually for at least a year in a dark bottle in cool, dark place. These can be used as is or mixed with other oils or creams to make beauty products.

A tincture of lemon balm is made by filling a jar three quarters full with fresh, washed leaves. Fill the jar with an 80% proof alcohol such as vodka, seal and leave in a cool, dark place for between four and six weeks, shaking occasionally. Strain and then store for up to a year.

This tincture, like many others, is taken at a dose of ¼ teaspoon or 1ml at a time. It is not recommended for children. Mix with honey to make it more palatable.

Glycerite

A glycerite is similar to a tincture but doesn't contain alcohol. They are used as ingredients in many beauty products such as toners, aftershave and lotions.

A glycerite can be made from lemon balm very easily. Fill a jar with freshly washed lemon balm leaves. Cover the leaves with a mixture of three parts vegetable glycerin to one part water. Seal and leave in a cool, dark place for three to four weeks. Strain and then store in a dark bottle in your refrigerator for several months.

The adult dosage is ½ to 1 teaspoon as required to help you relax and stay calm.

Herbal Vinegar

Herbal vinegars have many uses at home, from beauty uses such as hair rinses and bath additives to use in the kitchen as salad dressings.

Lemon balm makes an excellent vinegar and is easily made. Fill a jar ¾ full with freshly washed lemon balm leaves. Cover it with apple cider vinegar. Seal and leave in a cool, dark place for four to six weeks. Strain and then use as required. This will store in a dark glass bottle for 9 to 12 months or even longer.

The flavor of the herb infuses into the vinegar, so that when you use the vinegar it will taste of the herb.

HERB DIRECTORY

There are hundreds, if not thousands, of different types of herbs, ranging from those that you grow in your kitchen garden to those that you collect from the wild. This section will focus on herbs commonly grown in the garden rather than those found in the hedgerow, but will include some that have made their way from the hedgerow into the garden. Many of these are culinary herbs, but most also have some healing properties or health benefits.

Each of the herbs detailed here have many varieties, often with different tastes or colored leaves or flowers, though sometimes with different environmental requirements. Some of these unusual cultivars are surprisingly attractive and will help make your garden look fantastic. I can recommend some of these varieties rather than the commonly grown cultivars as they have a great taste.

Aloe Vera

Aloe vera, *Aloe Barbadensis*, is one of the most popular herbs in the world, used in a wide variety of health and beauty products. It is used for everything from treating sunburn, easing skin complaints and in detox drinks.

At a Glance Facts

~~Annual~~ / ~~Biennial~~ / **Perennial**	
Position:	Full Sun
Soil:	Sandy, free draining
Hardiness	None
USDA Zones:	8-11
Sow:	Not usually grown from seeds
Harvest:	Any time

This desert plant is surprisingly easy to grow at home in containers and incredibly useful. I use a leaf of my plant if I ever burn myself, though many people use it to treat their hair and as part of a healthy, detoxifying diet.

The origins of the aloe vera plant are a little unclear, but researchers believe it to have come out of Africa, probably Sudan. The earliest written record of its use dates back to Mesopotamia in around 2100BC, though the Egyptians also wrote about it around 1550BC. The ancient Greeks were also big fans of aloe vera and in 70AD, the Herbal of Dioscorides described the plant in great detail. This plant has naturalized itself in virtually every tropical area of the world. In fact, in many hot areas, growing aloe vera is a very profitable business.

If you do not live in a hot climate, you can still grow aloe vera at home as a house plant and its size will only be limited by the size of the container you put it in! I live in the middle of England where it is definitely not tropical, getting very cold in winter, yet my aloe plant grew to about three feet across when put in a large container and kept inside. You can easily find aloe vera plants in many health stores or garden centers, but when they get to a certain size, they start to produce baby plants that people often give away.

It is worth growing one of these at home, even if you live in a cooler area, as it is such a useful plant. It is fabulous to have on hand in case of burns or sunburn and is a very easy plant to look after.

Growing Instructions

Aloe vera is a dream plant to grow because it is so tolerant of a variety of conditions. Although it prefers bright sunlight, it will grow well in low light. It does not like watering very often and the number one problem people have with this plant comes from overwatering it! If the aloe gets a bit chilly or too dry, the leaves flatten a little and turn a red color, but in most cases, it bounces back again as soon as you remedy the problem.

This plant is rarely grown from seed; usually it is grown from the baby plants that form from underground runners. Plant in a very sandy, well-drained soil that is not going to be soggy or damp. You can buy specialist cacti soil mixes which the aloe will grow well in, though you can make your own from a mixture of sand, fine gravel and good quality soil.

If growing in containers, then an unglazed clay pot is perfect because it allows the soil to dry out more rapidly than a glazed or plastic pot. Whichever container you use, ensure there are plenty of drainage holes in the bottom, as the aloe plant does not like sitting in water. Unless you are encouraging baby plants to form, use a container that is a little bit bigger than the roots of the plants and large enough to support its weight.

Position your plant on a bright, sunny windowsill or in a sunroom. Although aloe vera will put up with low light conditions, it can become dormant and stop growing until it gets more light again.

Aloe vera is a dryland plant so it likes to be heavily watered and then allowed to completely dry out. It only needs watering every couple of weeks or less, particularly in winter or low light conditions when it does not grow as fast. Do not water every day and do not try to keep the soil moist as this will rot the roots and kill the plants. If the leaves start turning brown or going limp, then you are watering your plant too much.

Transplanting an aloe vera plant or potting up a plant is very easy. Fill your container about a third full of your potting mix, then stand the plant in the soil. Holding the plant upright, continue to fill the pot, pushing the soil down gently, until the soil level is about ½ to ¾ of an inch from the top of the pot. The bottom leaves should be just above the soil level. Now, put the plant on a sunny, warm windowsill and ignore it. Yes, you heard me right, ignore it! Do not water it for at least a week and leave it be. It will send out new roots and establish itself and once it has, then you can water it. Watering it too early will encourage a weak root system and root rot.

Although you can grow aloe vera from seed, it is more commonly grown from the 'pups' or suckers that come from the main plant. Let these baby plants get to a reasonable size with several sets of leaves and then you can cut them from the mother plant using a sharp knife at the point of attachment. Transplant them into their own pot and water once and then leave them to establish a strong root system. The pups require watering to help establish themselves, as they do not have the root system a larger plant has.

In the summer months, move your aloe vera plants outdoors and allow them to enjoy some fresh air. Be careful about putting them directly in bright sun if they are not used to it as this can damage the plants. Instead, put them in a slightly shady location and move them further out into the sun over the course of a few days.

Plant Care

Aloe vera plants do not require a great deal of care so are easy to grow at home. Water every couple of weeks, or less frequently and just leave the plant to it. So long as it is warm and gets plenty of light, it will continue to grow quite happily without your intervention.

If the plant starts to look like it is too big for its container, then you can repot it into a larger container, and it will continue to grow. If you do not want it to grow any larger, leave it in its container. If it starts to struggle, then take it out of the pot, trim the roots and put it back in again, but generally, it should be ok. Just be aware if you keep moving it into bigger pots, it will continue to grow to fill them! These do grow into large plants if given the chance.

Culinary Uses

Aloe vera is more commonly known for its health and beauty properties, but it can also be used in cooking. It is popular in a number of different cuisines, most notably Latin American and Asian. The plant is high in protein and several vitamins, including zinc, calcium, and magnesium as well as vitamins A, B-12 and C.

When preparing it for cooking, wash the leaves thoroughly, ensuring there is no dirt on them. The skin is not eaten but needs cleaning so there is no contamination of the inner flesh which is eaten.

Slice the bottom of each leaf and prop them up in a bowl. Leave them to sit for a couple of hours so the gooey substance from the leaves can drain out. This is not used in cooking.

Cut off the outer skin carefully as the leaf can be slippery and discard. Some people prefer to fillet aloe vera leaves like they would fillet fish and cut into the side. The flesh is then cooked.

Cut the flesh into 1" cubes and boil with a cup of sugar and the juice of one lemon/lime to make a sweet treat, add the cubes to a stew or soup or simmer for 30 minutes with your favorite spices.

Health Uses

The aloe vera plant is so useful that entire books and industries have built up around it. With so many uses, this is a summary of some of the most common health benefits. Additional information can easily be found online.

- Aids Digestion – smooths and cleanses the digestive tract, which boosts digestion. Taken internally, it also helps constipation and diarrhea as well as regulating your bowel movements. It has been taken for acid reflux and it helps promote healthy gut bacteria. As well as this, it has anti-microbial and anti-parasitic qualities and is considered useful in purging parasites from your system. Many people will drink some aloe vera gel every day to gain these benefits.
- Wound Healing – used topically, aloe vera has a long history of treating burns and sores, particularly sunburn. Using aloe vera on wounds accelerates the healing process significantly, by as much as 9 days.
- Dental Plaque – aloe vera can be used to reduce the build-up of plaque on your teeth. According to research performed in 2014, an aloe vera mouth rinse was just as effective as a chlorhexidine mouthwash.
- Treats Constipation – barbaloin, a compound found in younger leaves of the aloe vera plant, has been found to have laxative properties. It helps the intestinal muscles to contract, allowing for easier and smoother bowel movements.
- Fights Wrinkles and Skin Aging – skin aging is caused by a lack of collagen and moisture in the skin which means the skin becomes less elastic. Aloe vera, applied topically, has been shown to reduce the early signs of aging. Dr. Soyun Cho performed a 90-day study in 2009 -https://www.ncbi.nlm.nih.gov/pmc/articles/PMC2883372/ on 30 women aged over 45. They applied aloe vera gel to their skin every day throughout the experiment. At the end of the experiment, the skin's collagen production had increased, and the skin was more elastic. The results were fewer wrinkles and younger looking skin.
- Lowers Blood Sugar – aloe vera supplements have been shown to reduce blood sugar levels in the blood stream and allow you to better utilize insulin. Studies such as this https://onlinelibrary.wiley.com/doi/full/10.1111/jcpt.12382, have shown that aloe vera can be beneficial in controlling blood sugar in diabetics and in pre-diabetics, though you should confer with your health professional before undergoing any treatment.
- Treating Mouth Ulcers – a 2013 study

(https://www.ncbi.nlm.nih.gov/pmc/articles/PMC4439686/) found that aloe vera was very effective in treating mouth ulcers. The polysaccharide, Acemannan, present in aloe gel, shrinks mouth ulcers and alleviates the pain from it.

- Boosts the Immune System – numerous studies such as https://www.ncbi.nlm.nih.gov/pmc/articles/PMC3410334/ and many more have shown that aloe vera neutralizes harmful bacterial and helps to strengthen the immune system by fighting off infections. If your immune system is low or you are feeling run down, then aloe vera will help give you a much needed boost. Remember though, if you are taking any medicine for immune system problems, consult with your medical professional before using aloe vera.
- Relieves Heartburn – this affects an awful lot of people and studies such as https://www.sciencedirect.com/science/article/pii/S0254627215301515 have shown that consuming one to three ounces of aloe vera gel can help reduce heartburn.
- Treats Psoriasis – aloe vera is good for a wide variety of skin complaints and is also very helpful in treating psoriasis. Studies such as https://www.medicalnewstoday.com/articles/320081.php have shown that it can reduce the itchiness associated with psoriasis, moisturize the skin and promote healing of affected skin areas.

As you can see, aloe vera has numerous health benefits and scientists are busy conducting trials and studies to determine its use in treating a wide variety of complaints. Research is underway looking at anti-cancer properties, hair re-growth properties and more. Over the next few years we can expect aloe vera extracts to appear in more health supplements as scientists understand the beneficial properties of this plant.

Beauty Uses

As well as many health benefits, aloe vera also has numerous uses in the beauty industry. We have already mentioned its ability to fight the signs of aging and reduce wrinkles, but it also helps to reduce the visibility of stretch marks by improving the elasticity of the skin and healing the tiny tears in the skin that cause stretch marks.

Aloe vera plants contain the hormones Gibberellins and Auxin that both help to heal wounds and reduce inflammation. Gibberellin also stimulates the growth of new skin cells, allowing the skin to heal faster and with less scarr1ing. The gel is soothing, reducing itchiness and skin inflammation, so helps to reduce the effects of acne. The antibacterial properties help reduce the bacteria in the pores that cause acne, while its astringent properties removes dirt and unblocks pores.

As a sunburn treatment, aloe vera gel is second to none because of its ability to heal the skin. It forms a protective layer on the skin that helps it to replenish moisture. The aloe vera promotes rapid skin healing and cell growth plus has a cooling effect. Many sunburn treatments now contain some aloe vera, though you can use aloe vera gel either straight from the plant or bought in a store.

Used as a moisturizer, aloe vera benefits your skin without leaving a greasy feeling behind, making it ideal for anyone with oily skin. It is very effective when applied as a moisturizer prior to putting on mineral based make-up products and is also very good as an aftershave treatment.

Pests, Problems & Diseases

Aloe vera plants are very easy to grow and suffer from few pests and problems when grown inside. Occasionally, problems can be encountered when growing outdoors, but unless you are growing the plants in large quantities or live where the plants grow in the wild, these are unlikely to occur. Most aloe vera problems occur when the plant is in conditions that are either too wet or too cold for it, meaning it is relatively easy to avoid many of these issues.

- Overwatering – the most common problem you will encounter, so make sure you water the plant every two to three weeks when completely dry and that it does not sit in water
- Alternaria Leaf Spot – symptoms include small, round or oval dark brown sunken spots on the leaves
- Aloe Rust – a plant fungus that creates black or brown spots on the leaves and does not tend to spread beyond the affected spots
- Sooty Mold – a fungal infection usually caused by mealy bugs or aphids infesting your plant. Treat the bugs as soon as you spot them to stop this infection from occurring.
- Basal Stem Rot – occurs when conditions are too wet or cold so the stem rots, turning reddish brown or black. You can take a stem cutting above the infected area and replant it to save the plant.

Water direct to the base of the plant in the morning to allow plenty of time for the soil to dry out during the day. Water less frequently during colder months as the plant grows more slowly. Ensure your aloe vera plant has good air circulation and gets plenty of sunlight. If your plant is infected, then you can spray it with fungicides but check how these affect your use of the plant. Catching diseases early on generally means you can save your plant and prevent it from dying or spreading the disease.

Recommended Varieties

There are over 400 members of the aloe family, with *Aloe Barbadensis* being the most commonly grown with all the health and beauty benefits discussed earlier. Many of the other members of the aloe family have some beneficial properties, but many are also purely ornamental and not good for growing outside of their hot, native areas.

Here are some of the most popular and commonly grown members of the aloe family, some of which also having health and beauty benefits.

- *Aloe arborescens* – growing up to ten feet tall, this aloe plant assists with healing wounds. It is known as the candelabra aloe because of the large, red/orange cylindrical flowers that it grows. Studies have shown this cultivar supports the immune system, aids in healing wounds and shows some action against harmful organisms.
- *Aloe ferox* – also known as the Cape Aloe, this variety can also grow up to ten feet tall with large, red flowers growing another two to four feet! Extracts from this plant are used as a laxative and it helps treat constipation. Oils from this aloe family member contain high levels of oleic, stearic and linoleic fatty acids, which are found in many cosmetics. Research is underway into its ability to rejuvenate and nourish skin.

- *Aloe striata* – this stemless aloe plant, known as the coral aloe due to the pink tint of its leaves has wide, smooth leaves, unlike the jagged leaves found on many other aloe plants. It thrives in very hot, dry areas and stores a lot of water in its leaves. It is very hardy if you live in hot areas and early results from research point to this variety aiding digestion.

- *Aloe aristata* – another stemless aloe also known as lace aloe with deep green, toothed leaves with white speckles on. Often confused with *haworthia*, another succulent, this aloe has large orange flowers loved by birds and bees. Ayurveda medicine uses this cultivar for wound healing.
- *Aloe marlothii* – known as mountain aloe, this plant grows up to 20 feet tall with spiky, grey/green leaves growing from a central head to up to five feet long. The flowers can be any color from yellow to orange to vibrant red. It is thought to promote skin health and moisturize the skin.

- *Aloe polyphylla* – known as the spiral aloe, overuse of this plant by the beauty industry has caused the population to decline sharply to dangerously low levels. It has a very distinctive five point growing pattern, leaves with serrated edges and pointed tips as flowers that are a variety of shades of red.
- *Aloe plicatilis* – another aloe plant decimated by overuse, this fan aloe is a very decorative variety. Growing to over ten feet tall, this plant has special protection because overuse by the cosmetic and therapeutic product industries has caused it to become endangered.

- *Aloe dichotoma* – known as the quiver tree, this aloe family member grows very tall and has branches similar to a tree. It was commonly used in landscaping as it supports the surrounding environment, but overuse has led to it being declared critically endangered.
- *Aloe petricola* – known as the stone aloe, this is a great environmental booster, providing benefits to the plants it grows alongside. It is popular in gardens with its red, yellow and orange flowers.
- *Aloe ciliaris* – known as the common climbing aloe, this is a thin plant that grows very fast. It has soft, hair like teeth and pretty, red, tubular flowers that attract bees and birds, making it popular with gardeners.
- *Aloe maculate* – known as the soap aloe because its sap makes a soapy lather in water, this plant is also sometimes referred to as the zebra aloe. It produces long, tubular flowers with spots that look like the letter 'H' and range from green to red in color.
- *Aloe humilis* – this plant has long, thin triangular leaves edged with white teeth. It produces yellow, orange and red flowers from the stem. Use the gel of the plant to relieve sunburn.
- *Aloe barberae* – growing up to 50 feet tall with rose pink flowers with green tips, this is a very popular tree aloe. It has very soothing properties and is very effective in killing harmful organisms.

Recipes

Aloe Vera Salsa Recipe

Everyone loves a good salsa, and this is one you can enjoy the taste of knowing it is benefiting your heath too!

Ingredients:

- 12½oz/350g Aloe vera leaves (skin remove and filleted)
- 1 cup fresh chives (chopped)
- 1 garlic clove (chopped)
- Juice of 1 large lemon
- 3 baby marrow or baby zucchini
- 2 tomatoes
- 1 tablespoon salt

Method:

1. Put the aloe gel, marrow/zucchini, garlic and tomatoes into your food blender
2. Blend until it has a texture like paste
3. Transfer to a bowl
4. Mix in the chives, salt and lemon juice
5. Thoroughly combine and serve

Aloe Vera Acne Gel

This is a simple to make gel applied to your face to treat acne or spots. It will help cleanse the skin and tighten it. It takes just a few minutes to make and should be stored out of the sun. Apply the gel twice a day for maximum benefit.

Patch test this on your inner forearm as the skin is delicate like your face, to ensure you do not have any adverse reaction to the oils used in this recipe. As with many essential oil recipes, this should not be used by young children, babies or pregnant women.

Ingredients:

- 7 tablespoons aloe vera gel
- 5 drops tea tree essential oil
- 5 drops lavender essential oil
- 1 drop cinnamon essential oil

Method:

1. Put the aloe vera gel into a bowl
2. Add the essential oils and mix until thoroughly combined
3. Store in an air-tight glass container out of the sun and use within 3 to 4 weeks

How to Use:

1. Cleanse your face using your usual facial cleanser
2. Soak a face towel in hot water and place it on your face for two to three minutes to open your pores
3. Apply the home-made acne gel
4. Once the gel has penetrated the skin, apply your usual facial moisturizer

Aloe Vera Lemonade

A delicious drink that is great for your digestive system too!

Ingredients:

- 17½oz/500g aloe vera leaf
- ½ cup coconut water
- 4 tablespoons agave nectar (raw is best)
- 10 ice cubes
- 1 large lemon
- 1 large orange

Method:

1. Fillet the aloe vera and extract the gel from the leaves
2. Slice the orange in half and extract the juice
3. Slice the lemon in half and extract the juice
4. Add everything to your blender and blender on high until the mixture becomes a slush
5. Serve immediately garnished with a slice of orange or lemon

Aloe Vera Candies

These are very tasty and relatively healthy compared to some candies. Store the finished candies in your refrigerator and eat within two or three days.

Ingredients:

- 17fl oz/500ml full fat milk
- ½ cup fresh cream
- ½ cup aloe vera gel (fresh or drinkable bought from a store)
- 2 tablespoons white (granulated) sugar
- 2 tablespoons pistachio nuts (rinsed and sliced)
- 1 tablespoon ghee butter

Method:

1. Pour the milk into a large pan and slowly heat on a low heat until it starts to froth, stirring regularly
2. Add the aloe vera gel and simmer, stirring often, until the mixture reduces to about a third of its original volume
3. Meanwhile, make a sugar syrup by heating ¼ cup of water with the sugar (a double boiler can prevent it from burning)
4. Pour the fresh cream into the milk and stir
5. When the milk begins to caramelize (this takes a few minutes), add the syrup
6. Evenly grease a large square or rectangular pan with the ghee
7. Pour in the aloe vera mixture, ensuring it is evenly spread out across the pan
8. Refrigerate for 1 hour, then cut into evenly sized squares
9. Serve or store in an airtight container in your refrigerator

Angelica

Angelica, *Archangelica officinalis,* also known as wild celery is a plant that is useful from root to flower. Believed to have originated in Syria, it has now spread across Europe and has naturalized as far afield as the Alps and Lapland.

At a Glance Facts

~~Annual~~ / **Biennial** / **Perennial**	
Position:	Semi-shade to full sun
Soil:	Moist, fertile soil
Hardiness	Yes to 14F/-10C to 5F/-15C
USDA Zones:	4-9
Sow:	Spring
Harvest:	Stems – April/May Leaves – May/June Roots – Late Fall

Preferring a cooler climate, this plant grows up to six feet tall. This herb has a powerful mystical tradition behind it and was shown to a monk in a dream as a cure for the plague in the Middle Ages, when it was given its name, Angelica. Originally, its name was the 'Root of the Holy Ghost' because of its appearance in this vision.

Angelica is unusual because it is one of the few aromatic plants that grows natively in colder climates such as Norway and Russia. According to tradition, Angelica was used to feed the people of Iceland when there was no other food available.

This plant may not always seed until the second growing season, hence its status as a biennial plant. However, it is very, very good at seeding itself and will self-seed all over your garden. If you remove the flower heads and prevent seed formation, the plant will live for several years, giving it the status of a perennial.

Popular in cooking, this is a great herb to grow and will produce a large display of flowers that are loved by pollinating insects.

Growing Instructions

Angelica can be grown from seed; though ensure they are fresh as germination is difficult. Seeds are viable for a year or possibly two if you are lucky, so using fresh seeds will give you a much higher germination rate. Plant the seeds on their edge, which helps to prevent rotting.

With all the problems germinating seeds, most people think it is easier to buy plants and then harvest your own seeds, which you can plant immediately for maximum germination. As a rule of thumb the bigger the seed, the higher the likelihood of it germinating.

Seeds are sown in the fall as they need cold in order to germinate. Keep weeds down between the plants, but once the plants are large enough to shade the ground, they can generally care for themselves as they crowd out the competition. Leave around three feet between plants to allow them to spread out without crowding each other.

As angelica produces a long taproot, it is very temperamental when it comes to transplanting young plants. Many people prefer to plant the seeds in their final location, though you can use long root trainers such as those used for growing sweetcorn.

Dill should not be planted near to angelica, as the plants do not complement each other.

Plant Care

This herb likes a cooler climate and does not mind being in a shady location. If you live in an area with a hot summer, plant angelica in an area that receives dappled shade to protect it from the worst of the heat.

It prefers a slightly acidic soil that is moist, fertile and rich in organic matter. It is not drought tolerant and must not dry out, though does not like standing in water. Planted where it gets plenty of sun and the soil drains well, angelica is a very easy herb to care for. Make sure you water from the base to prevent fungal diseases taking hold.

To encourage flowering in the second year, cut the stalk back in the fall of the first year. This will force the plant to bush out and create multiple flower heads.

In the wild, angelica would grow in leafy groves near to running water, so mirror this type of environment to keep the plant happy. Mulch it a couple of times a year to provide nutrition and to aid water retention. In windy areas, angelica needs staking to support it due to its height.

Culinary Uses

Angelica is best known for its candied stem, popular in cookery. The seeds are used as a flavoring, commonly used in gin, Chartreuse and vermouth. The leaves provide flavor to stews, soups, fish and poultry. Eat the stems like asparagus or chop up and stew with apples and rhubarb. Mince the stems and they make them into a marmalade. This incredibly versatile plant is a great addition to any herb garden.

The leaves have a lovely aroma to them and can freshen a room. However, they are excellent as an herbal tea that also helps to reduce gas, fight colds and reduce motion sickness. The roots, although not used in the kitchen, produce a gummy substance when cut which is used as a fixative in potpourri.

Health Uses

Angelica has a slightly bitter taste and herbalists use it to improve digestion. It is thought to help relax the muscles of the intestine and release boating, gas and mild cramps. Of course, like many herbs, the scientific jury is still out and waiting for funding to research the plant in more detail.

Angelica tea is easy to make by steeping a teaspoon of dried angelica (leaves and stem) in a cup of boiling water for ten minutes.

It has been used traditionally for centuries not only to treat the bubonic plague, but to treat many other complaints too. Traditionally, a compress of angelica leaves helps rheumatism and gout and bathing in water steeped with angelica calms the nerves. Oddly enough, herbal practitioners use angelica tea to cause a dislike for liquor and treat alcoholism, which is strange when you consider how this herb flavors many alcoholic drinks.

If you are pregnant, then you should not use angelica as a herb. It can also increase the sensitivity of your skin to light, so use sunscreen if you are taking angelica and want to go out in the sun.

Research into angelica has been limited and as it can affect the light sensitivity of your skin, it is important that you consult with your medical professional before starting to take this as an herbal supplement.

Beauty Uses

Angelica is not widely used as a beauty product, but it can benefit your skin.

As a face wash, angelica will make your skin clearer, healthier and softer. It helps your skin to heal faster by allowing it to absorb nutrients better. It will help treat acne and spots, particularly when used twice a day. Simply mix two cups of aloe vera juice with ten drops of angelica root tincture to make a great face wash. The aloe vera provides a great deal of benefit here too.

Add two cups of angelica tea into your bath water to help soften the skin, and relieve the symptoms of eczema. Add some coconut oil for additional benefits.

Chinese medicine uses angelica to treat hair loss. High in Vitamin E, this herb helps stimulate oxygen circulation in both the scalp and body. By oxidizing the blood, it also oxidizes the hair cells and helps damaged hair cells regenerate themselves.

Pests, Problems & Diseases

Angelica is a fairly hardy plant and will generally be okay growing in your garden. Young plants are at risk of damage from slugs and snails, and older plants can attract aphids, leaf miners and even red spider mites. Although the plant does attract many beneficial insects, it can need a helping hand from you to keep the pest population under control. Be careful using chemical sprays if you are planning on using any part of the herb to eat or on your skin.

Recommended Varieties

There are many varieties of angelica that are grown across the world for ornamental and health purposes. The most commonly grown variety for use in the kitchen and for healing is *Archangelica officinalis*, which is easy to find.

Recipes

Candied Angelica Stem Recipe

This is incredibly simple to make and once cooked, you can roll the stems in sugar to make them even sweeter. For decoration or eating, roll the candied stems in sugar, but if you are using them in baking or cookies, just cook the stems in syrup.

Ingredients:

- Angelica stems (as much as you want to candy)
- Equal parts of sugar and water, e.g. two cups of water and two cups of sugar, depending on the quantity of angelica used
- White (granulated) sugar to coat the cooked stems

Method:

1. Peel off the outer layer of the stem
2. Cut the stem into ½" pieces
3. Put the stem in a saucepan and cover with the sugar and water solution
4. Simmer for around 10 minutes until tender and aromatic; the angelica should be translucent and candied
5. Leave overnight for the stems to absorb the sugar solution
6. Freeze or can the candied stems or dry them for storage in a glass jar

Candied Angelica Leaves Recipe

These are another very tasty snack. Blanch older leaves in boiling water for around 10 seconds to tenderize them; younger leaves just need dipping in the mixture below.

Ingredients:

- ½ cup white (granulated) sugar
- 2 egg whites
- 1 tablespoon water
- 1oz young angelica leaves (washed and dried)

Method:

1. Whisk the egg white and sugar until it becomes fluffy and doubles in volume
2. Use a pastry brush to coat the leaves with this mixture
3. Place on a non-stick tray and air dry or dry in a dehydrator

Anise

Also known as aniseed, *Pimpinella anisum*, is a popular flowering herb in the parsley family with a licorice taste. Anise usually refers to the seeds, which are used in cooking while the leaves are used as a herb. Sometimes referred to as aniseed, it has a very distinctive and popular taste.

At a Glance Facts

Annual / ~~Biennial~~ / ~~Perennial~~	
Position:	Full sun
Soil:	Well-drained
Hardiness	None
USDA Zones:	4-9
Sow:	2 weeks after last frost
Harvest:	Early fall

Having been cultivated in Europe, Northern Africa and the Middle East for centuries, it is popular not just for its flavor, but also as an aid to digestion and its ability to help prevent gas and flatulence.

Growing Instructions

As a warm season herb, anise does not like the cold, requiring a frost-free growing season of around 120 days. In cooler areas, late frosts often catch growers out, though young plants can be protected from light frosts with horticultural fleece. Sow seeds no earlier than two weeks after the last frost date in your area.

Anise is a bright green, bushy plant that grows one or two feet tall, and about the same across. The upper leaves are feathery, the lower leaves are broader and in the middle of summer, the plant will produce umbrellas of small, yellow/white flowers.

Unless you are using a lot of anise, one or two plants should be more than sufficient for your needs.

Plant in well-drained, organic matter rich soil in full sun, though anise will tolerate poor soils. It prefers a soil pH of between 6.0 and 6.7, but is relatively tolerant of minor variations in this.

Anise is another plant that does not transplant well, so I recommend planting directly in its final position or in containers. Water in and then keep moist until the seedlings appear. Keep the weeds down and avoid watering in the heat of the day, as this plant is susceptible to scorching damage.

When the flower heads, or umbels, have developed brown seeds, remove the flower head completely before they fall off and scatter the seeds. Allow to dry in direct sun and then remove the seeds from the flower head. Store in an airtight container where they will last for many years. If you wish to plant the seed, and then use it within a year otherwise the germination rate drops significantly.

Plant Care

If your garden is windy, then stake anise to protect it from wind damage. It does not like competition, particularly when young, so keep the base of the plant free from weeds.

Water regularly throughout the growing season, particularly just before harvesting. Anise does not require specific feeding, but does appreciate a dressing of good quality, aged compost in the middle of the growing season.

Culinary Uses

The primary use of Anise is as a flavoring in everything from food and toothpaste, to alcoholic drinks such as ouzo and anisette. Often referred to as aniseed, use the seeds whole or ground in cooking.

Although its name is similar to star anise (*Illicium verum*), the two spices are completely different. It is also not the same as fennel, which does have a very similar flavor (they are from the same family, but not the same species). Fennel is typically served as a vegetable or its leaves and seeds used as herbs, but anise is used purely as a spice.

Health Uses

Anise has a wide range of health benefits and is traditionally used as a diuretic, to stimulate appetite and to calm an upset stomach. It is also used to treat intestinal gas and as a cough expectorant. Aniseed is a common flavoring in anti-acid products because of its natural effects on reducing gas.

Note that if you are allergic to plants such as dill, fennel, cumin, celery, cilantro, asparagus or caraway, there is a chance you may also be allergic to anise. If you have any of these allergies, check with your doctor first before starting to use anise to make sure you are not putting yourself at risk.

Early research is showing that a tea of anise, saffron, caraway, cardamom, licorice, fennel, German chamomile and black seed can help people with allergic asthma to sleep better and reduces their coughing.

Research has also shown that a spray of ylang ylang oil, anise oil and coconut oil is helpful in getting rid of head lice and is as effective as commercial, chemical based products.

Be aware that in some cases, anise can act like estrogen, which means if you are taking any birth control, cancer treatment or have any hormone sensitive conditions, you must not use anise. It has been known to render the birth control pill ineffective and hinder certain cancer drugs from working. Medical advice is that pregnant women should avoid this herb.

Beauty Uses

Anise is not a common ingredient in beauty products as it can cause dermatitis and photosensitivity in some people. It is commonly confused with star anise, which is used in many beauty products.

Pests, Problems & Diseases

Anise does not suffer from any serious diseases or pest problems. Anise oil is currently being researched as an insect repellent and insecticide.

Recommended Varieties

There are few cultivars of anise, the main difference being variegated leaves. Anise is rarely grown as an ornamental plant and is purely grown for its aniseed flavor. The main variety you will find in the shops is *Pimpinella anisum.*

Recipes

Anise Biscotti

These are a delicious Italian biscuit with a hint of licorice. Store in an airtight container for four to six weeks.

Ingredients:

- 4½ cups all-purpose (plain) flour
- 2 cups white (granulated) sugar
- 1 cup butter (softened)
- 1 cup slivered almonds
- ⅓ cup brandy
- 4 eggs
- 4 teaspoons baking powder
- 1½ teaspoons anise extract
- 1 teaspoon vanilla extract
- ¾ teaspoon salt

Method:

1. Preheat your oven to 350F/175C
2. Line two cookie sheets with parchment paper
3. Beat the sugar and butter in a large mixing bowl until light and fluffy
4. Add the eggs, one at a time, beating well after each one
5. In a separate, small bowl, mix the vanilla, brandy and anise extract
6. In a medium sized bowl, sieve the baking powder, flour and salt together
7. Add the dry ingredients and the brandy to the butter mixture, starting with the dry ingredients and then alternating with the brandy mixture, ending with the dry ingredients
8. Stir in the almonds
9. Drop spoons of the dough onto the cookie sheet to form two 13" long strips per sheet
10. Smooth the dough with wet fingers
11. Cook for 30-35 minutes, until firm to the touch and golden brown
12. Allow to cool completely
13. Reduce the oven to 300F/150C
14. Cut the cool logs diagonally into ¾" slices using a serrated bread knife
15. Place the slices onto cookie sheets and back for 10 minutes, turn and back for another 10 minutes until slightly brown and dry
16. Cool and enjoy

Anise Extract Recipe
This is an easy way to make your own aniseed extract to use as a flavoring.

Ingredients:

- 8oz/240ml vodka
- 2 teaspoons/4g dried anise seeds

Method:

1. Put the seeds and vodka into a glass Kilner style jar and seal tightly
2. Shake well, then shake several times in the first three or four days
3. Leave in a cool dry spot for 2-3 months, shaking once a week
4. Strain the seeds off to prevent it from getting stronger or leave the seeds in as you use the liquor to allow the flavor to strengthen

Pastis

This anise flavored aperitif is easy for you to make at home. The recipe takes about ten minutes to prepare and then needs nine days for the flavors to mature before using it. This recipe makes enough for two cups and will store at room temperature for four months.

Ingredients:

- 1½ cups vodka
- ½ cup water
- ⅓ cup white (granulated) sugar
- 10 star anise pods
- 1 tablespoon licorice root
- ½ teaspoon anise seeds
- ½ teaspoon fennel seeds
- ¼ teaspoon whole cilantro (coriander) seeds)

Method:

1. Grind the herbs in a mortar a pestle until they are roughly broken up
2. Pour the vodka into a sealable glass jar
3. Add the herbs, then seal and shake
4. Store in a cool, dark place for 5 days, shaking a couple of times a day
5. Boil the sugar and water to make a light syrup (takes about 7 minutes)
6. Strain the spices out of the vodka using cheesecloth (strain twice if necessary to remove all the sediment)
7. When cool, add the syrup to the vodka and shake well
8. Leave for 4 days for the flavor to develop and then use

Basil

Basil, *Ocimum basilicum*, is a fragrant, warm-weather herb popular in Italian and Mediterranean cuisine. Basil is the main ingredient in the famous Italian sauce, pesto and famously combines well with tomatoes in a mozzarella and tomato salad. Sweet basil is the most commonly grown variety, though there are many other varieties with different properties; some with purple leaves, a lemon flavor or even a licorice flavor in Thai basil.

At a Glance Facts

Annual / ~~Biennial~~ / Perennial	
Position:	Full sun
Soil:	Loamy
Hardiness	None
USDA Zones:	10 and above
Sow:	Indoors – 6 weeks before last frost and outdoors after last frost
Harvest:	Summer onwards

With winter temperatures above 50F/10C, basil is a perennial herb, but in most areas, the winters are too cold, so basil is grown as a tender annual. Once the temperature starts to fall below 50F/10C, the plant can suffer cold damage if the temperature does not kill it. In cooler areas, grow basil in containers and move it inside during the winter months, and then put back outside again once the risk of frost has passed.

Growing Instructions

Although basil grows from seed, many people prefer buying pre-grown plants rather than wait for seeds to germinate. Start seeds off indoors six weeks before the last frost (find your local frost dates here:

http://www.almanac.com/gardening/frostdates). Sow a fresh pot of basil every two weeks for a continuous crop throughout the season. If you are planting outdoors, wait until the soil temperature has reached 50F/10C before sowing in the ground, though if you can wait until the soil temperature reaches 70F/21C you will have a higher germination rate. Basil, being a Mediterranean herb, likes heat and requires plenty of it to grow, which is why many people grow it in a greenhouse.

Position your basil plants somewhere that gets a minimum of 6-8 hours of full sun every day. Plant in a moist, but well-drained soil. Water freely during dry periods as basil suffers very quickly when it dries out.

When flowers start to appear, pinch them out so the plant continues to focus its energy on producing leaves. Plant basil with tomatoes as they complement each other, with basil improving the flavor of the tomatoes and helping to protect them from a variety of pests. Put two to three basil plants around the base of each tomato plant for the best results.

Plant Care

Basil loves a moist soil, but does not like to sit in water. If you live in a warmer area, then mulch around the base of your basil plants to help retain moisture and prevent the soil drying out. This is particularly important if you are growing basil in containers.

When your basil seedlings have six sets of leaves, prune the plant back to just above the second set to encourage bushy growth. Every time a branch gets to six to eight leaves, prune the branch back to the first set of leaves. About six weeks later, pinch off the center shoot as that should stop the plant from blooming too early. However, if more flowers appear, then remove them too so the plant concentrates its energies on producing the leaves you are growing it for.

Basil flowering – pinch out the flowers to maintain leaf growth

Once the plant reaches between six and eight inches tall, start to harvest the leaves. As the temperature reaches 80F/26C, the plant will grow very quickly, producing a lot of leaves. Harvest regularly throughout the summer to encourage the plant to continue to produce leaves, even if you do not need them, they can be stored. To give you an idea of yield, a dozen basil plants will produce somewhere between four and six cups of usable leaves per week in the summer if harvested regularly.

The best way to store basil is by freezing, which prevents the leaves from losing their flavor. Freeze whole sprigs of basil in airtight plastic bags. Although you can dry basil, connoisseurs feel some of the flavor is lost through this method of preservation.

Culinary Uses

Basil has a use in a wide variety of dishes, being particularly popular in Mediterranean, specifically Italian, cuisine. Fresh herbs are put in dishes towards the end of cooking to add flavor, and the dried herb is used either by itself or in a herb mix. It is commonly served with most dishes containing tomatoes and is popular served fresh with Mozzarella cheese and tomatoes. It is used in the popular mixed herbs, bought in stores and used in many dishes.

Health Uses

As you tend to use basil in large quantities, you benefit a lot from the health properties of this herb. It is a good source of many vitamins such as Vitamin C, calcium, potassium and iron and contains Vitamin A, manganese and magnesium in smaller quantities.

Basil has sedative and soothing properties, calming the digestion or nervous system. In herbal lore, it is believed to protect cells from damage and oxidation, acts as an anti-inflammatory and relieves both arthritic and rheumatic conditions. Herbalists use basil to help the symptoms of colds and flu as well as to treat chest and respiratory problems.

Basil also improves the blood flow through your body, eases stomach cramps, helps to protect again heart disease, relieves migraines, increases the production of breast milk and treats tiredness and depression. As it is so frequently used and in such large quantities in the Mediterranean diet, it is strongly linked to the longevity and good health of people native to these areas.

Beauty Uses

As well as tasting good and having a host of health benefits, basil has been used in beauty treatments for thousands of years. Basil is packed full of antioxidants, so is great for fighting the signs of aging and making your skin look younger. It is an excellent skin cleanser, particularly for anyone who as clogged pores or oily skin. Cool some basil tea and apply to your face for an excellent toner. You can make a simple face mask with egg whites, sea salt and basil leaves that will leave your skin looking younger and feeling fantastic.

Basil tightens pores and reduces acne, spots and blackheads due to its antiseptic properties. It reduces the appearance of fine lines and wrinkles as well as soothes the skin, reducing itchiness.

Wet basil leaves placed under the eyes will reduce dark circles and alleviate puffiness.

Pests, Problems & Diseases

Aphids will be the most commonly encountered problem with basil plants, so pick these off by hand if you catch them early on. In more severe infestations, spray them off with jets of water from a spray bottle; though be careful not to damage your plant. In worse cases, remove the infested plant material and destroy it or use a food-safe spray.

Slugs and snails can be a problem, particularly for young plants. Although you can use slug pellets, these risk harming beneficial wildlife. Beer traps are an effective way to catch slugs and snails, though picking the pests off by torchlight at dawn and dusk is by far the most efficient method of removing them.

Fusarium wilt is a disease that often affects basil, most commonly the sweet basil varieties though it does sometimes affect other basil cultivars. Symptoms of this disease include stunted growth, wilting and/or yellow leaves, brown spots on the stem, leaf drop and twisted stems. This fungal infection either comes from the soil or was already in the seeds you grew your basil from. There is no cure for this disease, so remove and destroy the infected plants and do not grow basil or mint plants again in that area for at least three years.

Basil shoot blight or bacterial leaf spot is a bacterial disease that exhibits symptoms of black or brown spots on the leaves and streaks of the same color on the plant. This disease occurs when infected soil splashes onto the plant's leaves from watering or the rain. There is no cure for this disease, but good air circulation can help to minimize the risk of it.

Downy mildew is another disease, evident by yellowing leaves that have a grey, fuzzy growth on the undersides. It occurs most often in wet conditions. Minimize the risk by watering directly to the base of the plant rather than from overhead, ensuring the soil drains well and that there is good air circulation.

As basil plants are very leafy, they often suffer from nitrogen deficiency that exhibits with yellowing or very pale green leaves. This is easy to remedy by regularly feeding your plants with a high nitrogen fertilizer.

Recommended Varieties

There are lots of different basil varieties on the market, check out online seed companies for the widest selection, though you can often find one or two varieties in your local garden stores. Supermarkets will typically stock live sweet basil plants, which are suitable for most culinary uses. Some of these other varieties though, are great variations with some wonderful, fresh flavors.

- Christmas Basil (*Ocimum basilicum* 'Christmas')– has a pleasant, fruity flavor from good-looking plants that grow up to 20" tall. The leaves are glossy green and large, around 2" long and the plant produces purple flowers.
- Cinnamon Basil (*Ocimum basilicum* 'Cinnamon)– – growing up to 30" tall, this cultivar has dark purple flowers and stems, with small, shiny leaves. The plant has a distinctive, pleasant smell and a unique spicy flavor.

- Dark Opal Basil (*Ocimum basilicum* 'Purpurascens') – growing up to 20" tall, this plant is completely purple, adding a splash of color to a salad or can be made into a tasty, colorful pesto.

Purple basil

- Holy Basil (*Ocimum tenuiflorum*) – also known as Tulsi or sacred basil, this is a revered herb in the Hindu religion, originating in India. It has powerful healing and beauty properties, often used as an immune system boosting tea. Growing to just 14" tall, this attractive plant has mottled green and purple leaves.
- Lemon Basil (*Ocimum × citriodorum*) – growing up to 24" tall, this plant has light green leaves up to 2½" long with delicate, white flowers. It has a subtle lemon flavor and is perfect in salads, served with fish or put in iced tea.
- Lime Basil (*Ocimum americanum*) - a short plant, growing up to 16" tall, this variety has small, green leaves and white flowers. It is particularly pleasant when served with fish and chicken.
- Spicy Globe Basil (Ocimum *basilicum) – this tiny plant, growing to just 10" in height, has small* leaves no more than an inch long. It grows as a small, mounded plant and is perfect for containers. The leaves have quite a punch to them and add a nice kick to any soup or sauce.

Spicy globe basil

- Purple Ruffles Basil (*Ocimum basilicum purpurascens*) – growing to a height of around 20" with leaves 2-3" long, this is a feathery version of Dark Opal. It has the same flavor as Dark Opal and is an attractive addition to any garden.
- Sweet Thai Basil ((*Ocimum basilicum var. thyrsiflora*) – a basil popular in Asia, this cultivar has a very distinct, spicy flavor that has hints of clove and anise about it. It has purple stems and flowers with green leaves and growing up to 16" tall. It is an essential component of Asian cuisine and looks great in your herb garden.

Thai basil flowers

Recipes

Basil Pesto

Pesto is a staple of Italian cuisine made with any variety of basil. Typically, chefs use sweet basil, but you can make it with Dark Opal or another purple variety for a variation in color or even make it with a flavored basil. Pesto darkens with air exposure, so cover tightly with plastic wrap to keep it greener for longer.

Ingredients:

- 2 cups fresh basil leaves (packed)
- ⅓ cup pine nuts (alternatively, use walnuts)
- ½ cup extra virgin olive oil
- ½ cup Parmesan-Reggiano or Romano cheese (grated)
- 3 garlic cloves (minced)
- ¼ teaspoon salt
- ⅛ teaspoon ground black pepper

Method:

1. Put the basil and pine nuts into your food processor and pulse a few times to chop

2. Add the garlic and cheese, pulse again a few more times, then scrape down the sides of the food processor
3. With the food processor running, slowly add the olive oil, which helps prevent it from separating. Stop occasionally to scrape down the sides
4. Add the salt and pepper to taste and stir well

Basil Face Cream

A great anti-aging cream that is easy to make. It will store in your refrigerator for up to two weeks in airtight, glass storage jars.

Ingredients:

- ⅓ cup witch hazel
- ⅓ cup fresh basil leaves/stems
- 2 teaspoons shea butter (substitute for another moisturizing butter if you prefer)
- 1½ teaspoons emulsifying wax pastilles
- 1 teaspoon almond or jojoba oil
- 7-10 drops rosehip oil
- Distilled or filtered water

Method:

1. Combine the witch hazel and basil in your food processor and blend well
2. Strain through muslin or a fine sieve into a bowl until you have ¼ cup of liquid, topping it up if required with distilled or filtered water
3. Use a double boiler to melt the shea butter, emulsifying wax and almond oil, heating until smooth
4. Add the basil liquid to the butter mix and stir slowly until well combined

5. Leave to cool and thicken
6. Add the rosehip oil and stir well; add 10 drops if you have very dry skin and 7 if your skin is not dry, the pour into a jar and refrigerate

Bay

Bay, *Laurus nobilis*, is a large evergreen shrub or tree that produces aromatic leaves popular in Mediterranean cooking. It will grow into a tree, given half a chance, but is often clipped into shape such as the well-known ball on a stick shape, making it an attractive addition to any garden. Used fresh or dry, the leaves are great in a wide variety of dishes from soups to stews and more.

At a Glance Facts

~~Annual~~ / ~~Biennial~~ / **Perennial**	
Position:	Full sun to partial shade
Soil:	Well-drained
Hardiness	23F/-5C
USDA Zones:	Evergreen in zones 8-10
Sow:	Not grown from seeds
Harvest:	Any time

Bay grows well in containers, which limit its height, but which does require a bit more care and attention. When planted in the ground, it can reach heights in excess of 23 feet (7.5m) if left unchecked. Bay is a popular topiary tree, usually in lollipop or pyramid shapes, and can be bought with plaited or spiraled stems. It is a great addition to a garden and is a wonderful herb to use in your kitchen.

Growing Instructions

Bay trees are quite hardy, though can withstand much lower temperatures in sheltered positions. When planted in containers, it is more susceptible to cold damage and should be brought indoors or moved to a more sheltered location for winter. When planted in the ground, bay is much hardier and able to tolerate colder weather. In extreme cold weather, fleece the plants as the leaves can be susceptible to cold damage. In USDA Zones 8 and higher, bay is an evergreen plant, though in cooler areas protect it from the cold with horticultural fleece to keep the leaves on the tree.

Bay trees are rarely grown from seed; usually you buy a small plant or a pre-trained plant in a shape such as the popular lollipop. This plant grows well in containers, though you need to be careful not to overwater it as this does cause root damage. Feed container grown bay trees every two weeks from the middle of spring to the end of summer.

Every two years, container grown bays need repotting. This replenishes the compost, aerates the soil and keeps the plant healthy. If you are unable to completely repot it, then remove the top 2-3" of soil every year and replace it with fresh compost. Every two years, lift the plant out of the container and trim the roots by around a third before replacing it and replenishing the compost.

In winter, wrap bubble wrap around the container for pot based plants as the roots can freeze, which causes damage to the plant.

Your bay tree will produce small green/yellow flowers in spring, which are loved by bees. On female plants, small berries will follow this which can be dried and used like the leaves, but have a stronger flavor.

Plant Care

Bay trees will grow quite happily with very little care and attention. Topiary trained trees require trimming with secateurs in the summer months to maintain its shape and encourage a dense habit. Prune any new shoots down to a bud that is facing in the direction you want it to grow. Remember to strip the leaves off any cuttings and dry them!

Shrubs and trees can benefit from pruning in the spring or summer to maintain their shape and prevent them growing too tall. Trim back to a lower leaf or bud on any branches that you want to remove. Once the tree goes over five or six feet, you may want to prune back the top leader to encourage bushier growth and prevent it becoming too tall.

You can collect seeds in the fall, remove the outer fleshy casing and sow immediately. If you buy bay seeds, soak them for 24 hours before sowing. In late summer, you can take semi-ripe cuttings and propagate your tree from these or in early summer, you can take softwood cuttings. Seeds are difficult to germinate and the resulting trees are slow to grow to a harvestable size.

They are rarely grown from seed and most people will buy part grown trees purely because they can usually start harvesting leaves within a year or two at the most.

Regularly feed and water your tree during the summer months, as necessary and harvest the leaves as and when you need them. You can harvest larger quantities of leaf in late summer to dry, or just remove leaves as you use them. Young leaves have a more delicate flavor whereas the older, larger leaves are considered to have the best flavor and are much stronger.

Culinary Uses

Bay leaves have been used as a flavoring for thousands of years, with documented use dating back to the Ancient Greeks. They are popular in American and European cuisine, and in particularly Mediterranean dishes. The leaves are usually added whole to a dish and then removed before serving, though sometimes they are crushed and wrapped in muslin to make a bouqet garni, which provides more fragrance. Ground bay has a much stronger taste and does not need removing from a dish.

Bay leaves are popular in a wide range of other cuisines over the world, including being a key component in Caribbean jerk chicken.

As well as culinary uses, bay leaves were traditionally scattered in a pantry to repel insects including mice, silverfish, cockroaches, flies and meal moths.

Health Uses

Bay leaves contain a good dose of vitamins and minerals, including Vitamins A and C, calcium, magnesium, potassium, iron and manganese.

A decoction of bay leaves (4-5 bay leaves in one liter of water) added to your bath water relieves aching muscles and rejuvenate your body. The same decoction used as a compress helps to heal skin infections due to its antibacterial and anti-fungal properties.

Rubbing bay leaf oil on arthritis inflamed joints helps to reduce the pain. It is also thought that bay leaves help to regulate blood sugar, something that has caught the imagination of research scientists.

According to cutting edge research, bay leaves contain powerful anti-cancer agents (https://www.ncbi.nlm.nih.gov/pmc/articles/PMC3357546/) and can even suppress the growth of leukemia cancer cell lines (https://www.ncbi.nlm.nih.gov/pubmed/12066204). Further research is underway as bay leaves appear to be useful in treating breast cancer (http://connection.ebscohost.com/c/articles/95212867/evaluation-volatile-oil-composition-antiproliferative-activity-laurus-nobilis-l-lauraceae-breast-cancer-cell-line-models) and colon cancer (https://www.ncbi.nlm.nih.gov/pubmed/23859043) too.

A bay leaf tea can also help to reduce the symptoms of coughs and colds by clearing congestion.

Beauty Uses

Although widely used in cooking, bay leaves have their place in beauty treatments. As they are high in flavonoids, antioxidants and tannins, they are bursting with goodness! The leaves have anti-fungal, anti-inflammatory, antibacterial and diuretic properties, so have plenty to offer any beauty regime.

Use bay leaves to give you silky, smooth hair and to help combat dandruff. Boil some leaves in a pan of water for 20-30 minutes until you can smell the bay. Then allow the water to cool and use it before shampooing to make your hair silky and after shampooing to combat dandruff.

This same mixture is also very helpful in combatting lice as it has a strong, bitter flavor that is suffocating for lice. They very quickly leave because they cannot stand the flavor of bay leaf water.

Bay leaf water also makes for an excellent skin toner. It tones and tightens the skin as well as evening out the pigmentation of your skin.

Bay Leaf Acne Busting Face Wash

A bay leaf tea is very good at combating acne and cleansing your skin. Boil four cups of water, and then add six large bay leaves. Simmer for around 20 minutes as the water colors and becomes aromatic.

Remove the leaves and allow the liquid to cool before use. It can be stored and used over several days. Use this bay leaf tea as a natural toner and cleanser as it is quite astringent and helps to clear your skin. Alternatively, add some bay leaves to your facial steamer to open your pores and draw out impurities.

Pests, Problems & Diseases

Pests ignore bay trees most of the time, though you can occasionally find aphids on new growth. It can suffer from the occasional disease, but in general they are healthy, easy to grow plants.

- Leaf Spot – usually caused the wet weather or waterlogged roots, more commonly found in container grown plants. This indicates the compost is depleted of nutrients and needs changing.
- Yellow Leaves – typically caused by nutrient deficiency and more common in container grown trees. The most common causes of this are waterlogged compost or damage from cold weather.
- Peeling Bark – usually found on the lower main stems, this is found after harsh winters and does not have an adverse effect on the tree, other than looking unsightly. If the growth above the damaged area is dead, then cut back to health wood removing the dead wood. Generally, though, this does not cause any long-term problems.

My bay trees, grown from 6" high cuttings

Recommended Varieties

There are not a lot of cultivars of the bay tree, with the main being:

- *Laurus nobilis* 'Aurea' – this bay tree has golden yellow leaves
- *Laurus nobilis f. angustiolia* – the willow leaved laurel has thinner leaves

than the bay tree, though they are still edible

Recipes

Cinnamon Bay Leaf Tea

This simple bay leaf tea is soothing and boosts your immune system. It takes just a couple of minutes to prepare and around 20 minutes to cook. Sweeten with some honey or other natural product if this tea is a bit too bitter for you.

Ingredients:

- 4 or 5 bay leaves (dried)
- 1 whole cinnamon stick or 1 teaspoon ground cinnamon
- 1 liter water

Method:

1. Add the leaves and cinnamon to the water and simmer for around 20 minutes
2. Make a weaker tea by chopping up the bay leaves and steeping them like regular tea

Vegetable Gravy

This is a lovely gravy made from vegetables and whatever herbs you have to hand. This recipe makes four servings and takes 40-60 minutes to make. Thicken by stirring in some mashed potato powder towards the end of cooking.

Ingredients:

- 1 medium carrot (finely chopped)
- 1 celery stick (finely chopped)
- 1 small onion (finely chopped)
- 1 bay leaf
- 18fl oz/500ml vegetable stock
- 2fl oz/50ml sweet sherry
- 1 tablespoon tomato puree
- 1 tablespoon all-purpose (plain) flour
- 1 tablespoon soy sauce
- 1 tablespoon vegetable oil
- 2 teaspoons chopped fresh herbs (a mix of any of parsley, sage, thyme, rosemary)

Method:

1. Fry the vegetables in the oil on a medium heat for 10 minutes until they soften and start to brown
2. Add the tomato puree, stir and fry for a further 30 seconds
3. Add the flour and cook for another minute
4. Pour in the stock, herbs and sherry, stirring well to ensure there are no lumps in the flour
5. Simmer for 5 minutes to thicken
6. Add the soy sauce, stir well and remove from heat
7. Strain through a sieve, return to a clean pan and season to taste

Bergamot

Bergamot, *Monarda didyma*, also known as bee balm due to its popularity with pollinating insects, is a highly aromatic, perennial herb growing up to three feet tall. The leaves, when crushed, have a similar smell to Bergamot Orange and are used in the manufacture of the famous Earl Grey tea.

At a Glance Facts

~~Annual~~ / ~~Biennial~~ / **Perennial**	
Position:	Full sun
Soil:	Loamy, moist, well-drained
Hardiness	Yes to 14F/-10C to 5F/-15C
USDA Zones:	4-9
Sow:	Spring or fall
Harvest:	Flowers – early to late summer Seeds – fall Stems – early summer

In summer, bergamot produces red, tubular flowers that are up to two inches long. It is a member of the mint family and has a citrus smell about it. It is very good at attracting pollinating insects to your garden and, as the flowers have a high nectar content, they attract hummingbirds.

There are many varieties of bergamot, some annual, some biennial and some perennial. Although they share some common elements, they are bred for ornamental purposes with different colored flowers, which can be purple, white, pink or red.

Flowering Bergamot

In the United States, bergamot is sold as Oswego Tea due to its association with the Oswego tribe of Native Americans. The Oswego people introduced bergamot to the settlers when black tea was scarce around the time of the Boston Tea Party. The Oswego tribe also use bergamot for perfume, medicine, food and as a preservative.

When buying bergamot in the United States, ensure you get the right plant as *Monarda fistulosa* is also referred to as bee balm but is a completely different plant and not suitable for making tea.

The first description of bergamot dates back to 1569 by Nicholas Monardes who gave the plant its scientific name. Its name came from the similarity in smell to *Citrus bergamia* (bergamot orange). Originating in the eastern parts of the United States, from Ohio to Maine, bergamot has spread and is now naturalized in the western United States as well as parts of both Asia and Europe.

Grown extensively as an ornamental plant, bergamot is a great herb in the kitchen and has numerous medicinal uses too. This variety and its cultivars are a great addition to any herb garden for its color and ability to attract insects.

Growing Instructions

Bergamot originates from a cooler climate where it would have thrived in the deciduous forests and lived on the banks of streams in moist soil conditions. For best results, plant your bergamot in a soil with plenty of organic matter. It does not like chalky soils and will struggle if the ground is too dry. Plant in a location that gets full sun, though it will tolerate partial shade. If you are growing it in a hot area, then planting it where it gets shade in the afternoon will help the plant to thrive.

This plant does not like a humid environment, so may struggle in warmer or tropical areas. It is also not frost tolerant and in winter can die back and become virtually dormant. However, it will bounce back in the spring. Even when it has died back, there are still small surface rootlets that give off the distinctive bergamot aroma.

In mid to late summer, bergamot flowers and produces seeds once the flowers finish. In the first year, cut the seed heads off to allow the plant to establish itself in the ground. The seeds are unreliable for propagation as they are easily hybridized and so may not be true to their parent. It is best to grow bergamot from cuttings or by dividing the roots in spring. The plant, once established, will send out creeping runners from the main clump that are removed and planted out to propagate this plant. If you want to contain bergamot and stop it from spreading, plant it in a large container sunk into the ground.

Bergamot Flower

Plant Care

Over time, bergamot forms a mat like growth, which is bare in the center as the plant concentrates its energy on the newer growth on the outside. Divide bergamot every three or four years to keep it looking great. In fall, prune to ground level to get plenty of fresh growth in the spring.

In dry conditions, bergamot can suffer from powdery mildew. If it does, remove and destroy any infected growth.

Because it attracts so many insects, it is a great companion for most plants, and in particular the tomato plant. Plant it around your vegetable garden to attract plenty of bees to pollinate your plants.

Bergamot is relatively drought tolerant, but prefers watering regularly. Try to keep the soil damp, but not wet. If the soil gets too soggy in winter, then it can rot the roots, so plant in a freely drained area. Wild plants are much more tolerant of soil conditions than the commercial cultivators that prefer richer soil.

Culinary Uses

Bergamot has a variety of different culinary uses that vary slightly depending on the cultivar. Lemon bergamot, for example, provides a hint of lemon to dishes which regular bergamot does not.

Use the flowers and young leaves in small quantities in salads, with the petals being a particularly colorful garnish for a salad. Both the flowers and leaves are said to bring out the flavor of pork. Fresh leaves are great for giving summer fruit drinks a bit of extra taste and are good as flavorings for jellies or wines.

The leaves and flowers can be brewed into a tea that tastes very similar to Earl Grey. A teaspoon of dried leaves or a half dozen large fresh leaves will produce a great cup of tea.

Health Uses

Where bergamot stands out is in its health qualities. Traditionally, bergamot was a medicinal herb for many Native American tribes who used Oswego tea instead of black tea and for treating sore throats and colds. Steaming the leaves and inhaling the fumes is great for clearing the sinuses. Just be aware that pregnant women should not use bergamot, as it has been known to stimulate uterine contractions.

Bergamot is also a strong antiseptic herb, used as a poultice for skin infections and wounds. Use the tea to treat mouth problems such as infections and gingivitis. Being a natural source of the antiseptic thymol, bergamot is commonly used as an active ingredient in modern mouthwashes.

The flowers have a higher flavonoid level than the leaves and so are valuable as a herb. Amongst its many other uses, bergamot is helpful treating digestive complaints, as a decongestant, a diuretic and to treat fungal or antibacterial infections.

Beauty Uses

Apart from as a scent, bergamot has few beauty uses. The oil is great for treating acne and keeping your hair looking fantastic. You can create a poultice from the leaves and flowers and apply that to your skin to treat skin complaints such as acne. Its strong antibacterial properties make it effective at killing the bacteria associated with this skin complaint.

Pests, Problems & Diseases

Bergamot is a generally hardy plant that does not suffer a great deal from pests and problems. One of the most likely issues will be powdery mildew, but minimize the risk by watering at the base of the plant and ensuring there is sufficient airflow around the leaves.

Stalk borers can be an issue with bergamot and are very difficult to diagnose and treat. As the larva hatch inside the stem, you often do not realize you have stalk borers until the plant starts to wilt, at which point insecticides will not work, as they cannot reach the pests. Check your plant for small holes in the stem, usually surrounded by yellow debris. If you see this, cut the stem and you should see the stalk borer caterpillar inside. You cannot save a wilted plant, which then must be removed and destroyed. Remove and destroy any weeds at the base of the plant as these can also harbor the caterpillars.

Spider mites are another tiny pest that can affect bergamot plants. These are very small and hard to spot, so you usually notice them when tiny spots start to appear on the leaves where the mites are feeding. In serious infestations, you will notice fine webbing on the plant. A liberal application of a fine horticultural oil or insecticidal soap will kill of spider mites, but you have to make sure it gets on the pests. Use a 1% solution of horticultural oil twice at seven to ten day intervals. Usually this will kill off the pests, but you may need to apply the oil again in severe infestations. Remove any weeds and plant debris from around your plants to help reduce the habitat for the mites to hide in.

The symptoms of a thrip infection is similar to those of spider mites, but without the webs. Hold a piece of white paper under your plant and shake it. If you have a thrip infestation, you will see them fall onto the paper. Insecticides are generally not effective in thrip control, but neem oil and insecticidal soaps can be effective if applied early.

Bergamot Seed Head

Recommended Varieties

There are many different *Monarda* varieties, with around fifty or so commercial cultivars available. Most of the bee balm varieties grow wild in the United States. Here are some of the more commonly grown cultivars.

- Eastern Beebalm (*Monarda bradburiana*) – with rich green foliage, lightly toothed leaves and stems tinged with purple, this plant is attractive even before it produces its light purple to lavender blooms. Native to the central and southeast United States, this cultivar produces a lot of nectar and attracts wildlife from hummingbirds to bumblebees.

- Lemon Beebalm (*Monarda citriodora*) – an annual cultivar found wild across much of the United States and Mexico. This plant has long, grassy like leaves with purple to purple/pink flowers on it. The leaves, when crushed, have a lemony scent as they contain citronellol and makes for a good insect repellent. Although known as 'lemon mint', this bergamot is not the same plant as the lemon scented mint.
- Basil Beebalm (*Monarda clinopodioides*) – a native of Texas, Louisiana, Oklahoma and Kansas, this is a woodier variety of bergamot with long, slender leaves around the flower stalks and more oblong shaped leaves at the base. The flowers are a pale purple color.
- Crimson Beebalm (*Monarda didyma*) – a popular ornamental cultivar native to the eastern United States but since naturalized throughout the rest of the country and in parts of Asia and Europe. This plant has lush, green leaves and produces large displays of tubular flower in colors ranging from white to purple, to pink and shades of red through to dark red.
- Wild Bergamot (*Monarda fistulosa*) – a gorgeous cultivar that produces a large amount of pink or lavender flowers with around 20 to 50 to each cluster. The foliage is a brilliant green and there are several different varieties of wild bergamot, each with a slightly different scent.
- Purple Bergamot (*Monarda media*) – preferring a wetter and swampier environment, this variety has square stalks and lance shaped leaves. Although not a true bergamot, it does have the bergamot scent and grows in the eastern United States and Canada.
- Spotted Beebalm (*Monarda punctata*) – also known as horsemint, this cultivar prefers a sandy, well-drained soil. It can be both a perennial and an annual, depending on its environment. The flowers are yellow with purple spots and, sometimes, purple tips to the petals. The leaves are slender and bright green with an aroma similar to thyme. This is a great plant to attract beneficial insects into your garden, particularly predatory wasps.

Recipes

Bee Balm Bread

This tasty bread recipe takes around two and a half hours to prepare and cook.

Ingredients:

- 4 cups flour
- 1 cup warm water
- 1 cup bee balm petals
- ⅓ cup warm water
- 3 tablespoons butter
- 1 teaspoon honey
- 1 egg
- 1 pack of dry yeast

Method:

1. In a large bowl, mix together the butter, honey, water and yeast
2. Add the flour and bergamot petals, stirring as you do
3. Once mixed into a dough, mold it into a ball and place in a greased bowl in a warm place for an hour to rise
4. Dust a surface with flour, then knead the dough for 10 minutes
5. Divide the dough ball into two and shape into two loaves
6. Place on a greased baking sheet, cover with a damp towel and leave for 20-30 minutes to rise
7. Brush the top with an egg wash and sprinkle over some more beebalm petals
8. Bake at 400F/200C for 45 minutes, until the bread is golden

Borage

Borage, *Borago officinalis*, is originally native to the Middle East and has a long history of use. Growing up to two feet tall, borage provides cucumber flavored leaves to use in teas and beautiful, star shaped flowers for use in salads. All of the plant, except the roots, have both culinary and medicinal uses.

At a Glance Facts

Annual / ~~Biennial~~ / **Perennial**	
Position:	Full sun to partial shade
Soil:	Well-drained
Hardiness	Yes to 14F/-10C to 5F/-15C
USDA Zones:	4-9
Sow:	Spring onwards
Harvest:	Any time

Less commonly grown now than in the past, this annual will quickly colonize an area of your garden by self-seeding. The flowers appear in June and July time and will attract butterflies and pollinating insects to your garden.

Growing Instructions

Borage is an easy plant to grow in both soil and containers. It prefers full sun, though tolerates partial shade. Depending on the cultivar, this plant can grow up to three feet tall and needs a rich, moist soil to thrive.

Start borage from seed between three and four weeks before the last frost or plant directly into the soil after the risk of frost has passed. Plant the seeds just below the surface and when germinated, thin the seedlings to 12-24 inches apart.

Generally, borage will grow with minimal assistance from you. It can benefit from being trimmed occasionally to keep it looking neat and growing upright.

Plant Care

Borage is susceptible to wind damage, so is best grown in sheltered areas or staked to prevent it from blowing over. Dig in lots of compost before planting to help condition the soil.

Culinary Uses

Borage has many uses in the kitchen as the flowers, stalk and leaves are all edible. When young and fresh, the leaves have a very mild cucumber taste and are often used in soups, stews, stocks, added to salad or brewed into a tea. Use young leaves in sandwiches instead of lettuce or chopped and added to yogurt or cream cheese. Cooked, borage leaves are a spinach substitute. Although the leaves do have fine white hairs on, these dissolve effortlessly in your mouth and disappear when cooked. The younger leaves are tasty raw, but older leaves should be cooked before eating as they can be a bit tough. Substitute mature leaves for spinach in virtually any dish.

The flowers a very attractive and look great in a salad. They can be candied or frozen in ice cubes and used in drinks.

Use the stems as a flavoring for alcoholic drinks such as Pimms No. 1. The Spanish parboil the stems and then fry them in batter. Eat raw in salads for a nice crunch and or chop the stems up and put in soup.

Health Uses

Borage is a great herb nutritionally, being high in essential vitamins, minerals and phytonutrients. It contains gamma-linolenic acid (GLA) in concentrations somewhere between 17-20%. This is one of the important omega-6 fatty acids and is beneficial in maintaining a healthy immune system, skin and joints. When eaten fresh, borage contains high levels of vitamin C, around 35mg per 100g typically, which is a powerful anti-oxidant, also good for boosting your immune system.

As well as all this, borage is extremely high in vitamin A, containing somewhere in the region of 140% of your RDA, plus it is very high in carotenes, which are strong flavonoid antioxidants that help fight harmful free radicals. Vitamin A is also important for maintaining healthy vision and skin.

The health and nutritional benefits of borage are significant, but it is also high in many minerals such as iron (containing 41% of your RDA), copper, magnesium, zinc, potassium, calcium and manganese. It is also rich in niacin (vitamin B-3) which helps to lower LDL cholesterol in your body. As well as all this, it contains thiamine, riboflavin, folates and pyridoxine which are important for a healthy body.

Eating borage fresh provides you with high levels of essential vitamins and minerals that are good for your health. Borage will help keep you healthy, boost your immune system and help combat the signs of aging.

Brew borage into a tea to help balance the adrenal glands after stress. It strengthens a patient after surgery and in particular when having received steroid treatment.

Making a tea from the flowers and leaves is beneficial in relieving a fever, promoting sweating, reducing the effects of a hangover and promoting lactation. It is a good treatment for chesty colds, dry coughs, bronchitis and sore throats. The tea also has a settling effect on your digestive system, helping treat irritable bowel syndrome and gastritis.

To make borage tea, pick a quarter of a cup of fresh leaves and then pour boiling water over them. Allow to steep for about five minutes, strain and drink or apply to your skin when cool enough.

Crushing the leaves and using them as a poultice helps relieve the pain from stings and insect bites as well as reducing bruising and swelling. It is also very helpful for treating boils and rashes.

Borage Oil

Make a poultice by chopping enough leaves and stems to cover the area you want to treat and then cover with cotton gauze to hold it in place. You can find the hairs on the leaves a little irritating to your skin and in sensitive people these hairs can cause skin rashes. Rinsing the leaves in hot water can soften them and prevent this irritation.

Beauty Uses

Borage oil is a golden yellow in color, and used in beauty treatments where it is called 'starflower oil'. The oil is very hydrating, used to treat inflammation, with very high levels of gamma-linolenic acid (GLA).

As this oil is so high in GLA, it is very hydrating for your skin and ideal to help relieve the symptoms of sensitive skin.

You can use the fresh leaves and flowers to make a nourishing face mask that will hydrate and rejuvenate your skin. Simply mix a handful of borage with an egg white (use a blender), then apply it to your face. Leave it for five minutes before carefully washing off. This is a little bit slimy, but it will make your skin look fantastic.

Pests, Problems & Diseases

Powdery mildew can affect borage, but ensuring these is sufficient spacing between the plants for the air to circulate can minimize the risks of this. Slugs do like to eat the leaves and you can sometimes get infestations of leaf mining flies. Apart from this, few pests or diseases bother borage.

Recommended Varieties

There are several varieties of borage commonly grown, including:

- Common Borage (*Borago officinalis*) – known as starflower, this is the most well-known of the borage species, with blue flowers and black stamens.
- Variegata (*Borago officinalis 'Variegata'*) – a variegated variety with mottled green and white leaves, but still the typical blue flowers.
- Alba (*Borago officinalis 'Alba'*) – known as white borage, this plant has sturdy stalks, stronger than regular borage and provides beautiful white flowers a little later in the season than the blue varieties.
- Creeping Borage (*Borago pygmaea*) – a sprawling plant that produces its blue flowers from late spring through to early fall. This is a short-lived perennial that grows well in USDA zones 5 and higher.

Recipes

Borage Ice Cubes

These are great to serve with drinks, as the flowers are attractive and look good in the ice cubes. A great conversation point for any party. This method ensures that the flower is in the middle of the ice cube otherwise they tend to float to the top.

Ingredients:

- Borage flowers
- Ice cube trays
- Cold water

Method:

1. Half fill the ice cube trays with cold water and freeze
2. Remove from the freezer and tip out the half cubes
3. Place a single borage flower in each division of the tray
4. Put the half blocks back in place and top up with water
5. Freeze until required

Borage Lemonade
A simple lemonade enhanced by the flavor of borage.

Ingredients:

- 2 cups water
- ¼ cup lemon juice
- 2-3 tablespoons white (granulated) sugar
- 3-4 medium borage leaves

Method:

1. Blend the ingredients together in your blender for 30 seconds
2. Strain into a tall glass, garnishing with borage flowers

Candied Borage Flowers
These are very attractive and a tasty, sweet treat.

Ingredients:

- Borage flowers (with a small stem, picked when dry)
- Egg white (beaten)
- Superfine (castor) sugar

Method:

1. Paint the flowers with the egg white using a small paintbrush
2. Dust them lightly with superfine sugar and place on waxed (greaseproof) paper
3. Leave in a warm place or in a cool oven to dry and set

Calendula

Calendula, *Calendula officinalis*, is a popular plant with light yellow to deep orange flowers appearing from early summer until the first frosts. These compact, sun-loving plants are often started inside and planted out after the last frost for an early display of color in the garden.

At a Glance Facts

Annual / ~~Biennial~~ / Perennial	
Position:	Light shade to ull sun
Soil:	Well-drained
Hardiness	Yes to 14F/-10C to 5F/-15C
USDA Zones:	Perennial in 9 and above
Sow:	Spring
Harvest:	Summer to fall

The flowers and leaves are edible and popular in salads and this plant has plenty of uses in your everyday beauty regime. In warmer areas, calendula is a perennial plant, but in most areas, treat it as an annual because it does not survive cold winters and does not appreciate very hot summers either. Grown in a sheltered area, calendula can grow late into the winter so long as the frosts do not get to it.

Growing Instructions

Although calendula likes full sun, it grows well in light shade in warmer climates. It grows in the ground or in containers. Seeds are either planted outside after the last frost, or started off indoors a few weeks before the last frost to plant out early. Typically, the seeds take between five and fifteen days to germinate.

Water well throughout the growing season and dead head spent flowers to encourage a longer flowering season. Fertilize regularly with a liquid bloom feed or any fertilizer that is high is phosphorus. Mulch well to help keep down weeds and prevent moisture loss.

Plant Care

Calendula plants are quite independent and do not need a lot of care. Seedlings will survive light frosts, but if there is a risk of a heavy frost, protect them with horticultural fleece.

Pick the flowers later in the morning after the dew has dried. Check daily for flowers and pick them as soon as you see them as they come and go very quickly. Use the flowers fresh or dry for later use. Pick the flowers regularly to simulate dead heading and encourage the plant to continue to provide more flowers.

Although calendula will self-seed, it does not become a nuisance like some other plants, which rapidly spread and take over an area.

Culinary Uses

Pick the flowers on a dry day, late in the morning. If you are eating them, only pick undamaged flowers and make sure you carefully shake off any insects. Remove the stems and pistils from the flower, reserving just the petals and wash before use.

The flowers have been used in cooking for hundreds, if not thousands, of years. They have a peppery, tangy taste that works well in both soups and salads, though they are versatile in the kitchen. Use the color from calendula petals as a substitute for the more expensive saffron and it is often used to color cheese.

The whole flowers can be dried and then added to stews and soups over winter to help boost your immune system. Add the flowers to breads and preserves to provide a welcome healthy boost over winter.

Pick the young, fresh leaves to use raw in a salad.

Health Uses

Calendula has many health benefits and the petals are used to treat conditions ranging from acne to burns to eczema. Brewed as a tea, this herb helps with sore throats and treating ulcers or urinary tract infections.

Gargling with calendula tea helps your mouth health and treats gingivitis and similar mouth disorders. As an anti-inflammatory, it helps to ease the symptoms of a sore throat and work to cure tonsillitis. The tea is also beneficial for your digestive system, treating stomach ulcers and calming upset stomachs.

With strong anti-fungal properties, calendula treats fungal infections such as athlete's foot and ringworm.

Beauty Uses

Calendula is very popular in beauty treatments due to its anti-inflammatory and antibacterial properties. The extract and oil is a common ingredient in many over the counter beauty treatments.

Use calendula oil to hydrate your skin. It is very good at healing damaging skin and making it look suppler and younger. It is a good oil to use around your eyes where it treats puffiness. The oil is also very good for your scalp and helps to treat dandruff.

With strong anti-bacterial properties, calendula is a very good treatment for acne as it deep cleans the pores and kills the bacteria responsible for acne.

It is excellent for treating dry skin, rashes and reducing the appearance of scars.

As a hair colorant, make a calendula flowers infusion to use on your hair to help provide a brunette or blonde highlight.

Pests, Problems & Diseases

Few, if any, diseases and pests affect calendula. Use calendula as a companion plant because it is good at repelling insects, most commonly paired tomatoes and carrots.

Older plants can suffer from fungal diseases such as powdery mildew. It is better to remove old plants and replace them with fresh ones as they will grow better and produce more flowers.

Recommended Varieties

There are many varieties of calendula with many different colored flowers. Here are some of the most popular and commonly grown cultivars.

- *Calendula officinalis 'Pacific Beauty Mixed Colors'* – has greater heat tolerance than the traditional orange and yellow plants
- *Calendula officinalis 'Sherbet Fizz'*– has softer tones and darker red undersides
- *Calendula officinalis 'Resina Calendula'* – has a higher resin content and is grown specifically for oil and tincture preparation.

An Ornamental Cultivar

Recipes

Honey Calendula Funnel Cake

Funnel cake is divine, but this version is even better, plus you get the health benefits of calendula! It takes about 20 minutes to make this.

Ingredients:

- 1 cup milk
- ½ cup fresh calendula flowers (or ¼ cup dried – just use petals, no stems, leaves or centers of the flower)
- 1 tablespoon white (granulated) sugar
- 1 tablespoon honey
- 1 teaspoon baking powder
- ¼ teaspoon fine seal salt
- 1 egg
- Powdered (icing) sugar and honey for drizzling
- Groundnut oil (or similar for deep frying)
- Calendula flower petals

Method:

1. Fill a pan with 1½" oil and heat to 350F/175C while you make the batter
2. Use a stick blender to mix the milk and flowers until tiny bits of flower are left
3. Add the honey and egg and blend well
4. Add the dry ingredients and continue to mix until thoroughly combined
5. Check the oil temperature and if it is hot enough, start making the cakes
6. Take your funnel and press your finger over the small opening to prevent batter from leaking out
7. Fill the funnel with batter
8. Hold the funnel over the pan and move your finger so the batter can flow
9. Distribute the batter around the pan in the size of the cake you would like, putting your finger back over the hole when you have enough batter in the pan
10. When the edges are golden brown, turn the cake and cook until brown
11. Remove from the pan and drain on a paper towel
12. Drizzle with honey and dust with sugar and calendula petal

Calendula Sugar Scrub

This is a great sugar scrub to use when you shower. Massage it gently into your skin and it will leave your skin feeling soft and glowing.

Ingredients:

- 2 cups white (granulated) sugar
- ½ cup calendula infused sweet almond oil
- ⅓ cup calendula infused coconut oil
- 10-20 drops of essential oil of your choice (for scent – optional)

Method:

1. Mix the coconut oil with the sugar
2. Slowly pour in the almond oil, while mixing, until you achieve the desired consistency
3. Stir in the essential oils
4. Store in a glass jar and enjoy

Calendula Cupcakes

Regular cupcakes but with calendula flowers! Very interesting to make and eat, these attractive cupcakes are bound to be a hit. This makes 16 cupcakes.

Ingredients:

- 3½oz/100g super fine (caster) sugar
- 3½oz/100g self-raising flour
- 3½oz/100g butter (softened)
- 2 eggs
- 2 tablespoons milk
- 2 tablespoons fresh calendula petals

Method:

1. Preheat your oven to 400F/200C
2. Put the flour, eggs, sugar and butter into a bowl and mix until full combined (quicker and easier in a food processor)
3. Gradually stir in the milk (pulse if using a food processor)
4. Fold in 1½ tablespoons of the calendula flowers
5. Spoon the mixture into paper cupcake cases
6. Sprinkle the remaining flowers on top of each bun together with a pinch of sugar
7. Bake in your oven for 15-20 minutes until cooked through
8. Cool on a wire rack

Caraway

Caraway, *Carum carvi*, known as Meridian Fennel or Persian Cumin, is a member of the carrot family. The leaves are aromatic and the seeds are popular in European cooking and can be chewed as an indigestion cure. This biennial herb grows up to two feet tall, with bright green leaves. The long taproot is edible and similar in taste and texture to parsnip.

At a Glance Facts

~~Annual~~ / **Biennial** / ~~Perennial~~	
Position:	Full sun to light shade
Soil:	Well-drained
Hardiness	Yes
USDA Zones:	3-9
Sow:	Spring or fall
Harvest:	In second year

In the second year, caraway will produce umbrella like clusters of pink and white flowers. The seeds will ripen about a month later, just before the plant dies off.

Particularly popular in Easter cuisines in Europe, the seeds are valued for their distinct, pungent flavor in anything from bread to cakes to soups and even cheese. Used for thousands of years in cooking, it was also a main ingredient in love potions as according to tradition, nothing that contains caraway can be stolen.

Growing Instructions

Caraway prefers a well-drained soil that has a lot of rich organic matter in it.

Add sand to improve drainage and make the plant happier. It grows best in a warm location with full sun.

Sow directly into the final location and cover with a ¼" compost. Leave about 6-8" between plants and then thin, removing weaker plants, to leave 12-18" between the remaining plants. Seeds are sown in spring around the date of the last frost, though can be started off indoors (in USDA zones 6 and lower) 2 to 4 weeks before the last frost. Keep the soil moist until the seeds germinate, then keep the soil moderately moist. For early spring plants, plant the seeds in early fall. Because caraway has a long taproot, it does not like being transplanted so if you do start it indoors, plant it out before it gets too big or start it off in a root trainer. It will reseed itself, but can also be propagated from new growth cuttings.

Caraway is slow and unreliable to germinate from seed; so many people will buy pre-grown plants.

Cut the leaves once established to use as required and harvest the seeds in the second year. Remove the seed heads once ripe and place in a paper bag to dry, and then thresh to extract the seeds. Harvest the seeds fully before the first frost.

Use caraway leaves fresh for the best flavor, though you can refrigerate them in a plastic bag for a few weeks. The dried seeds will store for months in an airtight container.

Plant Care

Seeds must not be allowed to dry out, as that will affect the germination and survival rates. Water regular until established and then continue to water often as they can dry out very quickly. Dig in aged compost prior to planting and then side dress with compost in the middle of the growing season.

Avoid getting the foliage wet, so water at the base of the plant or use a drip hose to irrigate your plants. In the fall, cut caraway back and it will re-sprout when spring comes. Plant every year for regular seed harvests.

Caraway is suitable for container growing, though you need a deep container to accommodate the taproot. Feed and water the plant regularly as this herb dries out quickly when grown in pots.

Culinary Uses

Caraway seeds have a strong scent and a very distinctive, aniseed flavor that gives a subtle licorice taste to dishes. The seeds have an earthy taste, with hints of pepper and citrus, though are actually fruit despite being referred to as seeds. In any recipe, you can substitute anise (not star-anise) seeds for caraway seeds, interchange ground caraway seeds for ground cumin and use whole caraway seeds instead of coriander seeds, though adjust the quantities as required to taste.

Rye and soda bread both use caraway seeds as does British seed cake. Use the seeds to flavor everything from sausages to soups and curries, pairing well with pork, cabbage and garlic.

Some ways to try caraway seeds include:

- Add to coleslaw or potato salad
- Put a pinch into any soup or sauce based on tomatoes
- Sprinkled over baked apples
- With any pork roast or pork chops
- In any cabbage dish
- In shortbread cookies

Toasted caraway seeds are great in salads and bread. Simple fry without oil in a skillet for a couple of minutes until the seeds become fragrant. Then remove them from the heat and cool before use. This really brings out the flavor of the seeds.

Use caraway leaves in a similar manner to its cousin, parsley. The root can be cooked and eaten like parsnip or carrot.

Health Uses

The seeds, fruit and oil all have a use as herbal medicines. It helps with digestive disorders, to relieve constipation and to kill bacteria. Do not use caraway oil if you are pregnant as it helps start menstruation and relieve the associated cramps. Nursing mothers traditionally use caraway oil to stimulate the flow of breast milk, though no research has been performed to back up this claim.

Caraway can reduce your blood sugar, which means diabetics must be careful when using this herb. Monitor your blood sugar carefully and adjust your medication as required, but speak to your medical professional and inform them you are using caraway.

Traditionally, caraway was used to relieve bloating and intestinal cramps. It helps with digestion and prevents flatulence. It has strong antimicrobial properties, which supports a healthy digestive system.

Caraway is proving of interest to the scientific community (https://www.ncbi.nlm.nih.gov/pmc/articles/PMC3210012/) as its traditional use to ease digestive problems appears to have a scientific basis. Another use of caraway is to treat Roemhild syndrome where panic attacks and anxiety come from chest pains resulting from a build-up of gas in the intestines and stomach. Chewing caraway seeds seems to be the most effective way to calm the stomach and gain digestive relief.

According to experts, 4oz/100g of seeds will provide you with your recommended daily intake of fiber, which is important for good digestive health. The fiber found in caraway seeds helps to reduce the risk of cancer by binding to toxins found in food and protecting the mucus membrane of your colon. This high fiber content also helps to reduce your levels of the bad cholesterol, LDL.

Caraway tea is excellent for treating coughs, colds, fevers, bronchitis, urinary tract infections and intestinal parasites, while boosting your immune system. The seeds act as an appetite stimulant, particularly in patients undergoing chemotherapy.

Beauty Uses

The carvones and caveols in caraway provide the recognizable taste and are responsible for the anti-flatulent, antioxidant and carminative properties of this herb. The seeds are also high in carotene, lutein, andzea-xanthin and crypto-xanthin, which help to remove free radicals and protect you against aging.

As a spice, caraway is high in Vitamins A, C, and E as well as many of the B complex vitamins. It is also high in vital minerals such as calcium, copper, magnesium, zinc, selenium, iron, manganese and potassium. These are very important for your health.

For hundreds of years, Caraway oil has been used as a poultice to reduce skin inflammation and puffiness. When added to a facial steam, it rejuvenates your skin, reduces wrinkles and acts as a disinfectant. The oil also helps combat skin eruptions such as boils, spots and acne. With strong regenerative properties, caraway oil can help to lighten scars, reducing their appearance.

The essential oil has strong antiseptic properties and treats hair lice, reduces hair loss and improves the texture of your hair.

Pests, Problems & Diseases

Few diseases bother caraway, but as a relative of parsley, it can be attacked by the parsley caterpillar. Remove these by hand and dispose of them.

Recommended Varieties

There are a few named caraway cultivars with 'Arterner' producing many seeds with a good concentration of the aromatic oil. Most caraway varieties found in stores or catalogs are generic, unnamed varieties.

Recipes

Potato and Cheese Fritters

A great way to use leftover potatoes, this taste dish takes 30 to 40 minutes to make and produces enough for a single serving. Serve with your favorite sauce or pickle.

Ingredients:

- 3½oz/100g leftover potatoes (grated)
- 1¾oz/50g Parmesan cheese (grated)
- 1¾oz/50g self-raising flour
- 2 spring onions (thinly sliced)
- 1 egg (beaten)
- 3½ tablespoons water or cold beer
- ½ teaspoon caraway seeds
- Sunflower oil (for frying)

Method:

1. Put the potatoes in a bowl, season with salt and pepper then add the caraway seeds and stir
2. Add the spring onions and cheese, stirring well
3. Add the egg and beer, stirring again, then add the flour and continue stirring to produce a thick batter
4. Heat 1" oil in a deep pan to 350F/180C
5. Lower tablespoons of the batter into the oil and cook for one minute, turn and cook until firm and golden
6. Transfer to kitchen paper to drain using a slotted spoon
7. Season to taste and serve immediately

Caraway Cabbage Soup

Both cabbage and bacon work very well with caraway, making this a tasty soup. Feel free to remove the bacon to make a vegetarian dish. This recipe makes 4 to 6 servings.

Ingredients:

- 14oz/400g potatoes (peeled and diced)
- 12½oz/350g green cabbage (cored and shredded)
- 7oz/200g streaky bacon (cut into ½" strips)
- 1oz/30g butter
- 2 onions (diced)
- 2 garlic cloves (minced)
- 1 bay leaf
- 1 liter chicken/vegetable stock
- 1 tablespoon caraway seeds
- Salt and pepper to taste

Crouton Ingredients:

- 4 tablespoons extra-virgin olive oil
- 2-3 slices country style white or sourdough bread (slightly stale and cubed)

Method:

1. Warm the butter on a medium heat in a large saucepan
2. Cook the bacon for a few minutes until the start to color
3. Reduce the heat to low, add the onion and bay leaf
4. Cook for about 15 minutes, stirring regularly, until the onion is translucent and soft
5. Add the caraway and garlic, cooking for 3-4 minutes, stirring often

6. Add the potatoes and cabbage and cook for another 5 minutes, stirring occasionally
7. Pour in the stock, season with pepper and bring to the boil
8. Simmer for 15-20 minutes until the potatoes are tender
9. Season to taste
10. Either serve as is, or blend some (or all) of the soup to make it smoother
11. Make the croutons by warming the oil on a medium heat and frying the bread cubes until golden
12. Serve the soup hot with the croutons on top

Catnip

Catnip, *Nepeta cataria*, is best known for the effect it has on cats. It is a perennial, dying back in winter and sprouting again the following year, and a member of the mint family. However, it is also beneficial to humans as a soothing tea.

At a Glance Facts

~~Annual~~ / ~~Biennial~~ / **Perennial**	
Position:	Full to partial sun
Soil:	Any, well-drained
Hardiness	Yes
USDA Zones:	3-9
Sow:	Spring
Harvest:	Anytime

Catnip is often grown by cat owners, as most cats will respond to it and act like kittens. When ingested, it acts as a sedative, but the scent drives cats crazy. Catnip has no effect on around a third of domestic cats, which is thought to be a hereditary trait. Many big cats including tigers, lynxes, cougars and leopards are affected in the same way by catnip; though require larger amounts of it.

The organic compound, Nepetalactone, is responsible for producing this amusing response in cats, but this compound is refined and used as a mosquito and fly repellent. Catnip also attracts lacewings, a beneficial predatory insect, as it contains the compound Iridodial.

Growing catnip, contrary to popular belief, does not deter cats from your garden and will in fact attract them. If you do not want the neighborhood cats to get high on your catnip, it should be grown in a cage or otherwise protected from them.

Growing Instructions

Catnip can be tricky to grow from seed as they have tough outer shells. Freeze the seeds overnight, and then put the seeds in a bowl of water for 24 hours. This will stratify the seeds and make them much easier to germinate. Plant out at a spacing of 18-20" between plants. Another way to propagate catnip is by dividing an established plant.

This herb is tolerant of most soil types, but prefers a well-drained soil. It will tolerate partial shade, but does best when grown in full sun.

Like most of the mint family, catnip, is very invasive and spreads quickly if allowed to go to seed. Remove the flower heads after they have flowered to prevent it from taking over your garden.

Harvest the leaves anytime in the growing season and air dry to maintain their scent, though you can use an oven or dehydrator if necessary. A stem tip with between four and eight leaves should be enough for a couple of cats to enjoy. If you are drying catnip, harvest the leaves in early summer, before the plant flowers.

Catnip is a good companion plant as it repels squash bugs, asparagus beetles, aphids and Colorado potato beetles. It also attracts lacewings, parasitic wasps and pollinating insects to your garden, so is worth planting.

Plant Care

Established catnip plants do not need a lot of care and only require watering if grown in containers or during a drought. They do not require feeding during the growing season as this reduces their flavor.

In late spring, pinch the plants back to delay flowering and keep the plant bushy.

Culinary Uses

Catnip is not widely used in cooking. Although catnip makes a good tea and tastes nice when added to a salad, it is mainly used for feline amusement.

Health Uses

The first documented use of catnip medicinally was in 1735 in the General Irish Herbal, where the plant was used to cause sweating, relieve indigestion, to increase appetite and to treat intestinal cramps. Although there is some lore relating to catnip, there is little clinical evidence for the benefits of catnip in humans apart from as an insect repellent.

However, herbalists use catnip to sooth and relax, saying it is particularly good for treating insomnia.

The herbal tea is useful, according to herbalists, for a variety of stomach complaints including soothing ulcers and treating acid attacks by regulating the secretion of both bile and gastric juices.

For women, catnip helps to regulate the menstrual cycle, reduce mood swings and ease stomach cramps.

According to research at the Iowa State University, the essential oil, nepetalactone, found in catnip, is ten times as effective at repelling mosquitos as DEET, which is used in commercial products. Research has also shown that catnip also repels cockroaches.

Beauty Uses

Catnip has a few beauty uses, as it is high in antioxidants. One use is to strengthen your hair and to promote hair growth. Pouring 16oz of boiling water over 2 teaspoons of dried catnip makes an excellent hair rinse to use after washing your hair.

Antioxidants fight free radicals, which cause many of the signs of aging. Drinking a couple of cups of catnip tea every day helps to battle the early signs of aging and keep your skin healthy.

An infusion of catnip acts as an antiseptic and is useful on small wounds where it helps speed up healing.

Pests, Problems & Diseases

The main pest to affect catnip is the local cat population. They will quickly find your plants and settle down on them. Grow indoors or in cages to protect catnip from cats.

Apart from cats, no other pests and diseases effect catnip.

Recommended Varieties

There are, surprisingly, over 250 different varieties of catnip. These are some of the most commonly grown cultivars.

- Common Catnip – the drug of choice for most cats, this plant grows up to three feet tall and produces white flowers. The leaves are heart shaped, gray/green in color, and covered in downy hairs.
- Camphor Catnip – not popular with cats, this cultivar smells of camphor rather than mint. It only grows to about 18 inches tall and the flowers have small purple dots in the throat.
- Greek Catnip – growing up to 18 inches tall, this variety has pink flowers and very pale green, almost white, leaves.
- Lemon Catnip – similar in size to common catnip but with purple spots on the flower. The strong, lemon scent puts off cats, but does make for a particularly lovely tea.

Recipes

Cat Treat Crackers

Catnip is not used much in cooking for humans, but you can make some special, home-made treats for your cats.

Ingredients:

- ¾ cup plain flour
- ½ cup whole wheat flour
- ½ cup yogurt
- 3 tablespoons vegetable oil
- 2 tablespoons dried catnip
- 1 tablespoon honey
- 1 egg

Method:

1. Preheat your oven to 350F/175C
2. Mix both flours and the catnip in a bowl
3. Stir in the egg, honey, oil and yogurt
4. Mix well and then press out the dough on a floured surface
5. Cut into cat mouth sized treats
6. Bake on a greased cookie sheet for 15 minutes until golden brown
7. Store in an airtight container in your refrigerator for a week or freeze for three months

Catnip Calming Tea

This tea uses catnip and peppermint to help you relax and to calm your nerves. Strain the herbs out before drinking the tea.

Ingredients:

- 1 heaped tablespoon of chamomile flowers
- 2 teaspoons catnip
- 2 teaspoons peppermint

Method:

1. Mix the herbs together in a bowl or cup until well combined
2. Pour boiling water over the herbs
3. Steep for 4-5 minutes
4. Strain and sweeten, if required, with honey

Chamomile

Chamomile has been popularized as a calming herbal tea. It is grown as single plants or can be planted en-masse to create an attractive, chamomile lawn. Non-flowing cultivars are best for a lawn, but the flowering varieties are better for culinary and health use.

At a Glance Facts

Annual / ~~Biennial~~ / **Perennial**	
Position:	Sunny
Soil:	Light, well-drained
Hardiness	Fully hardy
USDA Zones:	3-9
Sow:	April/May
Harvest:	Summer

There are two types of chamomile, Roman and German. The former is a perennial plant and the latter is an annual that self-seeds so much so that you will never be rid of it and most people assume it is a perennial.

German chamomile, *Matricaria chamomilla*, is native to Europe and western Asia. This sweet smelling plant grows to a height of one or two feet. The flowers are very similar to those of a daisy, but have the distinct, chamomile scent.

Roman chamomile, *Chamaemelum nobile*, grows to about a foot high and has flatter, thicker leaves than its German cousin. The flowers are similar to German chamomile, though there are non-flowering cultivars such as 'Treneague' and some double flowered varieties. Roman chamomile is native to western Europe, growing as far north as Northern Ireland.

Growing Instructions

Named cultivars, i.e. those grown for ornamental purposes, do not grow true when started from seed, so you will need to buy ready grown plants. Roman chamomile is started from seed or grown from root division or cuttings while German chamomile will grow from seed.

Sow seeds in late spring into containers and cover over with a thin layer of vermiculite. Germinate on a sunny windowsill or in a heated propagator. When the seedlings are big enough to be safely handled, transplant them to individual pots.

Once they have developed a strong root system, plant your chamomile into a well-drained, light soil in a sunny location. Plants in chamomile lawns should have around 4" of space between them. Hand weed until the chamomile has established itself.

Plant German chamomile early in the spring where they will germinate in around 7-10 days. Germination starts at a temperature of about 45F/7C and the young seedlings are able to withstand mild frosts, but need fleecing in hard frosts. The seedlings grow slowly initially, but after four or five weeks will have a growth spurt. Seedlings up to two inches tall are easy to transplant, but once they grow bigger than this they rarely survive being moved.

Plant Care

Water chamomile regularly, particularly when grown in containers. Clip it throughout in the growing season to maintain a compact, bushy aspect, otherwise it has a tendency to get leggy.

If you are growing chamomile in containers, then raise the pots up onto pot feet to prevent excessive moisture rotting the plant during winter.

Chamomile lawns benefit from occasional treading or rolling to keep the surface even.

Culinary Uses

Tea is one of the most popular uses for chamomile, but it has a multitude of culinary uses from desserts to savory dishes to cocktails! Top chefs such as Mina Pizzaro at Juni in Manhattan infuse chamomile flowers into ice cream for a sweet flavor with floral notes.

It has a very delicate flavor and can be infused into a simple syrup, which can then be used on fruit. Infused into cream, it provides a gentle flavor. Although most commonly used as a tea, you can use chamomile flowers in cookery, though they have not gained the popularity of many other herbs.

Health Uses

Chamomile is best known for its medicinal properties. It is considered the European counterpart of ginseng for its healing properties. German chamomile is probably the most researched medicinal herb in Europe, though its cousin, Roman chamomile, has been less researched. Use it for rinses and compresses for treatment of skin, mouth and gum irritations or inflammations as well as for haemorrhoids.

A tea of two or three grams of chamomile per cup of water is excellent for peptic ulcers and intestinal tract inflammations. The tea is probably best known for its ability to promote sleep, particularly in children.

German chamomile is the most used of the chamomile family and, so far, over 120 different chemical components have been identified in it. It is antimicrobial, antispasmodic and anti-inflammatory as well as mildly sedative. Through a breeding program set up in the 1970s and 1980s, scientists have bred more stable varieties of German chamomile for commercial growing with higher and more consistent levels of the active components.

Bisabolol, one of the main active components in chamomile, has strong anti-inflammatory properties. Drinking chamomile tea helps to relax the lining of the digestive track and calm upset stomachs. Remember when you are brewing the tea to cover the cup, as many of the active compounds are lost in the steam.

The cooled tea can be used as a mouth wash to help calm irritated gums and sooth mouth ulcers. Mixing chamomile with aloe vera also makes for an excellent cooling spray for treating sunburn.

Beauty Uses

As a strong anti-inflammatory, chamomile is excellent at reducing skin inflammation and helping wounds to heal, which it has been used for centuries to do. A chamomile tea compress will help reduce the appearance of scarring, whether from acne or wounds, though use fresh or dried flowers rather than purchased tea bags. Steep a tablespoon of dried chamomile flowers in 8oz of water for 5 minutes, allow to cool until it is a comfortable temperature and then soak a cloth and place on clean skin for 10-15 minutes.

If you have blonde hair, strong chamomile tea, used after shampooing as a rinse, can help to brighten it.

Chamomile tea bags have another use once you have made tea with them. Cool them and use them as eye compresses to reduce dark circles under your eyes and calm puffy or tired eyes.

Pests, Problems & Diseases

Not many pests and diseases affect chamomile, though a lack of water weakens this plant. Aphids may attack fresh growth and plants can occasionally suffer at the hands of mealybugs or thrips. Use chamomile as a companion plant because it has a strong smell that repels many pests.

Recommended Varieties

There are a number of chamomile varieties on the market, though most people just grow Roman or, more commonly, German chamomile. The variety 'Treneague' is popular to make a chamomile lawn as it has strong scent, does not flower and only grows to about 4" tall.

Recipes

Strawberries and Chamomile Cream

A nice take on the traditional strawberries and cream with the delicate flavor of chamomile infused into the cream.

Ingredients:

- 2 pints fresh strawberries (hulled and quartered)
- 1 cup heavy cream (divided)
- 3 tablespoons sugar (divided)
- 2 chamomile tea bags or 2 teaspoons dried chamomile flowers

Method:

1. Heat ½ cup of cream over a medium heat until the edges start to bubble
2. Remove from the heat and add the chamomile, stirring it in
3. Leave for 20 minutes to steep, then transfer to a medium sized bowl, cover and chill for 2 hours until cold
4. At the same time, toss the strawberries in 2 tablespoons of sugar until coated and then leave to let juices form
5. Strain the cream through a fine mesh sieve into another bowl
6. Add the rest of the cream and 1 tablespoon of sugar
7. Beat, using an electric mixer, until soft peaks form
8. Divide the berries between 4 to 6 bowls and cover with cream

Chamomile Shampoo Recipe

A very simple recipe for a shampoo that reduces scalp irritation, fights dandruff, strengthens your hair and makes it look glossy and shiny. Store the finished shampoo in an empty, washed out shampoo bottle and use it instead of your usual shampoo. Store in your refrigerator between uses. This will last for 4 to 6 weeks.

Ingredients:

- ½ cup distilled water
- ¼ cup unscented liquid castile soap (baby wash is ideal)
- ½ tablespoon vegetable glycerine
- ¼ teaspoon jojoba oil
- 5 chamomile tea bags
- 7 drops chamomile essential oil (can substitute for lavender if you prefer)

- 4 drops lemon essential oil

Method:

1. Place the chamomile tea bags in a bowl
2. Boil the water and pour over the tea bags
3. Steep for 20 minutes, then remove the tea bags
4. Once cool, pour the tea into a shampoo bottle using a funnel
5. Add the liquid soap and the vegetable glycerine, then drip in the essential oils
6. Shake gentle to mix the ingredients together
7. Store in your refrigerator and use as required

Chervil

Chervil, *Anthriscus cerefolium*, is a biennial herb with a mild aniseed flavor, used in potato, fish and egg dishes, salads and is a main ingredient in 'fines herbes'. If cooked for too long, the flavor of chervil is lost, so always add it right at the end of cooking.

At a Glance Facts

Annual / Biennial / ~~Perennial~~	
Position:	Partial to full shade
Soil:	Any, well-drained
Hardiness	Yes to 23F/-5C to 14F/-10C
USDA Zones:	3-8
Sow:	Spring to summer
Harvest:	Summer to fall

Chervil originated in the Caucasus area on the border of Asia and Europe, between the Caspian and Black seas. There is little recorded history of this herb, particularly from a medicinal standpoint, although its culinary use dates back hundreds of years. It is thought that people preferred stronger smelling and tasting herbs and chervil was just a little too delicate to be popular.

Known as the 'Lenten Herb', chervil has long been associated with the Christian festival of Lent due to its restorative and blood cleansing properties. Christians then and now use it throughout Lent and make a special chervil soup for Maundy Thursday. As it smells and tastes similar to myrrh, brought by the wise men to the baby Jesus, it became firmly linked to the Christian Easter celebrations.

This herb is considered by some to be a biennial, though is perhaps better classified as a hardy annual. A late sowing in August will generally keep you supplied with fresh chervil throughout the winter and into spring.

Chervil seeds do not store well and germination rates from seeds more than a year old is very low. Buy fresh seeds every year or allow your chervil plants to self-seed once they have flowered.

Growing Instructions

Plant chervil outside anytime from March through to August. Sow in ½"/1cm deep trenches and cover with soil. Leave 12"/30cm between rows. It can take up to three weeks for the seedlings to push their heads above the surface. Once they are big enough to handle, thin out to one plant every 6"/15cm.

Alternatively, start the seeds out in pots and plant out when large enough to handle. Chervil will grow in containers; though do not put too many plants in a single container.

Around nine weeks after sowing, the young leaves will be ready to harvest. Use fresh as required or freeze for use over winter. Once the plant flowers, the leaves are no longer suitable for use.

Chervil is a good companion to both broccoli and lettuce and best planted close to them. It will help to repel aphids from other plants and grows well with most other shade tolerant herbs. Plant chervil near radishes to give them a spicier flavor.

Plant Care

Chervil is an easy to maintain herb, preferring a cool, shady spot in your garden. Although it will grow in full sun, it runs to seed if it gets too hot, too dry or has too much sun. Since the leaves are unusable after flowering, plant chervil in shady spots to delay flowering as long as possible.

This herb requires regular watering, particularly during hot, dry spells. It will grow over winter, though needs protecting from the frost with cloches.

Chervil is often mistaken for a perennial because it is a prolific self-seeder. To prevent chervil taking over your garden, remove some of the flower heads, leaving a few to seed and provide new plants.

Culinary Uses

Chervil looks very similar to its relative, flat-leaf parsley and has a mild flavor, somewhere between tarragon and parsley with a hint of anise or licorice. Combined with chives, tarragon and parsley, it makes 'fine herbes', which is commonly used in French cooking.

Add chervil to an omelette or garnish scrambled eggs with it. It is also popular in salads where it provides a gentle kick. It is a key ingredient in béarnaise sauce, usually served on steak. It enhances other foods such as white fish and chicken.

Chervil wilts and loses its flavor in cooking, so add it right at the end of cooking, just before serving to retain its flavor.

Some of the common uses of Chervil in the kitchen include:

- Use the young leaves in soups, salads and stews
- Substitute for parsley to flavor fish and chicken
- Substituted for tarragon due do the similarity in flavor
- Often used in sauces such as ravigote and béchamel

Chervil has a very delicate flavor and one that is certainly to be enjoyed. It is worth growing and using, but remember to add it at the end of cooking so it retains its lovely flavor and aroma.

Health Uses

Chervil contains high levels of Vitamins A and C, as well as a number of B vitamins. It is also a good source of minerals including iron, calcium, selenium, potassium, manganese and copper, amongst others.

Herbalists use this herb to treat a variety of different ailments, including high blood pressure. Over the years, its uses have ranged from a diuretic to a digestive aid and an expectorant. Many people take chervil as a tea; though make sure you cover the cup while brewing to retain the volatile oils.

Beauty Uses

Chervil is not commonly used in beauty treatments, though it is used as a poultice to reduce cellulite. The cooled tea is very good for bathing tired or irritated eyes. Wet a cotton wool ball in cool chervil tea and then place for ten minutes on a closed eye.

Pests, Problems & Diseases

One of the main problems you will encounter is aphids on new growth. Remove these by hand or use organic, food safe sprays in serious infestations. Slugs and snails can also be a problem, particularly with young seedlings.

The main problem with chervil is that it bolts if it gets too hot and dry. There are some bolt-resistant cultivars on the market now, but sowing at the right time of year, in a cool spot of the garden and keeping the plant moist will help prevent flowering too early.

Recommended Varieties

There are two main varieties of chervil, common chervil and a variety with curled leaves. Root chervil is a relative of common chervil and the roots are eaten, which are similar to carrots or turnips. Due to its small comparative yield, root chervil is not commonly cultivated any more.

Wild Chervil

Wild chervil is not cultivated or commonly used in cooking. Although a relative of common chervil, it has a more unpleasant taste and is easily confused with poisonous plants such as hemlock and giant hogweed. Wild chervil is native to the UK and Europe, where it is a common sight in hedgerows and by rivers. In many areas of the United States it is designated an invasive species and the sale of it is banned.

Recipes

German Maundy Thursday Chervil Soup

This recipe is for a chervil soup traditionally eaten on Maundy Thursday in Germany.

Ingredients:

- 1¾ pints/1 liter vegetable/chicken stock
- 3½fl oz/100ml heavy cream
- 2oz/60g fresh chervil (finely chopped)
- 2 shallots (finely chopped)
- 1 large potato (peeled and finely diced)
- 2 tablespoons unsalted butter

Method:

1. Melt the butter in a large pan on a medium to low heat
2. Add the shallots, cooking for around 10 minutes until soft
3. Add the potato and cook for 5 minutes, stirring occasionally
4. Add the stock and bring to a simmer
5. Simmer for 10-12 minutes until the potato is tender
6. Remove from the heat and stir in the chervil
7. Blend until smooth
8. Return to the heat and add the heavy cream
9. Reheat on a low heat, careful not to let the soup boil
10. Season to taste with salt and pepper
11. Serve immediately garnished with chervil leaves

Chives

Chives, *Allium schoenoprasum*, is a low maintenance perennial herb in the *allium* or onion family. The leaves have a distinct, but not too strong onion taste and are great in salads. In the UK, cut fresh chives are added to potato salad and to egg mayo sandwiches. Although the leaves are the most commonly used part, the attractive pink flowers are edible and often used as a garnish on salads.

At a Glance Facts

~~Annual~~ / ~~Biennial~~ / **Perennial**	
Position:	Full sun or partial shade
Soil:	Well-drained, moist
Hardiness	Yes, down to -4F/-20C
USDA Zones:	3-10
Sow:	Early spring
Harvest:	Summer

Chives are native to China, where they have been used for over 5000 years. Marco Polo is credited with bringing this herb back to Europe from his travels in the Middle Ages. It now grows wild all across Europe and is popular to grow at home. During the Middle Ages, bundles of chives were hung in houses to keep disease and evil away.

Growing Instructions

Seeds are sown early spring on the surface of containers filled with seed compost. Cover them with a thin layer of vermiculite, then water and put somewhere warm to germinate.

Grow chives in containers or plant out into well-drained, moisture retentive soil in a sunny or partially shaded position in your garden. Chives will typically grow up to a foot tall in clumps.

If you want a faster harvest, then buy ready-grown plants. Chives easily grow on the kitchen windowsill where they are cut as needed.

Plant Care

Chives are very easy to maintain, requiring little attention from you. During long dry spells, water them well, otherwise give them plenty of water and they will perform well throughout the growing season until they die back in fall.

Every three years, lift and divide your chives to stop them becoming congested and to rejuvenate the plant. In containers, either move them to a larger container or divide the root ball into two and plant in separate pots.

Remove the flowers when they start to fade so that the plant remains productive for longer. As this is a perennial, you do not need to allow the plant to go to seed. Cut the leaves as you need them with a sharp pair of scissors at the base of the plant. The more you cut a chive plant, the more leaves will be produced.

Chives are best fresh, though you can freeze them. People commonly freeze chives in ice cube trays half filled with water, though these are only good for cooking.

Store the unwashed leaves in your refrigerator in a plastic bag, ideally in the door where they will last for a few days, if not a week.

Culinary Uses

Chives tend to lose their flavor when they are dried, so use them while they are fresh. This is one of the ingredients of the French, 'fines herbes' together with tarragon, chervil and parsley.

Some of the common culinary uses of chives include:

- Added to scrambled eggs
- Mixed with cottage cheese
- Thrown onto salads
- Mixed in with mayonnaise
- Added to plain yogurt to become a salad dressing
- In stews or soups
- To add flavor to omelets or mashed potato

Due to its delicate flavor, chives are popular in uncooked food where they provide a gentle onion flavor, without the over-powering scent and taste that comes from raw onions. Although used in cooking, chives do lose their flavor if cooked for too long so add just before serving.

Health Uses

Chives are a very mild, if not the mildest, member of the onion family and have high levels of vitamins A and C. They also contain good levels of vitamins B1 and B2 as well as the minerals iron, calcium and phosphorus.

Studies are underway on chives for their ability to reduce the risk of cancers, including stomach, colon and prostate. Regularly eating members of the *allium* family helps to reduce the risk of these cancers. The Journal of the National Cancer Institute published a paper showing that men who ate plenty of vegetables from the onion family had the lowest risk of prostate cancer, particularly when it was localized. Research continues as scientists work to develop treatments for cancer from this intriguing family of plants.

As they contain vitamin K, chives are helpful in maintaining bone strength and density. This herb also contains choline, which is a nutrient aiding memory, sleep and learning. Choline also works to help absorb fat, reduce chronic inflammation and maintain the structure of cellular membranes. *Allium* vegetables increase the body's production of dopamine, which helps to boost your mood and combat depression.

If you have an allergy to any member of the *allium* family such as onions or garlic, then you should be careful about eating chives as they may trigger an allergic reaction. Eating an excessive amount of chives can upset your stomach, though using at the usual quantities should have no negative effects.

Beauty Uses

Like other *alliums*, chives have a natural antibiotic effect and are beneficial for your skin, hair and scalp.

Some experts believe that chives will help slow hair loss and boost hair growth as it helps stimulate blood flow to the scalp. While research has yet to be published, herbalists from the past always recommended garlic, chives and onions for hair growth.

You can use chives on your hair by either adding chive oil to your shampoo or mashing or pureeing chives and applying them directly to your hair of scalp. It helps strengthen your hair and stop it breaking while giving your hair a glossy shine and body.

Make a simple overnight scalp mask by putting a small handful of fresh chives in boiling water for 30 seconds. Remove the chives and cool them in iced water for a couple of minutes. Then drain then, squeeze out water and puree them with ½ cup of extra virgin olive oil. Strain the mixture and use the chives or the oil as a face, scalp or hair mask. Put on your hair an hour before bed, massage it in and then put on a shower cap and go to bed. In the morning, wash your hair to remove the scalp mask and repeat for a week or two for the full benefit.

Many people use this treatment to help itchy scalps and to stop hair loss.

A quicker version involves juicing some chives and massaging the oil directly into your scalp before leaving it for an hour then washing it off.

Pests, Problems & Diseases

Chives, generally, do not suffer from many problems. Occasionally you will find aphids on chives, but this is a rare occurrence due to the shape of the leaves.

The fungal disease, leek rust, can occur during long, wet spells. This causes bright yellow spots to form on the leaves. Mild infections do not harm your plant, so just remove and destroy infected leaves. In serious infections, the leaves will shrivel. Unfortunately, once established, there is no treatment for rust. Leave plenty of space between plants for air circulation to help prevent rust becoming a problem and remove and destroy infected leaves as soon as you spot them. If your chives are badly infected, then remove the plants and destroy them. Avoid growing any member of the *allium* family in the same area for at least three years to prevent re-infection.

Recommended Varieties

There are a few varieties of chives cultivated, though common chives are the most often cultivated variety. Some of the other varieties include:

- Black Isle Blush – very similar to common chives but with light mauve colored flowers with a pink center
- Forescate – pale pink flowers and leaves with a hint of garlic to them
- Fine Leaved – has thinner leaves and a milder taste than common chives
- Garlic/Chinese Chives (*Allium tuberosum*) – a white flowered cultivar with leaves that taste of garlic. Deadhead this variety as it is a prolific self-seeder. The flowers are eaten in the bud stage and popular as a stir fry ingredient in China
- Giant Siberian Chives (*Allium ledebourianum*) – often used in flowerbeds, this is much taller than the common chive and has distinct, blue green foliage. It has a rich, chive taste and is strongly recommended by gardeners

Recipes

Blue Cheese Potato Salad

This is a great variation on the normally potato salad, but feel free to change the cheese for your personal favorite.

Ingredients:

- 2lb/900g red potatoes (cut into chunks)
- ¾ cup sour cream
- ½ cup blue cheese (crumbled)
- ½ cup celery (diced)
- ½ cup red onion (diced)
- ½ cup fresh chives (chopped)

- 2 tablespoons apple cider vinegar
- 2 tablespoons whole milk
- ½ teaspoon fine sea salt
- ¼ teaspoon ground black pepper

Method:

1. Put the potatoes in a pan, cover with water and boil for 8-10 minutes
2. Drain the water and put the potatoes in a large bowl
3. Allow to cool until warm, not hot
4. Add the celery, chives and onion, tossing well
5. Whisk the sour cream together with the milk, salt and pepper
6. Stir the cheese into the sour cream mixture
7. Pour the dressing over the potatoes
8. Cover and chill until ready to serve

Cheesy Bacon Muffins

These are a lovely snack, great with soups or on their own. Feel free to leave out the bacon to make a vegetarian version. This recipe takes about 45 minutes to make and produces 12 muffins.

Ingredients:

- 6 slices of thick bacon
- 1 egg (beaten)
- 2 cups all-purpose flour
- 1 cup sharp Cheddar cheese (shredded)
- ½ cup milk
- ½ cup vegetable oil
- ½ cup cream of mushroom soup
- ⅓ cup Parmesan cheese (grated)
- 1½ tablespoons white (granulated) sugar
- 4 teaspoons dried chives
- 2 teaspoons baking powder
- 1½ teaspoons garlic powder
- ¼ teaspoon salt

Method:

1. Cook the bacon until evenly brown, then crumble and put to one side
2. Preheat your oven to 400F/200C
3. Lightly grease a 12 hole muffin pan
4. In a medium bowl, mix the egg, soup, oil and milk

5. In a large bowl, mix together the rest of the ingredients
6. Add the wet ingredients to the dry ingredients, and stir together to just moisten
7. Divide the batter evenly between holes in your muffin pan
8. Bake for 20-25 minutes until a toothpick inserted into a muffin comes out clean

Glazed Parsnips and Carrots

This is a delicious dish, ideal for any holiday meal. Substitute turnips for parsnips if required. It takes about 35 minutes to make and produces enough for 8 servings.

Ingredients:

- 4 large carrots (cut into 3" x ½" pieces)
- 4 large parsnips (cut into 3" x ½" pieces)
- ¾ cup chicken or vegetable stock
- ¾ cup orange juice
- ¼ cup butter
- 3 tablespoons fresh chives (chopped)
- 2 tablespoons lemon juice
- Salt and pepper to taste

Method:

1. Melt the butter in a large skillet on a medium heat
2. Cook the carrots and parsnips for 8-10 minutes until the edges are lightly browned
3. Stir in everything except the chives
4. Bring to the boil, reduce the heat and cover
5. Simmer for 10-12 minutes, stirring often, until the liquid has reduced to a syrup
6. Season to taste, sprinkle with chives and serve

Zucchini and Chive Dip

This is a delicious dip with the combination of zucchini and chives working very well. Serve with vegetable batons or chips. This recipe makes 20 servings and takes about 1¼ hours to make.

Ingredients:

1. 8oz cream cheese (softened)
2. 1 cup zucchini (shredded)
3. 3 tablespoons milk
4. 3 tablespoons fresh chives (chopped)

5. 1/8 teaspoon salt

Method:

1. Mix the milk and cream cheese until well blended
2. Add the chives, salt and zucchini and stir well
3. Refrigerate for 1 hour before serving

Comfrey

Common comfrey, *Symphytum officinale*, is a very popular plant with gardeners as it makes a very potent liquid fertilizer, but is also highly prized for its healing properties.

At a Glance Facts

~~Annual~~ / ~~Biennial~~ / **Perennial**	
Position:	Full sun to partial shade
Soil:	Moist, but well-drained
Hardiness	Fully hardy
USDA Zones:	3-9
Sow:	Spring
Harvest:	Late summer/early fall

Common comfrey is extremely difficult to get rid of once established, but non-invasive cultivars are available such as Bocking 14. If you are planning on growing this at home, always buy a non-invasive cultivar otherwise comfrey will quickly take over your garden.

Use the leaves of the plant to make a liquid fertilizer, as they are high in nitrogen, phosphorus and potassium, plus the dead leaves make for an excellent mulch or leaf mold. Many gardeners will have some comfrey growing in their garden to make a liquid feed.

Comfrey will grow anywhere from three to five feet tall and spread anywhere from two to four feet wide.

Comfrey, a relative of borage, is found growing in the wild, usually in damp locations, often by streams and rivers. The flowers appear in late spring and early summer and the leaves are harvested several times throughout the growing season. It will die back in late fall and grow back in the spring.

Growing Instructions

Start comfrey seeds indoors or sow them directly in their final location. Sow from March to June, bearing in mind that comfrey does require a winter chill to germinate properly. It will often be two years from sowing before you see any germination, which is why most people start from a pre-grown plant or from root cuttings.

Plant root cuttings, which are two to six inch pieces of root, horizontally between two and six inches deep. In clay soils, plant closer to the surface, and in sandy soils, plant deeper. You can buy crown cuttings, which grow faster than root cuttings, but they are a little bit more expensive.

Common comfrey is a very vigorous plant and will grow in containers, but does not achieve its full potential. Because it is such a difficult plant to get rid of once established, most people grow the Bocking 14 variety which is less invasive. Comfrey does not require a lot of maintenance, but regular feeding and mulching helps to produce a stronger plant. Remove the flowering stems in the first year for more leaf growth in the second.

Plant Care

Comfrey roots, used in ointments and skin creams, can be harvested throughout the year, but it is best to dig them up in early winter. The leaves can be cut in early summer and then again in early fall. Avoid cutting after September to allow the plant to conserve its energy for winter.

When handling comfrey, wear gloves as the stems have stiff hairs on which can cause irritation for some people. I would recommend wearing long sleeves too as even brushing against the leaves could irritate the skin.

Once it has established itself, comfrey is self-sufficient. Every year the plant grows larger and the root system becomes bigger and denser. Once established, comfrey is extremely difficult to get rid of because the roots are very brittle and snap when you try to dig it up. The plant will then grow from each piece of root. Comfrey has a very deep taproot, so is very drought tolerant. This makes it extremely hard to remove, and I have dug comfrey up with roots three feet long. Covering comfrey in black plastic, cardboard and manure, which would normally keep down weeds does not work as comfrey just keeps on growing regardless!

Use bruised comfrey leaves in your compost heap to help with decomposition and speeding up the composting process. The leaves are also suitable for adding to leaf mold where they will help make the final leaf mold more nutritious and speed up the decomposition process.

A popular use for comfrey leaves is for lining the bottom of runner bean and potato trenches. The leaves break down and provide a potassium rich fertilizer for your beans and potatoes. Use the leaves as a mulch on the soil surface to help control weeds and provide nutrients to your plants.

Culinary Uses

Comfrey has no culinary uses as it contains toxins that damage the liver if taken internally and the official recommendation is to not consume comfrey. It is only used medicinally and then only topically.

Health Uses

Comfrey was known in Old English as 'knitbone', though its modern name derives from the Latin '*con fera*' meaning to knit together. Comfrey has long been prized because of its ability to heal. Historically, herbalists have used it for everything from healing wounds to fixing broken bones and treating tuberculosis.

There are many stories of how comfrey heals broken bones and speeds the healing of wounds. This plant had such a good reputation that in World War II, first aid packs contained comfrey tablets to speed the healing of wounds and broken bones.

Modern research has shown that this comfrey deserves its reputation due to the high levels of allantoin and rosmarinic acid it contains. Allantoin accelerates new tissue growth (cellular mitosis) and rosmarinic acid relieves inflammation and pain. When a foetus is developing, allantoin is present in the placenta and it is even present, in smaller quantities, in breast milk.

Comfrey is also high in Vitamin C, magnesium and calcium, all of which help to strengthen bones.

Before using comfrey topically, make sure the wound is completely clean. Then apply a comfrey ointment or poultice. Wounds have been known to heal very rapidly and trap debris in the wound, which is why it is important clean them thoroughly first.

Studies have proven that comfrey can relieve pain and inflammation due to arthritis as well as healing bruises, sprains and other joint and muscle aches. In studies, comfrey has frequently outperformed its pharmaceutical equivalent, , and experts recognize it as a safe treatment for these conditions.

There are high levels of antioxidants in comfrey, so it is excellent in fighting free radicals. Allantoin is also very soothing for the skin as well as being hydrating, exfoliating and repairing. Allantoin reduces keratinisation or abnormal thickening of the skin, so leaves your skin feeling smooth after use.

Use topical applications of comfrey to treat skin irritations such as stings, sunburn and rashes.

Beauty Uses

Comfrey has its beauty uses, though it is recommended not to apply anything made from comfrey to your face, anal or genital area, as there is a risk of absorbing toxins or an allergic reaction in sensitive people.

Use poultices and ointments to nourish and moisturize your skin so it becomes soft and supple. The leaves also have an astringent property, so it helps your skin feel more toned.

The high levels of allantoin in comfrey smooths out rough skin, removes dead skin cells and helps reduce blemishes and dark spots on your skin. Comfrey poultices help relieve the symptoms of psoriasis and eczema, reducing inflammation and itchiness.

Overall, comfrey is a very helpful plant that is excellent at healing wounds and broken bones. The roots were mashed into a powder, which was turned into a cast for broken bones in the Middle Ages to speed healing. It is not a herb to be taken internally, but used externally it has a whole host of benefits.

Pests, Problems & Diseases

Pests or diseases do not particularly bother comfrey. In rare occasions, you may encounter comfrey rust, which can overwinter in the roots and makes the plant less vigorous. However, this is not common and you are unlikely to see it.

Recommended Varieties

There are many varieties of comfrey, all with slightly different characteristics. These are some of the most commonly cultivated varieties. If you are growing comfrey for medicinal purposes, then you are best growing common comfrey. Grow Bocking 14 for composting and Bocking 4 is best grown as an animal feed.

- Creeping Comfrey (*Symphytum grandiflorum*) – also known as dwarf comfrey, this creeps along the ground rather than growing upright. It is sometimes referred to as ornamental comfrey, but can quickly become a weed and take over your garden.
- Bocking 14 – a cultivar of Russian Comfrey (*Symphytum x uplandicum*), which is a cross between rough and common comfrey. This has a

high potassium content and is sterile, so does not set seed and take over your garden. Although suitable for growing in containers, it will still increase in size so needs dividing every few years. This variety is popular for composting and is not suitable for use as an animal feed. It is lower in beneficial compounds and not well suited for medicinal use.

- Bocking 4 – another cultivar of Russian Comfrey that is better for medicinal use and animal fodder. It runs wilder than Bocking 14 and is not as good for composting as Bocking 14.

Recipes

Comfrey Compost Tea

This highly nutritious fertilizer is excellent for your plants as a diluted liquid feed. This is not for internal consumption. Tomatoes, cucumbers and peppers will particularly appreciate this feed as it will encourage the formation of plenty of healthy fruits.

Requirements:

- Lots of comfrey leaves
- A large bucket
- Stone or brick (to weigh leaves down)
- Plastic bottles (for storage such as used milk bottles)

Method:

1. Wear gloves to protect your hands from the hairy leaves and harvest the leaves from lower down on the plants
2. Remove the flowers and any stems, placing those on your compost pile
3. Chop the leaves up and pack them into the bucket as tightly as possible
4. Put a brick in the bucket to weigh the leaves down
5. Cover the bucket to prevent insects getting in and the smell escaping
6. Place the bucket somewhere out of the way and not anywhere people frequent due to the aroma that will come from your comfrey tea
7. Check the mixture every couple of weeks, the leaves will break down leaving a smelly, brown liquid which is what you collect and use, storing in a cool, dark place
8. Top up with fresh leaves as required
9. Dilute at a ratio of 10 parts water to 1 part comfrey and use on your plants. Note that the darker the fresh liquid is, the stronger it is and the more you will have to dilute it

Cilantro (Coriander)

Cilantro, *Coriandrum sativum*, or coriander as the Europeans call it, is a hardy, annual relative of parsley grown for its leaves and seeds. It is popular as a garnish and grows well outside or in containers.

At a Glance Facts

Annual / ~~Biennial~~ / ~~Perennial~~	
Position:	Full sun to partial shade
Soil:	Moist but well-drained
Hardiness	Fully hardy
USDA Zones:	3-11
Sow:	Summer
Harvest:	Later summer to fall

Documented use of this herb dates back 7,000 years where it is mentioned in Sanskrit texts, but it was likely in use for thousands of years before this. Cilantro seeds were discovered in the Nahal Hemar cave in Israel and have been dated to 8,000 years ago. In the United States, this herb is referred to as coriander when it is grown for seeds and cilantro when grown for its leaves.

The Chinese believed cilantro seeds granted immortality. Both the ancient Egyptians and the Peruvians used the seeds and leaves to flavor food. Cilantro seeds have been found in Egyptian tombs dating back 3,000 years.

Cilantro even has a mention in the Old Testament of the Bible, "When the children of Israel were returning from slavery in Egypt, they ate manna in the wilderness and the manna tasted like coriander seeds."

The Romans were responsible for bringing cilantro to Britain, where it soon naturalized. The native British used cumin, vinegar and cilantro to preserve meat while the Romans used it in bread. For the Romans, cilantro was a high status herb and considered exotic.

Although a hardy annual, this plant is often mistaken for a perennial as it is a prolific self-seeder.

Growing Instructions

Cilantro is one plant you will find on the shelves of your local supermarket, pre-grown and ready to sit on your kitchen windowsill. These are great starter plants and I have planted these in the ground where they have produced a great crop of leaves over the year.

You can grow this herb from seed, sown directly into the ground or in pots. It takes anywhere from seven to twenty days for the seeds to germinate. Planting new seeds every three or four weeks will give you a constant supply of fresh leaves over the growing season.

If you are growing for the seeds, then thin the plants to about 4"/10cm between plants and position them in a sunny location.

Sow in early fall for early winter seeds, though protect the seedlings with cloches or small polythene tunnels.

Cilantro will tolerate a light frost, but it struggles in hot and humid climates. In cooler climates, USDA zones 3 to 8; sow in the spring whereas in the warmer zones, 9 to 11, it is sown in fall or winter. Cilantro has a tendency to bolt in hot weather and then go to seed. Unfortunately, once this herb flowers, the leaves become bitter and less palatable.

Plant in a full sun or a partially shaded location in a well-draining soil. It does not grow in waterlogged, compacted soils and can develop root rot if the soil is too wet. Cilantro has a long taproot so prefers not to be transplanted.

According to companion planting, cilantro will grow well with most herbs, but do not plant it near fennel, as they do not grow well together.

Start harvesting the leaves after about four weeks. They are best harvested early in the day and eaten fresh, though you can freeze them. Seeds appear approximately 90 days after sowing. Collect the seeds by cutting the plant, hanging it until dry and then shaking the seeds into a paper bag. Rub the dried fruits with your hands to extract the seeds. Store seeds in airtight containers and use whole or grind into a powder.

Plant Care

This herb does not require a great deal of care beyond weeding around the plant to stop weeds competing with it and the occasional liquid feed to give it a boost. Keep the soil around it damp, but do not overwater. Make sure the soil does not dry out as this can cause the plant to bolt.

Culinary Uses

Cilantro is a herb used in a wide variety of cuisines and dishes. It is popular in salsa and guacamole, but also used in many other dishes. Some of the more common uses are:

- Mix into sour cream and top chilies, soups or stews with it
- Stir into rice or use as a garnish for a bit of spice
- Mix with lime juice for a pleasant dressing for salad or rice
- Add to any salad dressing, particularly vinaigrettes or citrus, for extra flavor
- Mix into coleslaw for a more interesting taste
- Add to a stir fry at the end of cooking for a fresh flavor
- Garnish pasta or rice salads for a unique flavor

Cilantro has a very distinct flavor, which makes it popular in cooking. Use the seeds, whole or crushed, to flavor dishes or add whole to pickling recipes. It is popular in Indian meals and most commonly seen as a garnish on just about anything!

Health Uses

As well as tasting great, cilantro is packed full of vitamins, minerals, antioxidants and beneficial phytochemicals. It contains high levels of vitamins A and K as well as C and E. Eating ½ cup of fresh cilantro a day provides you with 16% of your daily-recommended amount of vitamin K. It is also high in minerals such as iron, potassium, calcium and magnesium and is a source of dietary fiber.

The high levels of vitamin K and calcium, link cilantro to strong teeth, bones and hair. Across Europe, people consider this a beneficial herb because it lowers blood pressure, bad cholesterol levels and supports a health heart.

Cilantro has a whole host of health benefits, including:

- Removes Harmful Heavy Metals – cilantro binds with heavy metals in your system, which allows your body to excrete them. Studies show it helps remove toxins such as lead from your body, so if you are concerned about heavy metal poisoning, you should be regularly consuming cilantro. See http://www.ncbi.nlm.nih.gov/pubmed/19902160 and http://www.ncbi.nlm.nih.gov/pubmed/8686573 for details of these studies.
- Supports Heart Health – The phytochemicals found in cilantro appear to reduce oxidative stress on the heart and can help prevent myocardial infarctions (http://www.ncbi.nlm.nih.gov/pubmed/22750725). Studies show that cilantro also reduces triglycerides and total cholesterol - http://www.ncbi.nlm.nih.gov/pubmed/22671941.
- Balances Blood Sugar – adding cilantro to your diet will help to balance blood sugar levels and can even help to reduce blood sugar, http://www.ncbi.nlm.nih.gov/pubmed/22671941. Research

indicates that eating cilantro during the day can help maintain a consistent blood sugar level.

- Reduces Anxiety and Aids Sleep – cilantro is shown to be a natural sedative which helps your sleep cycle and calms nerves. In a study by the Indian Journal of Pharmacology, they found that cilantro extract had the same effect on anxiety as Valium but without the potentially dangerous side effects.
- Prevents Food Poisoning – consuming cilantro with a meal can help reduce your chances of getting food poisoning. The International Journal of Food Microbiology published a study that showed cilantro was particularly effective in fighting listeria - http://www.ncbi.nlm.nih.gov/pubmed/11929164.
- Reduces Neurological Inflammation – inflammation of the brain is linked with a number of neurodegenerative diseases such as Alzheimer's and Parkinson's. Research published in Molecular Neurobiology found that a diet high in garlic, ginger, clove, cinnamon, pepper, cilantro and turmeric helped prevent inflammation associated with these diseases - http://www.ncbi.nlm.nih.gov/pubmed/21360003.
- Protects Against Colon Cancer – research, http://www.ncbi.nlm.nih.gov/pubmed/10940583, shows that cilantro reduces cholesterol levels and increases bile and sterol compound excretion. This decreases the levels of toxicity in the colon, which reduces the risk of colon cancer.
- Eases Skin Irritations – used internally or externally, cilantro is a good remedy for a number of skin irritations, including sunburn, hives and poison ivy. Cilantro naturally contains anti-histamines, which help calm your immune system when it is responding to allergens. Blend cilantro with coconut oil to apply to your skin for a moisturizing effect. Alternatively, blend with water, strain and apply to your skin while drinking the left over juice for maximum effect and a fast response.
- Settles Stomachs – cilantro is very good at settling your stomach, reducing gas and preventing bloating. It is also used to reduce indigestion and heartburn. Serve cilantro with hot dishes such as curries and Thai noodle dishes for a cooling effect that can prevent heartburn.
- Prevents Urinary Tract Infections – as cilantro is high in antibacterial compounds, it can help keep your urinary tract healthy and infection free. Soak 1½ teaspoons of cilantro seeds in two cups of water overnight then strain and drink. This will help to relieve the symptoms of a UTI and speed your recovery from it.

Beauty Uses

As well as its health uses, cilantro has many beauty uses because it is high in antioxidants and vitamin C. It is a strong antiseptic, anti-fungal, anti-inflammatory and antibacterial agent that has a disinfecting effect as it soothes and cools your skin.

Pests, Problems & Diseases

Cilantro suffers from few pest and disease problems. Slugs and snails will attack young seedlings, which need protecting from these voracious pests.

In hot, dry weather, cilantro will bolt and set seed too early, making the leaves bitter and unpalatable. Sow bolt-resistant varieties or at the right time of year, keeping the soil moist.

Recommended Varieties

Coriandrum sativum is the most commonly grown cilantro variety, though a cultivar known as Leafy Leisure is grown for its large volumes of leaves and that it is slower to bolt than regular cilantro. One cilantro cultivar has a hint of lemon flavor to the leaves and is worth growing.

Recipes

Spicy Slaw

This is a great vegetable coleslaw that has a nice kick to it. It only takes about ten minutes to make and produces six servings.

Ingredients:

- 1 cup mayonnaise
- ½ cup fresh cilantro (minced)
- 3 garlic cloves (minced)
- 14oz pack of coleslaw mix
- 1 teaspoon Sriracha hot chili sauce
- ¼ teaspoon salt
- ⅛ teaspoon cayenne pepper

Method:

1. Mix everything, except the coleslaw mix and cilantro, together in a small bowl to make the dressing
2. Put the cilantro and coleslaw mix into a large bowl
3. Add the dressing and toss well
4. Refrigerate until ready to serve

Smoothing Face Mask

This will help your skin look smooth and feel great.

Ingredients:

- ½ cup oatmeal
- ¼ cup chopped cucumber
- ¼ cup milk
- Handful of fresh cilantro

Method:

1. Blend the ingredients together in your food processor for about a minute until it looks smooth
2. Spoon into a glass bowl
3. Apply liberally to your face and leave until hard, around 20 minutes
4. Rinse your face and pat it dry

Acne Treatment

This is a good treatment for acne, spots or blackheads as it has a strong cleansing effect as well as being an anti-bacterial agent.

Ingredients:

- 1 cup boiling water
- 1 teaspoon chamomile
- 1 teaspoon cilantro
- 1 teaspoon lemongrass

Method:

1. Add the ingredients to a pan and leave it to cool for an hour
2. Blend in your food processor until the mixture has the consistency of a paste
3. Apply to your skin, after cleansing it
4. Leave for 20 minutes then wash with warm water, splashing your face, once clean, with cold water

Blackhead Buster

Another very effective mixture for cleansing your skin and combatting blackheads.

Ingredients:

- 1 teaspoon lime juice
- 1 teaspoon cilantro juice

Method:

1. Mix the juices together until well combined
2. Apply to your face
3. Leave for an hour then wash off with warm water

Cilantro Lip Balm

After a few days use, this lip balm will give you smoother, pinker lips.

Ingredients:

- 2 teaspoons cilantro juice
- 1 teaspoon lemon juice

Method:

1. Mix together well
2. Apply to your lips and leave overnight
3. Wash off in the morning and repeat every night for several days

Itch Relief Paste

A simple paste that will help to relieve itchiness on your skin. Mix some coriander seeds with a teaspoon of honey and a little water, and then apply to the skin for rapid relief!

Cilantro Body Oil

A great body oil for treating sunburn, wounded or scarred areas of skin.

Ingredients:

- 1 tablespoon powdered cilantro seeds
- 1 cup of oil (olive, almond or sunflower works well)

Method:

1. Mix the powdered seeds with the oil
2. Leave to infuse for a week in a sealed container, shaking regularly
3. Apply to affected skin at night, rinsing in the morning

Anti-Hair Loss Oil

A simple oil that helps to prevent hair loss and stimulate new growth.

Ingredients:

- Hair oil
- 1 tablespoon powdered cilantro seeds

Method:

1. Mix the ingredients together in a glass container
2. Seal and leave for a week to infuse, shaking regularly
3. Massage into the scalp two or three times a week

Cilantro Detox

A good mixture for detoxifying your system, being particularly good at removing heavy metals from your body.

Ingredients:

- 1 tablespoon cilantro seeds
- ¾ pint/½ liter water
- 1 teaspoon honey or sugar

Method:

1. Bring the water to the boil in a small saucepan with the cilantro seeds
2. Stir in a teaspoon of honey or sugar to sweeten
3. Remove from heat and leave to cool until drinkable

4. Drink, while warm
5. Repeat two or three times a day for a thorough detox

Roast Ham

I love this dish. This makes an incredibly tasty ham that your friends and family will really enjoy. When cooking the ham, try replacing some (or all) of the water with apple juice to make a really tender ham with a fruity taste. Serve hot or use cold. It takes a couple of hours to cook, though does require some soaking time, so best to start the day before it is needed. This size ham will serve 8 to 10 people. Adjust the quantities and cooking time depending on the size ham you are using.

Ingredients:

- 11lb/5kg raw, smoked ham (boned or boneless)
- 10 black peppercorns
- 2 leeks (halved)
- 2 bay leaves
- 1 onion (halved)
- 1 carrot (cut into large chunks)

Glaze Ingredients:

- Whole cloves (for decoration)
- 3 tablespoons demerara sugar
- 3 tablespoons light muscovado sugar
- 2-3 tablespoons English mustard powder
- 1 teaspoon cilantro (coriander) seeds
- 1 teaspoon orange zest (grated)
- Honey to drizzle

Method:

1. Test how salty the ham is (fry a small piece in oil). If it is too salty, soak it in cold water overnight, changing the water once
2. Put the joint in a large pan, cover with cold water (or a mixture of apple juice and water) and add the onion, carrot, leeks, peppercorns and bay leaves
3. Bring to the boil, cover and simmer for 20 minutes per 1lb/450g
4. Leave the ham to cool for 15-20 minutes in the liquid, then remove and transfer to a cutting board, leaving until cool enough to handle
5. Cut the skin from the ham, but leave behind an even layer of fat
6. Score the fat in a diagonal criss-cross pattern then cook immediately or refrigerate for no more than 2 days before cooking

7. Preheat your oven to 400F/200C
8. Grind the coriander seeds in a pestle and mortar
9. In a separate bowl, mix the sugars and orange zest
10. Add the ground coriander seeds and mix well
11. Evenly sift the mustard powder over the ham
12. Coat the fat with the sugar mixture (roll the ham in it or sprinkle it on by hand)
13. Push a whole clove into the middle of each cut diamond on the fat
14. Drizzle the honey over the ham
15. Cover the exposed end of the ham with foil, leaving the fat exposed
16. Place in a roasting tin and bake for 15 minutes until the glaze is crispy, sticky and even a little charred
17. Serve immediately or cool and refrigerate until required

Cumin

Cumin, *Cuminum cyminum*, is a warm season annual, grown for its seeds, which are popular in a range of cuisines from Mexican to Indian to Middle Eastern. The plant also has a number of medicinal uses.

At a Glance Facts

Annual / ~~Biennial~~ / ~~Perennial~~	
Position:	Full sun
Soil:	Any, well-drained
Hardiness	Not frost hardy
USDA Zones:	5-10
Sow:	Late spring to early summer
Harvest:	Fall

Use of cumin dates back thousands of years, mentioned in both the Old and New Testaments in the Bible and used by the Ancient Egyptians, Romans and Greeks. It was such a valued commodity that at one point in history, people used it to pay off debts and taxes!

The Romans and Greeks used cumin in almost every meal because it could be substituted for black pepper, which was difficult to get and very expensive to buy. In Biblical times, cumin was a very effective antiseptic, though more recently it is used to settle stomachs and aid digestion.

Growing Instructions

Start the seeds indoors about 6 to 8 weeks before the last frost date. If planting outside, sow a week or two after the last frost when temperatures have started to warm. Plant four seeds together at a depth of about ¼", with spacing of 4-8" between plants. When the seedlings reach 2" tall, remove the weaker plants, leaving the strongest plant in each cluster. The seeds will typically germinate in one to two weeks and the mature plants will grow up to two feet (60cm) tall. If planting multiple rows of cumin, leave 18" between the rows.

Improve the germination rate by soaking the seeds for eight hours before sowing.

The seeds are ready to harvest when the pods have ripened and turned brown. Remove them from the plant and allow to dry fully. Rub the pods in your hands to remove the seeds. Alternatively, hang the stems upside down in paper bags where they will dry and the seeds fall out.

Use cumin seeds fresh or dry fully and store in an airtight container for up to six months.

Plant Care

Cumin does not need a lot of care. Water it regularly, particularly in dry weather, ensuring you do not overwater. Allow the soil to almost dry out between watering, and then give it a good soaking.

Culinary Uses

Cumin seeds have a very interesting flavor, being bitter but sweet, and are a common ingredient in spice mixtures, stews and curries. In the United States, Mexican and cuisine from the South West use a lot of cumin. Although the spice was originally native to the southwest of Asia, it has made its way around the world and has become a staple in Indian, Middle Eastern and North African cooking.

Cumin Powder

The cumin plant is a relative of parsley and the seeds have a nutty, smoky flavor that works well when combined with cilantro, cinnamon and chilies.

Use cumin seeds either whole or ground. Toast the whole seeds before use to bring out their aromatic flavor. Cumin is mostly used in savory dishes and is a key part of many curry powders. Any chili con carne will benefit from the addition of cumin.

Some of the other culinary uses include:

- Rub on lamb or pork
- Use in marinades and barbecue sauces
- Add whole seeds to bread
- Fry with onions and serve with lentils
- Use ground cumin in omelets
- Add to rice or couscous to give them some taste
- Use in lamb or pork stews or casseroles
- Gives pickles and chutneys a bit of a kick
- Compliments vegetables such as eggplant and zucchini
- Key component in falafel
- Very tasty on roast potatoes

Cumin is a versatile spice and worth trying in your kitchen. It has a very interesting flavor and can really spice up a dish without becoming overpowering, like some of the hotter spices.

Health Uses

Humans have used cumin for thousands of years medicinally and it has a number of benefits. Modern day researchers have begun to investigate cumin and the beneficial effects it has on the human body.

Cumin is high in iron, which has many beneficial effects, including transporting oxygen to the cells in your body. It also assists in absorbing nutrients from food. In larger quantities, cumin acts as a diuretic.

This herb treats digestive and stomach disorders such as relieving bloating, gas and flatulence. Research is underway into the anti-carcinogenic properties of cumin as early research is showing it can prevent stomach and liver tumors forming in animals.

The high levels of Vitamin C found in cumin together with its anti-fungal properties make it very effective at fighting colds and respiratory problems. Early research is showing promising results in using cumin for maintaining healthy kidneys – http://www.ncbi.nlm.nih.gov/pmc/articles/PMC3642442/.

The high levels of thymoquinone, dithymoquinone, thymohydroquinone and thymol found in cumin seeds has proven very interesting to anti-cancer researchers as they appear to help treat both breast and colon cancer - http://www.ncbi.nlm.nih.gov/pmc/articles/PMC3252704/.

Beauty Uses

This aromatic spice also has its beauty uses, containing over one hundred different chemical compounds. The Islam culture believes that cumin can heal any disease, apart from death, while the Bible refers to cumin seeds as 'curative black seeds'.

Cumin has many benefits for skin care. Eating cumin in your meals helps to keep your skin free from pimples, rashes and boils as this herb is high in compounds such as cuminaldehyde, which is a good detoxifying agent. Herbalists use a mixture of vinegar and ground cumin seeds to treat boils and acne.

With high levels of vitamin E, disinfectant and anti-fungal properties, apply cumin topically to help a wide range of skin complaints including eczema and psoriasis. It also acts as an antioxidant and combats the free radicals that cause aging, helping to firm your skin.

A simple facemask can be made from a mixture of three parts ground turmeric to one part ground cumin, mixed in honey or water and applied to the skin. Leave it until it has dried and then wash it off for smooth, glowing skin. Mix this with plain yoghurt instead, and it is an ideal treatment for sunburnt, blotchy or spotty skin.

Pests, Problems & Diseases

Aphids are most like to attack cumin, so regularly check new growth and treat as appropriate.

The adult plants can be susceptible to blight and powdery mildew, so ensure adequate spacing between plants and keep weeds down so there is sufficient air circulation. Water the plants in the morning to prevent the foliage from being wet at night.

If the soil becomes too wet from either rain or overwatering, then cumin plants can suffer from root rot.

Recommended Varieties

There are no named varieties of cumin available in seed catalogs. This plant is often confused with caraway; to which it bears a resemblance. Many of the European languages use the same or similar words to describe these two plants. Many of the Slavic languages refer to cumin as 'Roman caraway' just to confuse matters. *Nigella sativa*, *Bunium persicum* and *Bunium bulbocastanum* are all referred to as black cumin sometimes, which causes further confusion as they are not the cumin used for cooking.

Recipes

Curried Potatoes

This is a simple dish to make that shows off the flavor of cumin. Use whatever curry powder you like; you can make these as hot or as mild as you want. Reduce the amount of curry powder if you prefer the other spices to shine through. It takes about 35 minutes to prepare and cook this dish.

Ingredients:

- 2lb new potatoes (cut into ¼" cubes)
- 3 tablespoons fresh cilantro (chopped)
- 2 tablespoons extra-virgin olive oil
- 2 tablespoons whole cumin seed
- 2 teaspoons curry powder (of your choice)
- 2 teaspoons coarse salt
- 2 teaspoons ground turmeric
- 1 teaspoon ground black pepper

Method:

1. Put the potatoes into a saucepan, cover with water and boil until just tender
2. Put to one side, cover and keep warm
3. Heat the oil in a large pan on a medium to high heat
4. Sauté the curry powder, turmeric and cumin for about a minute
5. Add the potatoes and cook until toasted, stirring regularly
6. Transfer the potatoes into a large bowl and toss with the salt, pepper and cilantro
7. Serve immediately

Dill

Dill, *Anethum graveolens*, is a large herb with ferny foliage with yellow flowers appearing in the summer. The leaves have a strong flavor and are popular in soups or salads. The seeds are a key ingredient in curry powder.

At a Glance Facts

Annual / ~~Biennial~~ / ~~Perennial~~	
Position:	Full sun
Soil:	Well-drained
Hardiness	Hardy to 14F/-10C
USDA Zones:	3-11
Sow:	Spring to early summer
Harvest:	Summer to early fall

Once harvested, dill will quickly start to lose its flavor, so use this herb when fresh.

Dill is native to the Mediterranean, found growing wild throughout Greece, where it is commonly used in a wide variety of dishes including Tzatziki. The Ancient Greeks used it in wine, as a fragrance, and winners in athletic contests were presented with a dill wreath.

Growing Instructions

Sow dill directly in its final position as it has a long taproot and does not like being transplanted or disturbed. It is suitable for growing in containers; though make sure they are deep so there is plenty of room for its roots.

Sow dill anytime from the middle of spring to the middle of summer in a fertile soil in full sun. Sow the seeds thinly in ½" deep trenches and lightly cover. When the seedlings are large enough to handle, thin the seedlings to 6"/15cm apart. In pots, thin them to about 4"/10cm apart. The seeds should germinate in ten to fourteen days. Shelter the adult plants from strong winds.

Dill Seedlings

Dill grows well with onions and cabbage, but do not grow it near to carrots or fennel. As dill is related to both of these plants, cross-pollination can occur which spoils their taste.

Plant Care

Water regularly, but do not allow to dry out. Support adult plants with canes as they do have a tendency to blow over in strong winds. Keep the weeds down around dill as it is not keen on competition and can be smothered by faster growing weeds.

Harvest the leaves as you need them throughout the growing season. Use fresh or freeze/dry for winter use. Regularly picking the leaves will help to encourage the plant to produce more leaves and delay flowering until later in the growing season. Gather the seeds when the seed heads start to turn brown in late summer. Cut the stalks, and then hang them upside down in a paper bag. Separate the seeds out from the stalks and store in an airtight container.

Culinary Uses

Dill is a popular herb in the kitchen, pairing particularly well with fish and seafood in general. It is popular with salmon, but is also used to garnish potato and egg dishes as well as being an ingredient in white sauces. Of course, one of the best-known uses for dill is in the famous dill pickles. Dill seeds are frequently used in breads and spice mixes.

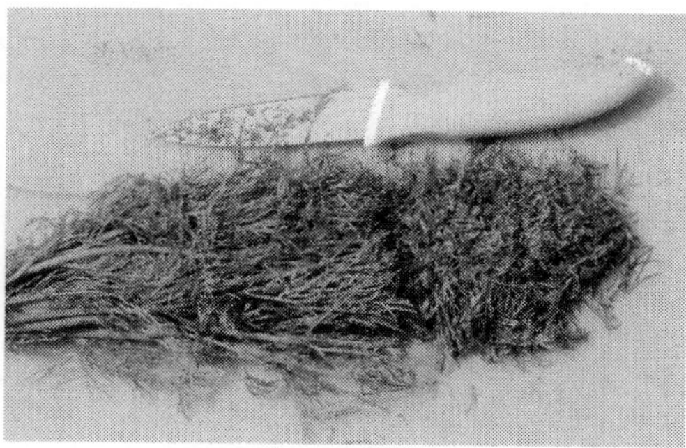

Like many herbs, the fresh leaves wilt and lose their flavor quickly when cooked, so are best added to a dish towards the end of cooking.

Make a simple dill sauce for salmon by stirring half a cup of chopped dill leaves into one cup of plain yoghurt. Squeeze in some fresh lemon juice, add a clove of minced garlic and season to taste with salt and you have a simple sauce!

Another popular use is to make roast dill potatoes. Cube some potatoes and lay out on a parchment paper lined cookie sheet. Coat the potatoes with olive oil, then sprinkle with dried dill and season to taste with salt and paper. Roast for about 45 minutes on 350F/175C until golden brown and tender. Garnish with fresh chopped dill and enjoy.

Health Uses

Dill is commonly used for digestion issues such as flatulence, liver problems and loss of appetite. Herbalists use it to treat urinary tract infections and kidney disease. It is traditionally helpful for a number of other complaints including infections, coughs and colds, fevers and bronchitis.

Do not use dill when pregnant or breast-feeding as it can start menstruation, which could lead to miscarriage. The safety of taking dill medicinally while breast-feeding has not been reliably researched and the official recommendation is to avoid dill as a medication while breast feeding, but it is safe to use in food.

If you are allergic to any of the plants in the carrot family, such as caraway, celery, fennel or cilantro, then you may also be allergic to dill as they are related. It is best to test how dill reacts with you in small quantities or avoid it completely if you are unsure whether you are allergic to it.

Research has shown that dill can be helpful for people suffering with depression by taking an aqueous extract of dill. The study (http://www.ncbi.nlm.nih.gov/pubmed/26872137) published in the American Journal of Therapeutics, indicates that this extract had a significant analgesic and anti-depressant effect comparable to sertraline and tramadol, but without any adverse effects.

Research has shown dill lowers cholesterol, http://www.scilit.net/article/10.1155/2015/958560. Anyone with high cholesterol will benefit from introducing dill into his or her diet.

Researchers have tapped into traditional knowledge to discover how dill can help with epilepsy and convulsions. Research is underway, http://www.ncbi.nlm.nih.gov/pmc/articles/PMC3957353/, which shows that the traditional use of dill as an anti-convulsant is justified and it appears to be effective.

Dill is also very high in antioxidants, which combat free radicals which cause the signs of aging and other damage to your body. Research has shown, http://www.ncbi.nlm.nih.gov/pubmed/15364640, that dill is effective in fighting free radical damage.

Beauty Uses

Dill appears to be able to influence elastin in your skin, an enzyme that helps rebuild the structural integrity of your skin. An extract of dill seed activates dermal fibroblasts to stimulate the creation of elastin. The same extract also increases the production of tropoelastin, which is the precursor of elastin. Scientists are researching dill seed for this ability to fight the signs of aging - http://www.ncbi.nlm.nih.gov/pubmed/16842595.

Pests, Problems & Diseases

Generally, dill is pest and disease free. You may find aphids on new growth and slugs and snails could attack your seedlings. In hot or dry weather, dill can bolt and set seed early. This can be avoided by regular watering and growing a bolt resistant cultivar.

Recommended Varieties

There are a few varieties of dill commonly available commercially, including:

- Bouquet – good if you want to focus on seed production
- Dukat – a vigorous dill that is very slow to bolt and has an excellent flavor
- Fernleaf – a bushy, dwarf variety, ideal for containers
- Herkules – a tall plant growing to over four feet tall that produces lot of leaves
- Mammoth – grows to around three feet in height and is good for seeds.

Recipes

Tomato and Dill Feta Salad
This nice, simple salad is easy to make. Feel free to swap the feta cheese out for another variety you prefer.

Ingredients:

- 1lb colored tomatoes (cut into chunks)
- 1 garlic clove (minced)
- 1 red bell pepper (de-seeded and cut into 1" pieces)
- ½ red onion (thinly sliced)
- 1 cup feta cheese (crumbled – or substitute for your favorite cheese)
- 1 cup Kalamata olives (pitted)
- ⅓ cup English cucumber (thinly sliced)
- ¼ cup extra-virgin olive oil
- ¼ cup fresh dill (coarsely chopped)
- ¼ cup fresh mint leaves (coarsely chopped)
- 2 tablespoons red wine vinegar
- Flaky sea salt

Method:

1. Put the onion into a bowl of cold water and put to one side for 15 minutes
2. Put the chopped tomato in a medium bowl
3. In a large bowl, add the garlic, a pinch of salt and the red wine

vinegar
4. While whisking, drizzle in the olive oil
5. Drain the onion and pat dry
6. Return to the empty bowl and add the bell pepper, red onion, dill, mint, olives and cucumber
7. Pour on the dressing and toss until well combined
8. Refrigerate for 10 minutes to marinade
9. Add the tomatoes and cheese, tossing again
10. Season to taste and serve using a slotted spoon so the juices are left in the bowl

Dill Pickles

One of the most common uses for dill, these are easy to make and very tasty!

Initial Ingredients:

- 2½ quarts water
- ¾ cup pickling salt
- ½ cup white vinegar
- Fresh dill
- Pickles (or other vegetables cut into 3-4" strips)

Ingredients for Packing Pickles into Jars:

- 4 quarts water
- 1 quart white vinegar
- ½ cup pickling salt

Method:

1. Put the initial ingredients into a large pan and heat to dissolve the salt
2. Alternate layers of pickles with fresh dill in a large ceramic bowl (garlic or chili peppers can be added for some extra kick)
3. Pour the brine over the vegetables and weigh down with a plate
4. Leave for 2 weeks, removing any scum that appears on top of the brine every day
5. After 2 weeks, drain the liquid from the pickles
6. Pack the pickles into hot sterile jars
7. Heat the second set of ingredients together until boiling
8. Pour over the pickles, leaving ½" headroom
9. Seal and process in a boiling water bath for 15 minutes

Echinacea

Echinacea, *Echinacea purpurea*, is a beautiful plant that attracted lots of attention for its healing properties. It has large, daisy-like flowers that have mounded heads and rose or pink petals on a single stem, clearly visible above the foliage.

At a Glance Facts

~~Annual~~ / ~~Biennial~~ / **Perennial**	
Position:	Full sun
Soil:	Well-drained
Hardiness	Hardy to 5F/-15C
USDA Zones:	3-8
Sow:	Late winter to summer
Harvest:	11-15 weeks after sowing

This perennial plant is great for attracting pollinating insects and butterflies love it. It has a long, deep taproot and is popular as an ornamental flower.

Growing Instructions

Sow the seeds in late winter through to spring. Space plants at least a foot apart, with the same distance between rows. Sow seeds ½" deep while there is still the possibility of a light frost to help with germination. Seeds will usually germinate in 10 to 20 days and will, if sown early enough, flower in the first year.

During the growing season, pinch off spent flower heads to encourage the formation of more. Leave some for the birds or for the plant to self-seed.

Plant Care

Echinacea plants are low maintenance and tolerate heat, drought, poor soil and humidity. Once established, avoid overwatering and only fertilize with a specific flower fertilizer otherwise you end up with leggy, floppy plants with poor flowers.

In late winter, once the flowers have gone to seed, cut the plants back to the ground. Leave some seed heads in place to self-seed or for the birds, which love them. If you want to collect the seeds, cover them with netting to prevent the birds from eating them all.

Echinacea benefits from a good mulch to help retain moisture and to keep down weeds.

Established Echinacea plants grow in clumps, which benefit from being divided every few years in the spring or fall. Plant these clumps separately for new growth. Be careful doing this as Echinacea does not like to be disturbed.

Culinary Uses

There are no culinary uses for Echinacea.

Health Uses

Some years ago, everyone hailed Echinacea as the cure-all plant with its ability to boost your immune system and fight infection. It was the most commonly used medicinal plant by the prairie Native Americans who used it to treat everything from cancers to colds. It was popular, until the invention of antibiotics, with doctors and in 1993; German doctors prescribed Echinacea over 2.5 million times!

Herbalists consider Echinacea to be good for fighting infections and to purify the blood. It is considered an aphrodisiac and herbalists use it as a decoction or tincture to treat sores, gangrene, infected wounds, acne, herpes, psoriasis and more.

Today, Echinacea is mainly used to treat and prevent colds and heal infections. This herb helps white blood cells fight foreign invaders such as the cold virus. As well as stimulating your immune system, it also accelerates healing of any infections.

A 1992 study in Germany showed that four drops of Echinacea extract decreased the duration and symptoms of colds. Research has shown that this herb can reduce the symptoms of a cold by 59% and the duration by as much as 1½ days! Further clinical studies are underway to determine the best way to use Echinacea to improve your health.

Echinacea contains phytochemicals that studies, https://www.ncbi.nlm.nih.gov/pmc/articles/PMC2668539/, have shown to be effective in fighting cancerous tumors. Initial research has been positive, but the expert recommendation is to use Echinacea to compliment cancer treatment rather than as a replacement.

Echinacea tea or a herbal supplement has been shown to help level out blood sugar, keeping glucose levels under control in both diabetic and pre-diabetic people. This research is very promising as it can stop blood sugar levels plummeting in the case of hypoglycaemia. https://www.researchgate.net/publication/312135104_Antioxidant_Antidiabetic_and_Antihypertensive_Properties_of_Echinacea_purpurea_Flower_Extract_and_Caffeic_Acid_Derivatives_Using_In_Vitro_Models.

Echinacea tea has proven to be useful in fighting inflammation, https://www.ncbi.nlm.nih.gov/pubmed/19107735. People who suffer from uveitis (eye inflammation) and inflammatory arthritis benefit from consuming this tea regularly.

With high levels of antioxidants and anti-inflammatory compounds, preliminary studies has shown Echinacea helps to lower blood pressure - https://www.ncbi.nlm.nih.gov/pmc/articles/PMC3924237/.

Many health products are available from stores containing Echinacea but you can make your own tincture or decoctions from the flowers at home. If you are using Echinacea for health purposes, do not use any chemical sprays on the plant for at least two weeks before harvesting.

Beauty Uses

Echinacea helps to reduce inflammation and has some antibacterial properties as well as being high in tannins. It is beneficial in fighting acne and smoothing the skin, reducing the visible signs of aging. The best way to use Echinacea for treating acne is as a tea - https://www.ncbi.nlm.nih.gov/pubmed/20830697.

Research is still underway about the effect of Echinacea during pregnancy and breastfeeding. Current advice is to avoid use of this herb during this time.

As Echinacea has an effect on the immune system, it can make some autoimmune conditions such as rheumatoid arthritis, lupus and multiple sclerosis worse. If you suffer from any autoimmune condition, do not use Echinacea without consulting a medical professional. Do not give this herb to children under 12 and sometimes it can react with caffeine and immunosuppressant's. If you are in any doubt about whether Echinacea is suitable for you or are taking any other treatment, speak to your doctor first.

Pests, Problems & Diseases

Echinacea does suffer from a number of different pests including aphids, leafhoppers and Japanese beetles. Keep weeds down around the plant and remove any debris from the ground to eliminate places where pests can live. Plant marigolds, nasturtiums and other plants that attract beneficial insects, which will help to keep the pest population under control.

If pests infest your Echinacea, try removing them by hand first. If they persist, use an organic pesticide or neem oil spray, which should take care of the problem.

This plant is susceptible to several diseases including aster yellows, powdery mildew and anthracnose. Proper spacing between plants and watering to the base will help reduce the incidences of these diseases. In serious cases, use an organic fungicide to treat the disease.

Recommended Varieties

There are many different varieties of Echinacea. These are some of the most commonly grown varieties:

- *Echinacea angustifolia* – growing up to two feet tall, this compact flower has 2" heads with 1" rose-pink colored petals. Suitable for USDA zones 3 to 8.
- *Echinacea pallida* – growing to normal size, this cultivar has large heads with pale rose petals. Suitable for USDA zones 4 to 8.
- *Echinacea paradoxa* – growing around three feet tall, this is an unusual variety in that the petals are bright yellow. Growing in USDA zones 4 to 8, this variety has attractive, lance shaped leaves.
- *Echinacea purpurea* – growing up to four feet tall and occasionally as tall as six feet, this shrubby plant has leafy stems and plenty of flowers. The petals are flat or drooping and range from rose pink to red-violet. There are many different cultivars such as Bright Star, which has rose-pink flat flower heads, Kim's Mop Head, which has white flowers, Magnus which has extremely large flower heads, Springbrook's Crimson Star with deep crimson flowers and more. This cultivar is hardy from USDA zones 3 to 8 and is particularly valued for its medicinal properties.
- *Echinacea tennesseensis* – growing up to three feet tall, the rose-purple petals on this cultivar are unique as they sweep upwards, giving them impression of a cup. This cultivar is being bred to create new hybrids, which will be released to market in coming years. This variety is hardy for USDA zones 4 to 8.

Recipes

Echinacea Tincture

Echinacea tincture is very easy to make and is very good for you. Most people make it with alcohol, though apple cider vinegar or glycerine are alternatives if you prefer.

Ingredients:

- Pint glass jar with lid
- 80% proof, food grade alcohol (vodka or rum)
- ½ cup dried Echinacea leaf and/or root

Method:

1. Fill the jar, without packing down, half full with the Echinacea
2. Add a few tablespoons of boiling water to damp the dried herb (this helps to draw out the beneficial compounds from the herb)
3. Fill the jar with alcohol and stir using a clean metal spoon
4. Seal the jar and leave in a cool dry place for a minimum of three weeks and maximum of six months, shaking daily
5. Strain through cheesecloth and store the tincture in dark glass bottles

Evening Primrose

Common evening primrose, *Oenothera biennis*, is a biennial plant growing up to 5 feet/1.5m tall with lots of bowl shaped, yellow, fragrant flowers opening in the evening during the summer and fall months. Each flower has four petals and cultivars can produce white or pink flowers, rather than the traditional yellow.

At a Glance Facts

~~Annual~~ / **Biennial** / ~~Perennial~~	
Position:	Full sun to partial shade
Soil:	Well-drained
Hardiness	Fully hardy
USDA Zones:	3-11
Sow:	Late spring to early summer
Harvest:	Varies – see below

Often cultivated for its roots, evening primrose is now more frequently grown for its seeds, which are high in omega-6.

This plant gets its name because its flowers open late in the afternoon, usually around 4pm and they remain open until the middle of the following morning. Evening primrose is native to North America where it grows wild in hedgerows and scrubland. Explorers took this plant to Europe in the 1600s where it has now naturalized, since being taken to many other parts of the globe.

Although common evening primrose is a biennial, other cultivars can be annual or perennial and grow as tall as six feet and two feet wide. *Oenothera* cultivars are used for ground cover, as ornamental plants and in containers, with some cultivars growing to just 6" tall.

You have probably seen evening primrose growing in the wild and wondered what the plant is. It is instantly recognizable and hugely popular for its health and beauty application. Preferring full sun, *Oenothera* does not hide in the shade and is clearly visible when it grows.

Initially, evening primrose was grown for its roots, which have a nutty flavor and were boiled like parsnips. Nowadays, people grow evening primrose as an ornamental or for its medicinal uses.

Growing Instructions

Evening primrose has adapted well to many different conditions and, depending on the cultivar, will thrive in full sun to partial shade. Common evening primrose, grown for medicinal use, prefers full sun. It grows well in poor soil, usually found growing wild on scrubland. *Oenothera* prefers well-drained soil that has plenty of organic matter dug into it. It is generally tolerant of high pH levels.

Seeds can be scattered on the surface of the soil and covered lightly. Do not plant the seeds deeper than 5mm otherwise they will struggle to germinate. Leave about 8" between plants and water in. Most evening primrose cultivars are drought tolerant and do not require a great deal of watering.

Grow *Oenothera* either from seed or by division. You can often find seedlings in garden centers. Plant later in spring when there is no danger of frost. Keep some horticultural fleece to hand and be prepared to cover young plants in case of a late frost.

In the first year, plants develop long taproots and rosettes of cold-hardy leaves. In the second year, branching stems appear and the plant will grow to its full height.

As well as being a useful medicinal herb, evening primrose is often used as a trap crop to attract Japanese beetles from other plants, including roses.

Plant Care

Evening primrose does not require a great deal of care; it grows like a weed in the wild and is more than happy to look after itself in your garden.

Pretty much all of this plant is used in one way or another. The stem is not eaten as it is too woody, but it is mashed into a poultice and applied to speed the healing of bruises. The leaves are tasty if harvested early on, though the older the leaves, the tougher they are, requiring boiling for longer.

The roots are harvested in spring and cooked like parsnips, which they taste similar to, though are slightly more peppery. The root is best when harvested in the first year as it dies at the end of the second season.

Harvest flowers when they open and use immediately to decorate salad or use in an infused oil. Flowers appear from June to September, opening later in the afternoon and dying within a day. The seeds, ready in mid-August, are dried out and kept for replanting or eaten. Once a plant has set seeds, it dies.

Evening primrose plants do not require regular feeding, though they do benefit from a layer of well-rotted manure in the spring.

Culinary Uses

The traditional use of evening primrose is as food, with the entire plant being edible. The leaves taste similar to spinach or kale, the flowers look great in a salad and the green seed pods are cooked like a vegetable. Use the ripe seeds in baking as you would poppy seeds. The roots have a pleasant, spicy taste, similar to rutabaga and parsnip.

Health Uses

The entire plant was used medicinally by the Native Americans to treat a wide variety of ailments. The roots were used to treat hemorrhoids and the leaves used to treat minor wounds, sore throats and gastrointestinal problems.

Today, manufacturers extract an oil from the seeds and market it in capsule form, used to help a wide variety of conditions include premenstrual symptoms, osteopororis, eczema and rheumatoid arthritis.

Evening primrose is very high in gamma linolenic acid (GLA) which is a type of omega-6 fatty acid. This helps to boost the immune system and regulate blood pressure. The seeds are very popular with birds, so to save the seeds you must net your plants to prevent birds eating the seed heads. The seeds are also very high in tryptophan, an amino acid that our bodies convert into the mood boosting brain chemical, serotonin. The leaves are high in quercetin, a bioflavonoid, which keeps your blood vessels healthy and eases the effects of asthma.

The use most people are familiar with is its ability to reduce discomfort associated with premenstrual syndrome (PMS). Many studies have shown that evening primrose oil reduces irritability, breast tenderness and evens out the mood changes that are frequent with PMS.

Recently, evening primrose has become popular because it is high in essential fatty acids, amino acids, vitamins and minerals that the body cannot make, but needs to remain healthy.

Beauty Uses

Evening primrose oil helps with many skin conditions that are usually hard to treat such as eczema and psoriasis due to its high omega-6 fatty acid content. Mix evening primrose oil with coconut oil and apply to sore areas and it will reduce the symptoms.

The high GLA content of evening primrose oil also helps your skin, including smoothing out wrinkles. The high levels of antioxidants neutralize free radicals and prevent oxidation. Apply evening primrose oil daily to your face and neck to reduce the signs of ageing or you can take two capsules a day for a similar effect.

Studies have shown that applying evening primrose oil to your hair helps slow hair loss and even help with hair re-growth, particularly when mixed with rosemary essential oil. Mix these with coconut oil and massage into your hair and scalp, https://www.umm.edu/health/medical/altmed/supplement/gammalinolenic-acid.

Early studies are showing that the high levels of GLA in evening primrose oil helps to regrow nerve damage, which is of particular interest to medical researchers. https://www.ncbi.nlm.nih.gov/pubmed/28620418

Taking evening primrose oil together with fish oil is proving helpful in treating the side effects of rheumatoid arthritis. The same mixture will also help with any inflammation related disease.

Pests, Problems & Diseases

Evening primrose is generally pest free, though can suffer from powdery mildew and leaf spot occasionally.

Recommended Varieties

There are a number of different cultivars, growing anything from six inches to six feet in height with a wide variety of colored flowers. These are some of the most popular cultivars:

- Common evening primrose (*Oenothera biennis L.)* – growing four to six feet tall, this biennial produces leafy stalks in its first year and flowers in the second.
- Mexican evening primrose (*Oenothera berlandieri*) – a spreading perennial growing up to 18" tall, native to Missouri, Kansas, Nebraska, Kansas, Mexico and Oklahoma. This plant thrives in poor soil with little water, but loves full sun.
- Showy (*Oenothera specious*) – likes heat, is drought tolerant and grows up to two feet tall with white and pink, pale lavender or just pink flowers.
- Pale evening primrose (*Oenothera pallida*) – native to the western states, this is a low growing biennial.

Recipes

All of this plant is edible. Harvest the seedpod in the fall and cook the seeds for 10 minutes at 325F/160C, then use like poppy or sesame seeds in breads, soups or salads. The young, green seedpods are great steamed and served with other vegetables.

Eat the flowers as they have a mild lemony/pepper taste, being particularly good as a garnish. Cook the young leaves like spinach and use in soups, salads or stews.

The roots are dug towards the end of the first year, as the older roots tend to be a bit too woody and tough to enjoy. The roots are prepared like turnip or parsnip and taste similar, though slightly more peppery.

Fennel

Fennel, *Foeniculum vulgare*, is a popular herb closely related to Florence fennel (*Foeniculum vulgare var. dulce*), also known as bulb fennel. The herb is a perennial covered in attractive yellow flowers early in the summer. The entire plant has a very distinctive aniseed taste and smell, used in a wide range of dishes, most notably fish. The flowers attract beneficial insects such as pollinators and predatory wasps that hunt harmful pests.

At a Glance Facts

~~Annual~~ / ~~Biennial~~ / **Perennial**	
Position:	Full sun to partial shade
Soil:	Light, free-draining
Hardiness	Yes to 23F/-5C to 14F/-10C
USDA Zones:	3-8
Sow:	Early to mid-spring
Harvest:	Spring to summer

Herb fennel is often referred to as sweet fennel. It is often confused with bulb fennel, though they are different plants. Although you can use the leaves from bulb fennel as you would from this fennel, doing so reduces the size of the resulting bulb.

Herb fennel grows wild on the Pacific coast of the United States. Humans have used it for thousands of years to flavor food. The Romans called it fenicularius, using the ground seeds and fresh shoots in their cooking. It appears the Romans were responsible for the spread of fennel as their armies conquered the then known world. Fennel has travelled to every corner of our planet, found as far afield as Australia, the Americas, India and China.

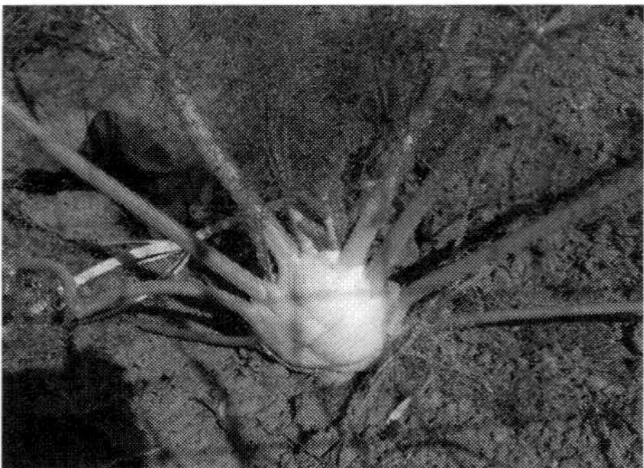

Bulb Fennel

It is valued not just for its taste, but also for its medicinal properties, and is an easy plant to grow in your garden.

Growing Instructions

Sow fennel in early spring in small pots or in the middle of spring in its final position. Fennel does not like its roots being disturbed, so must be transplanted before it gets too big or sown direct in the ground. Once seedlings reach 6" tall, do not transplant them, as they will struggle to recover.

Once established, fennel is relatively tolerant of drought and requires little maintenance. Plant herb fennel in a sunny spot in a light, free draining soil. Although herb fennel is a perennial in warmer areas, it is treated as an annual in colder areas.

Sow on top of the soil and cover with a thin layer of soil. Leave about a foot between plants, as fennel grows very tall.

Fennel attracts a wide range of insects when allowed to flower including pollinators and predatory wasps. It is best grown at the edge of your garden as it can impact the growth of other plants.

Plant Care

Harvest leaves as needed from spring through to fall. Use the seeds fresh in summer or harvest in late summer and dry for use over winter.

As a perennial, the plant grows into a clump over several years and ends up with very woody stems. Divide large clumps in late winter and transplant to a new location. Make sure you dig out the deep roots. Replant shoots with lots of root hairs immediately. Those with few root hairs are potted up, put somewhere shady for two weeks and then replanted. Water regularly until they are established.

Culinary Uses

Fennel is popular in cooking. Look for healthy, perky leaves that are a good shade of green, or bronze in the case of bronze fennel. The stalks are also edible. Wash, chop and use! Wrap fresh fennel in damp kitchen paper, place in a perforated bag and refrigerate where it will last for up to three days.

Roast fish on a bed of whole fennel fronds to give it a delicious flavor, or add chopped leaves to sauces or soups.

Use the leaves of the bulb fennel plant in the same manner as herb fennel. There are also bronze varieties of fennel that have a similar flavor, just a different colored foliage.

The seeds, whole or crushed, are popular in breads and Italian sausages. Fennel seeds also work well in curries, with any dish containing pork, in pasta sauces, in pickling vinegars and in any salad or salad dressing.

This is a very popular herb for use in your kitchen and is a common ingredient in a wide variety of commercial products from toothpastes to mouthwashes and move.

Fennel Seeds

Health Uses

Most of the research into fennel's health benefits has focused on the seeds, which contain high levels of antioxidants and have anti-inflammatory properties. Herbalists have traditionally used fennel seeds to relieve intestinal gas and cooks add them to water when cooking beans, asparagus, cabbage and other gas inducing foods.

As a nutritional substitute, fennel seeds reduce many of the symptoms experienced during the menopause as this research indicates - https://www.ncbi.nlm.nih.gov/pubmed/28509813.

Fennel has a long association with weight loss. As far back as 1650, William Coles, an English botanist, described fennel as "in drinks and broths for those that are grown fat, to abate their unwieldiness and cause them to grow more gaunt and lank." Modern research has shown that drinking fennel tea before meals encourages you to eat less - https://www.ncbi.nlm.nih.gov/pmc/articles/PMC4525133. According to this Korean study, sipping tea made from fennel leaves or seeds throughout the day helps reduce your appetite.

Fennel is high in many beneficial vitamins such as Vitamin C, B1, B2, B3, B7, A, E and K as well as plenty of trace minerals. It contains antioxidant, antibacterial and anti-inflammatory flavonoids such as apigenin and quercetin.

Fennel also contains a compound called anethole that mimics the function of estrogen in your body according to research, https://www.ncbi.nlm.nih.gov/pmc/articles/PMC4137549/. Be careful taking this herb if you are using any birth control pills or on any tablets that influence estrogen levels. Breast feeding mothers should avoid fennel, as it may not be safe.

Other research is indicating that proteins contained in fennel seeds cause cancer cell death. Although still in early stages, this research looks promising for future cancer treatments. Read more about the research here https://www.ncbi.nlm.nih.gov/pubmed/21212515 and here https://www.ncbi.nlm.nih.gov/pubmed/28745237.

Anyone allergic to celery, mugwort or carrot must be careful with fennel as it can cause an allergic reaction. Fennel appears to slow blood clotting, so anyone with a bleeding disorder needs to take medical advice before taking this herb.

Beauty Uses

Fennel is a popular beauty treatment. A fennel seed infusion is great for cleansing your skin, removing excess sebum and dead cells as well as unclogging your pores. With its antiseptic and anti-inflammatory properties, it works very well against acne. Make a simple skin cleansing infusion by steeping a tablespoon of fennel seeds in a small pan of hot water for twenty minutes. Cool, then add a couple of drops of tea tree essential oil and store in a sealed glass bottle. Use by soaking a clean cotton wool ball and wiping your face. This simple infusion also acts as an astringent, tightening pores and firming skin.

A fennel seed infusion is an excellent treatment for cellulite. Grind fennel seeds and mix with water to make a paste, then apply to your skin to reduce the signs of cellulite.

Being high in antioxidants and vital vitamins, fennel seeds are very good for your hair. Rinsing hair in fennel water helps to cleanse and strengthen it as well as stimulating hair growth.

As a diuretic, fennel helps detox your body and stop water retention. This helps with making your skin look good. The fennel infusion mentioned previously works well as a natural detox drink. Use the same water as a cold compress on your eyes to relieve irritation and reduce puffiness.

Fennel seed powder is an excellent skin exfoliator. Grind a tablespoon of fennel seeds, mix with a teaspoon of water and use as a facial scrub to remove dead cells and excess sebum.

Pests, Problems & Diseases

Fennel is very disease resistant and few pests bother it. Aphids can be an issue on new growth and slugs and snails will attack young seedlings.

Recommended Varieties

There are two types of fennel; herb fennel detailed here (*Foeniculum vulgare*) and the bulb type Florence fennels (*Foeniculum vulgare var. dulce*).

Some popular varieties of both types of fennel include:

- Purpureum – ornamental bronze leaf herb fennel
- Rubrum – ornamental bronze/red leaf herb fennel
- Rhondo – fast maturing bulb fennel with good, round bulbs
- Cantino – early planting, slow to bolt bulb fennel
- Mantavo – high yield, slow bolting bulb fennel
- Victoria – vigorous bulb fennel, slow to bolt

Recipes

Fennel Pesto

This unusual take on pesto uses fennel leaves from either herb fennel or bulb fennel to make this traditional Italian condiment. Very quick and easy to make, taking just ten minutes, you can use this fresh or freeze it.

Ingredients:

- 3 cups fennel fronds (loosely packed)
- 1 cup walnuts (toasted)
- ½ cup extra-virgin olive oil (plus a little extra)
- 1 garlic clove
- Juice of 1 lemon
- 1 teaspoon sea salt

Method:

1. Toast the walnuts until golden brown, about 3-5 minutes, then put aside to cool
2. Put the garlic, lemon juice, fennel and walnuts into your food processor together with half the olive oil
3. Blend until incorporated
4. Continue blending while drizzling in the rest of the olive oil until you achieve your preferred consistency (add more oil/water a teaspoon at a time if you want your pesto thinner)

5. Use or refrigerate/freeze in an airtight container

Fennel Tea

An easy way to gain the many benefits of fennel from a simple to make tea. Drink this after meals to help digestive problems

Ingredients:

- 1 teaspoon dried fennel seeds per cup
- Hot water

Method:

1. Put a teaspoon of dried fennel seeds in each cup
2. Fill the cup with hot water and cover (take care not to boil the seeds as this reduces the nutrients)
3. Steep for ten minutes, then drink
4. Repeat 3 times a day

Feverfew

Feverfew, *Tanacetum parthenium*, is a daisy like herb best known for its ability to alleviate headaches. This is a short-lived perennial whose leaves have a very distinct aroma. The flowers are up to an inch across, with white petals and bright yellow disks in the middle.

At a Glance Facts

~~Annual~~ / ~~Biennial~~ / **Perennial**	
Position:	Full sun
Soil:	Well-drained
Hardiness	Yes, down to -4F/-20C
USDA Zones:	5-10
Sow:	Spring
Harvest:	Summer to fall

Although herbalists use this plant to treat headaches, its attractive flowers make it a popular ornamental plant.

Originating in south eastern Europe, feverfew has spread across Europe, North America and Australia where it can be seen in gardens or growing wild in the hedgerow. Confusingly, feverfew is a perennial in most areas, but acts as an evergreen in warm areas such as the southern United States. In cooler areas, like the northern States, it behaves like an annual.

While this is a valuable medicinal herb, it is incredible invasive and self seeds prolifically. Pharmaceutical researchers are investigating the active ingredient, Pathenolide, due to its ability to ease arthritis, fever and headaches.

Growing Instructions

Feverfew is easy to grow from seed in spring or is taken by division or basal cuttings. This herb does not tolerate heavy, wet soils, preferring a light, well-drained soil with full sun.

Start the seeds indoors in late winter or sow direct in the final position after the last frost. Seeds take between 10 and 14 days to germinate.

Seeds are easily available online or in garden centers. Seed packet labelling is confusing as it is often referred to by its Latin names, which are *Tanacetum parthenium* and *Chrysanthemum parthenium*. Luckily, most seed packets also include its common name and a picture.

The seeds are very small and you sow them by scattering them on top of the soil. Spray them with water rather than using a watering can as too much water can disperse and lose the seeds. Keep them moist, but not wet, until they have germinated. When 3" tall, transplant them into individual pots or outside, watering regularly until established. Avoid covering the seeds with soil or compost as they require sunlight to germinate.

Plant Care

Feverfew requires very little care, growing like a weed in the wild. Dead head throughout the growing season to encourage more flowers and prevent self-seeding. Once flowering has finished, cut the plant down to ground level where it will regrow in spring. This herb is self-pollinating and does not require insects for pollination.

Each spring, apply a good, balanced fertilizer. As the plant does not tolerate dry conditions, keep the roots moist throughout the year.

In very cold winters, mulch your feverfew to protect the roots from the cold. Mulching in summer helps to conserve moisture and reduce the frequency of watering.

Feverfew leaves are best when harvested at the start of the flowering season, though can be picked at any time while the plant has flowers on it. Dry or use the leaves within a few days. Use the dried herb within four months otherwise it loses its potency and has fewer benefits.

Culinary Uses

There are no known culinary uses for feverfew; it is grown either as an ornamental plant or for its medicinal properties

Health Uses

Despite its name, the main use of feverfew is to treat headaches, though herbalists also use it to treat digestive issues and arthritis. Herbalists use both the leaves and flowers, though commercial products only use the leaves. Numerous studies have agreed that headaches, including migraines, are effectively treating by feverfew - https://www.ncbi.nlm.nih.gov/pubmed/16232154 and https://www.ncbi.nlm.nih.gov/pmc/articles/PMC3210009/. Research is still underway to identify and extract the active components.

Other uses for feverfew include cooling the body down after fevers and treating inflammation of the joints, particularly when caused by allergies as it inhibits histamine secretion. This herb encourages menstrual flow, eases menstrual cramps and relieves gas and bloating.

Pet owners will like feverfew as it contains compounds called pyrethrins that paralyze fleas. A strong infusion of feverfew is excellent at managing fleas on both cats and dogs. As an oil, it acts as an insect repellent and reduces the symptoms of bites.

Feverfew could slow blood clotting, so anyone with bleeding disorders should avoid this herb. Before and after surgery, avoid this herb as it could inhibit healing. People who are allergic to ragweed, daisies, marigolds or chrysanthemums may also be allergic to feverfew.

Beauty Uses

As a natural anti-inflammatory, feverfew helps with redness or swelling of the skin and also treats scratches, patches and ringworm. Regularly drinking feverfew tea, which is high in antioxidants, protects your body from harmful free radicals, helping your skin to look great.

Some people can experience side effects from using feverfew such as an upset stomach, heartburn, constipation, flatulence, tiredness, weight gain and trouble sleeping, although these usually occur with excessive use. Pregnant women and breast feeding mothers should avoid feverfew.

Pests, Problems & Diseases

Generally, feverfew is disease free. Most problems are environmental, usually down to the soil being too waterlogged. Feverfew can suffer from aphids, slugs, spider mites and powdery mildew. Planting geraniums and garlic near feverfew helps reduce the incidences of these problems.

Recommended Varieties

There are a number of ornamental varieties of feverfew, though the common variety is best for medicinal use. Some popular varieties include:

- White Wonder – has half inch, white flowers
- White Stars – an exotic cultivar with long, thin petals that have hooks on the end and pale yellow centers
- Golden Ball – grows up to 18" tall with double, creamy yellow flowers
- Crown White – grows up to 28" tall with bright white, tiny flowers
- Ultra Double White – grows up to 2 feet tall with double white flowers, popular with florists and with flower growers
- Aureum – grows up to 12" tall with golden leaves and small, white flowers

Recipes

Feverfew Tea
Put one to two teaspoons of Feverfew leaves (fresh or dry) in a cup. Fill with boiling water and leave for up to 10 minutes to steep.

Ginger

Common ginger, *Zingiber officinale*, is an aromatic root very popular in cooking for its distinct flavor. Usually a tropical plant, ginger grows as an annual in other areas such as the UK and much of the United States.

At a Glance Facts

~~Annual~~ / ~~Biennial~~ / **Perennial**	
Position:	Full sun to partial shade
Soil:	Moist, well-drained
Hardiness	No
USDA Zones:	7-10
Sow:	Spring after last frost
Harvest:	After at least 8-10 months

Native to south east Asia, the name is thought to derive from the Sanskrit word 'singabera' which means horn shaped. Most people are familiar with ginger, but few people grow it, even though it is relatively easy to grow in a single season.

Ginger has a long association with cooking and is mentioned in writings from ancient India, China and the Middle East. The Romans prized ginger so much that they imported it at great expense from China. Today, this aromatic root grows as far afield as Fiji, India, Australia and Jamaica.

As well as its taste, ginger has numerous medicinal applications, used to reduce gas, stomach cramps and nausea. Double blind studies have shown ginger to be more effective than store bought medicines in treating motion sickness! Pregnant women use ginger to alleviate the nausea and sickness that comes with some pregnancies.

Ginger tea is one of the most popular ways of benefiting from this root. It is simple to make, just steep a couple of slices of fresh root in a cup of hot water for up to five minutes.

Growing Instructions

Ginger grows outdoors in USDA zones 7 and above, though unless you live in zone 10, the leaves will die in winter. In zone 6 and below, ginger needs to be grown in a container and brought indoors in winter or grown outdoors as an annual.

Ginger roots specifically for planting are available, or ginger roots from the supermarket will grow. The variety sold in stores for use in your kitchen is *Zingiber officinale* and is safe to grow. Look for a rhizome that is plump and has small eyes. Ideally, these eyes will have started to turn green. The rhizome can be planted whole or cut into pieces for multiple plants. If dividing, each piece should be at least 1½" wide and have one or more eyes. However, pieces with three or more eyes are far more likely to sprout.

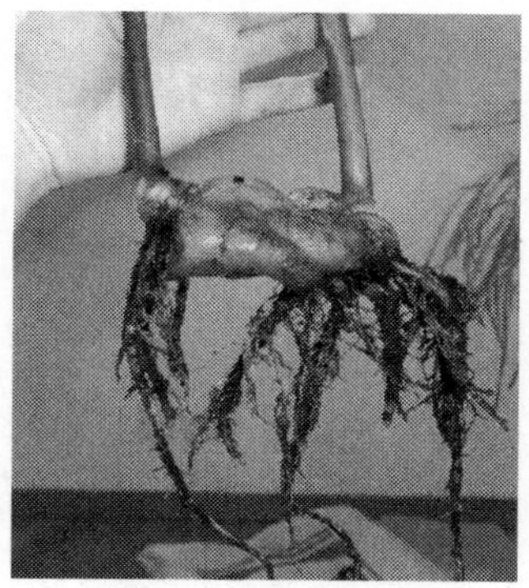

Leave the pieces somewhere dry for a few days for the root to callus over the cuts, reducing any risk of infection. Then plant out, leaving about 8" between rhizomes. Initially, the plant will grow a few leaves over where the rhizome is located and over time, if you do not harvest it, then it will become a dense clump. The foliage above ground will only grow between two and three feet tall. A 14" wide, 12" deep pot will comfortable hold three average sized rhizomes.

Ginger likes a high quality, well-drained soil. It prefers a slightly acidic environment with a pH of between 6.1 and 6.5, though will tolerate normal garden soil. Pick a site with morning sun and partial shade that is well away from large roots and sheltered from the wind.

The rhizomes germinate at a soil temperature of 71-77F/22-25C.

You can grow ginger indoors in containers following a similar process. Plant it in a wide pot that is about 12" deep with rich, well-draining soil. Position the rhizome so the eyes are facing upward and cover with a couple of inches of soil before watering lightly.

Position the pot in a warm location that does not get too much light and keep the soil moist. After two to three weeks, shoots should start to appear; ginger is not a fast growing plant. A few months later, you can start harvesting small pieces of ginger.

Plant Care

When growing outside, cut back the stems in the fall as it dies back.

Keep the soil around ginger moist, but not wet. Check how wet the soil is and before it has completely dried out, water your ginger rhizomes.

In colder months, when the temperature drops below 50F/10C, you can dig up the rhizomes and bring them indoors, storing in a warm, dry location. Alternatively, cover with a thick layer of mulch if the temperature is not going to approach freezing.

Ginger is ready to harvest around eight months after planting once the leaves die down. Dig up the entire rhizome, or just remove pieces. The flavor improves and grows stronger as it matures in the ground; so many people leave their ginger in the ground all year round, harvesting what they need when they need it.

If the air is dry where you live, then ginger can have an issue with spider mites, as it prefers a humid environment. Mist the plant regularly to help keep it moist and provide it with the environment it needs.

Weed regularly around the ginger. It is a slow growing plant so weeds very easily overtake it.

Culinary Uses

Ginger is highly prized as a culinary spice and has been for thousands of years. It is used in a wide variety of dishes either as the whole rhizome (chopped or grated) or as a dried powder.

Ginger is a key component in Chinese cuisine and is popular powdered in the West for baking and sweet dishes such as pumpkin or apple pie. Ginger pairs particularly well with garlic as seen in many stir-fries and for a sweet dish, pairs well with ground cinnamon, cloves and nutmeg.

One reason ginger is so popular in the kitchen it that it naturally aids digestion, reducing and eliminating nausea, cramps and flatulence. This is why ginger is often found in Indian curries.

Ginger tea or non-alcoholic ginger ale is a great drink that settles the stomach and reduces nausea.

In the West, ginger is common in sweet dishes such as gingerbread men or apple pies. Powdered ginger is best for baking, but fresh can be used by substituting six parts fresh ginger for one part ground ginger.

Health Uses

Ginger is a close relation of cardamom and turmeric, being in the same family. Originating in China, it has long been used for its medicinal properties, not just in its homeland, but also everywhere else it is used. Medicinally, ginger is used fresh, powdered, dried, juiced or as an oil.

The most important oil in ginger is 'gingerol', which has healing properties and gives ginger its unique smell and taste. It is a powerful antioxidant and has a strong anti-inflammatory effect, see https://www.ncbi.nlm.nih.gov/pubmed/25230520 for details of the research into this oil.

Ginger is extremely effective in treating all forms of nausea, including morning sickness and seasickness to the point it is as effective as, or more effective, as over the counter remedies. Research, https://www.ncbi.nlm.nih.gov/pubmed/10793599, has shown how powerful ginger is in combatting nausea whereas https://www.ncbi.nlm.nih.gov/pubmed/9815340 has shown how effective ginger is for seasickness. In a study with pregnant women, researchers found ginger helped with nausea from morning sickness but had no effect on vomiting episodes – https://www.ncbi.nlm.nih.gov/pmc/articles/PMC3995184/. As with taking any herbal supplement, please speak to your physician, particularly if you are pregnant.

Cancer patients receiving chemotherapy and people who have just had surgery can both benefit from the anti-sickness properties of ginger. Research is promising as you can see in these papers - https://www.ncbi.nlm.nih.gov/pubmed/16389016 and https://www.ncbi.nlm.nih.gov/pubmed/20842754.

Ginger is effective at reducing muscle pain caused by exercise. In a study, https://www.ncbi.nlm.nih.gov/pubmed/20418184, consuming two grams of ginger every day for eleven days reduced muscle pain from people performing elbow exercises. Researchers think this is due to the anti-inflammatory properties of ginger.

These anti-inflammatory properties are beneficial for sufferers of osteoarthritis. In a controlled study of 247 people with osteoarthritis of the knee, https://www.ncbi.nlm.nih.gov/pubmed/11710709, researchers found that ginger extract reduced pain, meaning patients required less pain medication.

A separate study, https://www.ncbi.nlm.nih.gov/pubmed/22308653, showed a topical application of mastic, cinnamon, ginger and sesame oil reduced both pain and stiffness.

Recent research indicates ginger may have powerful anti-diabetic properties. In 2015, researchers had 41 type 2 diabetics take two grams of powdered ginger every day. The fasting blood sugar levels for these people were 12% lower than usual - https://www.ncbi.nlm.nih.gov/pmc/articles/PMC4277626/. Further, the HbA1c marker for long-term blood sugar levels dropped 10% over a twelve-week period. In addition, there were significant reductions in two major risk factors for heart disease; a 28% reduction in ApoB/ApoA-I ratio and a 23%

reduction in oxidized lipoprotein markers.

Ginger has a long history of use for treating dyspepsia or chronic indigestion, which is normally indicated by pain and discomfort in the upper area of the stomach. Ginger speeds up the time it takes the stomach to empty, which helps reduce indigestion. Eating ginger soup reduced the time for the participant's stomach to empty from 16 minutes down to 12 - https://www.ncbi.nlm.nih.gov/pmc/articles/PMC3016669/. A separate study with 24 participants showed that consuming 1.2 grams of ginger powder before eating sped up stomach emptying by 50% - https://www.ncbi.nlm.nih.gov/pubmed/18403946.

A traditional use of ginger is to relieve pain, including dysmenorrhea or menstrual pain. In this study, https://www.ncbi.nlm.nih.gov/pubmed/19216660, 150 women took one gram of ginger powder for three days at the start of their menstrual period. The results showed ginger to be as effective as ibuprofen in relieving pain.

Ginger powder is linked to reducing bad cholesterol (LDL) levels. In a study of 85 people over 45 days, a daily intake of 3 grams of ginger powder significantly reduced cholesterol markers – https://www.ncbi.nlm.nih.gov/pubmed/18813412. In another study on rats, ginger extract proved to be as effective as atorvastatin, a drug used to lower cholesterol - https://www.ncbi.nlm.nih.gov/pubmed/23901210. This shows ginger to be very effective at treating high cholesterol and could be introduced to the diet to prevent cholesterol becoming a problem.

Ginger has powerful antibiotic properties and studies showed it to inhibit bacteria - https://www.ncbi.nlm.nih.gov/pmc/articles/PMC3609356/ and https://www.ncbi.nlm.nih.gov/pmc/articles/PMC3418209/. Gingerol is effective at treating gum inflammation such as periodontitis and gingivitis - https://www.ncbi.nlm.nih.gov/pubmed/18814211.

Plenty of other research is underway into ginger and its active components. It has uses ranging from treating respiratory infections to cancer. Like many herbs, research is targeting the active components of this plant to create effective medicines.

Beauty Uses

As ginger is packed with antioxidants, it is very effective at fighting wrinkles and reducing the visible signs of aging. Add the powder to beauty treatments or consume it orally for a similar effect. Try applying sliced fresh ginger root to your face to revitalize your skin and leave it glowing.

With powerful antiseptic properties, ginger kills bacteria on the skin and in your pores that are responsible for spots and acne. A face mask made from grated ginger and any store bought face mask will moisturize and soften your skin, leaving it looking fantastic.

Fresh ginger applied to scars for 30 to 40 minutes once a day for at least a week will help bring color back to the scarred area and reduce the whiteness of the scars.

Ginger is also very good for your hair, helping to strengthen hair roots, reduce hair loss and stimulate hair growth. Being a natural antiseptic, it also combats dandruff. The antioxidants in ginger are good for repairing dry hair and split ends. Just make a fresh ginger infusion and use it on your hair.

Pests, Problems & Diseases

Ginger is generally trouble free, though is sometimes affected by red spider mites when grown under glass.

Recommended Varieties

Common ginger, also known as Chinese ginger, is the variety most commonly found in stores. These plants grow up to four feet tall, spreading two or three feet wide. It is not a showy or attractive plant, but there are many ginger cultivars available. However, to buy these you will have to find specialist suppliers as most stores only stock common ginger.

India grows over fifty different cultivars, including 'Rio de Janeiro' and 'Nadia'. Chinese grows even more, with 'Shandong', 'Laiwu' and 'Gandzhou' being some of the more commonly grown plants.

Japanese gingers have smaller rhizomes than Chinese gingers, but have a much more intense flavor. Use them exactly as you would use regular ginger. 'Sunti' and 'Kintoki' are strong flavored cultivars with small rhizomes whereas 'Sanshu' has a medium sized rhizome. For a larger rhizome, try 'Oshoga'.

Ginger does have a number of relatives that are much more attractive above ground; some even have tasty rhizomes too. *Zingiber mioga* "Dancing Crane" is a hardy cultivar able to survive through the winter in USDA zones 5 to 10. *Zingiber zerumbet* or pinecone ginger, produces pinecone shaped flower bracts and grows up to seven feet tall. The flowers are very attractive and this cultivar is often grown as an ornamental, though only grows in USDA zones 8 to 11.

Recipes

Ginger is very popular in cooking, used in both sweet and savory dishes.

Ginger Cookies

These are delicious cookies made using both crystallized and fresh ginger to give them a unique taste. The dough can be frozen for up to a week and the finished cookies will store in an airtight container for around five days, though usually they are eaten way before this!

Ingredients:

- 2 cups/10oz unbleached all-purpose flour
- 1 cup/7oz white/granulated sugar
- ½ cup/3½oz white (granulated) sugar – used for rolling the dough
- 16 tablespoons/2 sticks unsalted butter (softened but firm)
- 2 tablespoons crystalized ginger (minced)
- 1 tablespoon light brown sugar
- 1 large egg
- 1½ teaspoons vanilla extract
- 1 teaspoon grated fresh ginger
- ½ teaspoon baking powder
- ¼ teaspoon table salt

Method:

1. Mix ½ cup of sugar and the fresh ginger in your food processor for 10 seconds until combined, then put to one side
2. Pre-heat your oven to 375F/190C, positioning the trays in the upper and lower middle positions
3. Line two baking sheets with parchment paper
4. In a medium sized bowl, whisk together the salt, flour and baking powder
5. Beat the butter, brown sugar and 1 cup of sugar with a hand mixer or in a standing mixer with a paddle attachment for around 3 minutes, until light and fluffy, scraping down the sides of the bowl as required
6. Add the vanilla essence, crystallized ginger and the egg, mixing again for 30 seconds
7. Add the dry ingredients and mix again for 30 seconds on a low speed
8. Place the ginger sugar in a shallow bowl (for use to roll the cookies)
9. Fill a medium bowl half full of water and dip your hands in, shaking off excess moisture (prevents the dough from sticking to your hands)
10. Roll a heaped tablespoon of dough into a 1½" ball in your hands
11. Roll the ball in the ginger sugar, then place on the parchment paper
12. Repeat with the rest of the dough, leaving 2" between the balls
13. Wrap the bottom of a glass with buttered parchment paper (or the butter wrapper) and flatten each ball to about ¾" thick
14. Bake for 15-18 minutes until golden brown at the edges and just set; reverse the position of the cookie sheets halfway through cooking
15. Cool for around 3 minutes on the baking sheet, then transfer to a wire rack to cool

Simple Ginger Beer

This easy to make, simple ginger beer produces about 3 quarts and takes about 20 minutes to make. If you find this to be a little too strong, dilute it with lemonade or fizzy water.

Ingredients:

- 3 quarts water
- 1 pound fresh ginger root (washed and grated)
- 1 to 1½ cups of light brown sugar (loosely packed)
- ½ cup lime juice

Method:

1. Bring the water to a boil in a large pan, then remove from the heat
2. Add the grated ginger, cover and leave to steep overnight
3. Strain through a fine sieve, pressing the ginger to extract all the juices
4. Add the lime juice and one cup of sugar, stirring vigorously
5. Adjust to taste with the rest of the sugar
6. Cover and store for 24 hours at room temperature
7. Decant into a bottle with a tight screw top and refrigerate for 3-5 days before drinking

Ginger & Pumpkin Soup

Pumpkin soup has to be one of my favorite types of soup. This recipe really makes for a special soup that is very popular around Thanksgiving time. This recipe serves 8 people and takes around 55 minutes to make.

Ingredients:

- 2 x 15oz cans pumpkin puree (not pumpkin-pie filling) or freshly cooked, pureed pumpkin
- 3 large garlic cloves (minced)
- 2 bay leaves
- 1 large, sweet apple (diced) – Pink Lady works well
- 1 yellow onion (diced)
- 4 cups/1 quart chicken/vegetable stock
- ⅓ cup heavy cream
- ¼ cup fresh ginger (minced)
- 3 tablespoons extra-virgin olive oil
- 2 tablespoons maple syrup
- 1 tablespoon salted butter
- 1 teaspoon + 1 teaspoon salt
- ½ teaspoon freshly ground black pepper
- ¼ teaspoon freshly grated nutmeg

Method:

1. Heat the butter and oil in a large Dutch oven on a medium to low heat
2. Add the ginger, onion, garlic, pepper, nutmeg, bay leaves and one teaspoon of salt and cook for 6 minutes, stirring often, until the onions are translucent
3. Add the apple, cooking for a further 5 minutes, stirring occasionally
4. Add the chicken stock, maple syrup and pumpkin puree, cooking for 20 minutes, stirring occasionally

5. Remove the bay leaves from the soup
6. Process in a blender until smooth, in batches if necessary. Freeze the soup at this stage if you wish to store it
7. Return the soup to the pan, stir in the cream and season to taste
8. Serve hot

Ginger Limeade

This great, alcohol free punch is delicious by itself or added to cocktails. It takes about 15 minutes to make this recipe that produces 8 servings.

Ingredients:

- 6 cups water
- 2 cups water
- 2 cups white (granulated) sugar
- Juice of 8 limes
- Grated zest of 3 limes
- 20 fresh mint leaves
- 2 tablespoons freshly grated ginger

Method:

1. Mix 2 cups of water and the sugar in a small pan and simmer on a medium to high heat
2. Stir until the sugar dissolves, remove from the heat and cool for 5 minutes
3. Pour this sugar water into a pitcher
4. Add the lime juice and zest, ginger and mint
5. Stir with a wooden spoon, pressing the mint leaves against the sides of the pitcher to release their flavor
6. Leave for 10 minutes
7. Strain through a fine mesh sieve into another pitcher
8. Add 6 cups of water, stir well and taste, adding more sugar as required
9. Serve garnished with fresh mint leaves and lime wedges

Horseradish

Horseradish, *Armoracia rusticana*, is a perennial plant valued for its long, hot taproot. It produces bright green leaves that look like dock leaves and small, white flowers appear in early summer

At a Glance Facts

~~Annual~~ / ~~Biennial~~ / **Perennial**	
Position:	Partial to full shade
Soil:	Any, well-drained
Hardiness	Yes, down to -4F/-20C
USDA Zones:	3-9
Sow:	Spring or fall
Harvest:	Fall to early spring

The root is the main ingredient in horseradish sauce, a British accompaniment to roast beef or added to coleslaw to give it a serious kick. The cooked leaves are associated, historically, with the Jewish festival of Passover as part of the Passover Seder Plate, known as Maror, which means bitter in Hebrew. The harshness of the leaves is symbolic of the struggle of the Jews in Ancient Egypt. Exodus 12:8 says, "with bitter herbs they shall eat it", so horseradish and four other herbs make the Seder Plate to represent this period of Jewish history. Prior to the 17th century, horseradish had few culinary purposes and was primarily used for its medicinal properties.

Horseradish is an invasive plant and can be very difficult to get rid of once it has established itself. Most people grow horseradish in containers to avoid this problem.

This plant is thought to come from the east or south eastern parts of Europe, though some experts believe it originated in western Asia. Evidence points to horseradish being one of the medicinal herbs prized by the ancient Greeks.

The medicinal uses of horseradish are extensive, used for anything from toothache to worms and venereal disease! Horseradish was mixed with white vinegar to remove freckles, though many people suffer an allergic reaction when horseradish is applied to the skin.

In 1597, John Gerard published a herbal book in England which suggested using horseradish as a food, "the horseradish stamped with a little vinegar put thereto, is commonly used among the Germans for sauce to eate fish with and such like meates as we do mustarde". His book was a translation of an earlier work by a Flemish physician called Rembert Dodeons. Experts believe using horseradish as food originated in Germany and central Europe.

Horseradish sauce became very popular and its use spread to the American colonies in the 17th century. As horseradish root is very high in vitamin C, sailors took it on sea voyages and ate it to prevent scurvy. Today, horseradish is a staple of the English Sunday Roast and popular as a condiment across Western Europe and America.

Growing Instructions

Grow horseradish in light, fertile soil that is moist, but well drained. It prefers a position in full sun and needs regularly watering in the growing season.

Although you can start horseradish from seed, it is much easier and quicker to grow it from pieces of root available in most garden stores. The roots are known as 'thongs' and sometimes are pre-grown in containers.

Growing in containers is easy. Fill a large container with a good quality, multi-purpose compost. Make some deep holes in it and then put the root pieces in the holes, so they are about 2"/5cm below the surface, then cover. A 12"/30cm container will comfortable hold three thongs. Water and leave in a sunny or partially shaded spot.

Follow the same process to grow in the soil, though keep the area free of weeds until the horseradish has established itself.

Horseradish is a good companion plant for most root crops as it boosts their disease resistance. Be careful handling horseradish roots as the juices are fiery hot and can hurt if you rub your hands on your eyes, nose or mouth. Wear gloves when handling the root to prevent any possible problems. Home-grown, raw horseradish is often much stronger and hotter than that bought in supermarkets.

Plant Care

Horseradish is a low maintenance plant once established. Water regularly during the growing season and in dry weather. Apply a balanced liquid fertilizer in the summer to give your plants a boost.

Cut off any damaged leaves and remove dead growth from the crown in fall.

Harvest in the fall once the foliage has died back, ideally after a frost as this improves the flavor of the roots. Harvest the roots the year after it is planted. Harvesting some roots every year helps to prevent the plant spreading and becoming invasive. Lift the roots and cut off what you need using a sharp pair of secateurs, it will grow back quick enough.

The roots are best fresh, but you can wash, grate and dry the roots if you have an excess. Alternatively, store them in a wooden box, covered with damp sand in a cool, dark area where they will last for several months. The washed roots will keep in a perforated plastic bag in your refrigerator for at least three months.

Culinary Uses

Horseradish makes a great condiment that is on a par with its cousin, mustard. The root is not cooked. When preparing horseradish, be very careful and wear gloves. It is extremely hot and the juices can burn your skin. Grating the root starts an enzymatic reaction, which releases extremely strong fumes that can be irritating to the eyes and nose. Work in a well-ventilated area or outside to minimize the effect of these fumes.

Wash, clean and peel or scrape the roots so the rough skin is removed, leaving the creamy white flesh of the root exposed. Like potatoes, horseradish discolors when exposed to air and becomes bitter, so use it straight away or toss it with lemon juice or vinegar to prevent discoloration.

Horseradish sauce is easy to make; the instructions are in the recipe section below. It is traditionally served with roast beef, but works well with cured meats, broccoli, seafood and smoked fish such as mackerel. Eat the leaves raw in salads or cook like a leafy vegetable. Make horseradish sauce milder by adding the vinegar as you grate or immediately after grating the root. To make a strong sauce, leave it three or four minutes before adding the vinegar. When you grate horseradish, you release isothiocyanates or volatile oils that give the root its heat. Adding vinegar stops this enzymatic reaction, so the longer you wait to add the vinegar, the hotter the resulting sauce will be.

Add the grated root to sour cream or yogurt to make a dip that is delicious with fresh vegetables. Try stirring some into mashed potatoes to give them a spicy kick. Just be careful not to add too much horseradish to anything as it can be overwhelming.

Health Uses

Horseradish contains more vitamin C than oranges and lemons though should not be eaten in high quantities because it is a laxative and diuretic. It also contains high levels of Vitamin K, which helps to maintain heathy bones and arteries. By encouraging perspiration, it helps to lower fevers. Horseradish peroxidase or HRP is an enzyme found in horseradish used in an antibody based test for HIV, AIDS and SARS. Scientists also use this enzyme to track harmful pathogens in air, food and water.

If you have a weak thyroid or take any medication for your thyroid gland, do not use horseradish as it contains chemicals that interfere in this gland's production of hormones.

Do not feed any of the horseradish plant to livestock or pets, as it can be fatal.

Horseradish has many health benefits. It contains manganese that helps boost energy production and defend your body against antioxidants. Its high levels of vitamin C are good for your immune system, skin and hair.

Containing vital amino acids and vitamins, including B9 (folic acid), horseradish can help to boost your nervous system and keep your brain healthy. With a wide range of B-vitamins, horseradish helps red blood cell formation and provides the folic acid pregnant women need to keep their babies healthy.

As horseradish helps to regulate your metabolism, it can reduce insomnia and improve your ability to sleep due to its high levels of magnesium.

The strong aroma from horseradish, although eye watering, can help to clear your nose and respiratory system when you have a cold or allergies.

Beauty Uses

Horseradish root can have some beauty uses, though be careful with it as some people do suffer from an allergic reaction to it. If you are unsure, patch test it on your skin before using any beauty product with horseradish in.

Horseradish will lighten skin discolorations. Grate a four-inch piece of fresh horseradish root and add it to a quarter cup of apple cider vinegar. Seal it in a glass jar and leave it for two weeks, shaking daily. Strain, then refrigerate and apply three times a day using a cotton ball to discolored areas of skin.

Mixing some grated horseradish root with buttermilk and glycerine, leaving it overnight before straining, makes a lotion that treats blackheads, acne and oily skin.

Make a facemask from grated horseradish root, sour cream and oatmeal to help reduce the appearance of freckles. Apply it twice a week to your skin, massaging it in with your fingers. Leave it for 15-20 minutes like a facemask and then wash off with warm water.

Mixing horseradish root with vinegar makes an effective treatment for dandruff. Apply a horseradish poultice to your scalp to help prevent hair loss and regrow your hair.

Pests, Problems & Diseases

Horseradish is generally pest free, though it can sometimes suffer from club root.

Recommended Varieties

Amoracia rusticana is the main variety of horseradish found in the shops, though there are over 30 horseradish cultivars according to the International Herb Association. The main difference between cultivars is usually the foliage and disease resistance levels.

- Maliner Kren or Common – crinkled leaves, rounded where they attach to the stem. High quality roots, but not favored commercially due to susceptibility to turnip mosaic 1 virus and white rust.
- Bohemian Type – smooth leaves, tapering at the base includes cultivars such as Bohemian Giant, Sass, Swiss and New Bohemian. Developed in Bohemia or the Czech Republic, these cultivars vary in disease resistance but have fleshy roots which are smaller than those of common horseradish.
- Big Top Western – a new variety bred for disease resistance, particularly to the turnip mosaic 1 virus. There are many numbered strains of this cultivar, but generally, it is of more interest to researchers and farmers.
- Variegata – large, wavy leaves that grow from the middle of the plant. Typically grown as an ornamental due to its appealing foliage, it will take two or three years for the plant to reach maturity.
- Wasabi – not a member of the horseradish family, but belonging to the *Wasabia japanoica* family from Japan. The root is similar to horseradish, but hotter and sweeter. It can be tricky to cultivate, but worth a try as an alternative to horseradish if you like hot food.

Recipes

Horseradish Sauce

This is an easy to make, tasty horseradish sauce that takes about ten minutes to make. Traditionally served with roast beef, it is also delicious with chips, fish cakes, salmon and in roast beef sandwiches! Refrigerate any leftovers in a sealed container.

Ingredients:

- 6fl oz/175ml double cream (whipped to soft peaks)
- 8 tablespoons freshly grated horseradish root
- 4 tablespoons mayonnaise
- 2 tablespoons Dijon mustard
- 1 pinch caster sugar (or to taste)
- Salt and pepper to taste

Method:

1. Mix the mustard, horseradish and mayonnaise together until well combined
2. Fold in the whipped cream
3. Season to taste using salt, pepper and sugar

Dill and Potato Beef Salad

A lovely salad by itself, but add the beef and this becomes a great main course meal. Cook the beef how you prefer it and serve warm or cold. This recipe makes enough for 4 people.

Ingredients:

- 14oz/400g small, waxy potatoes
- 12½oz/350g rump/sirloin steak or cold roast beef
- ½ red onion (finely sliced)
- 3 tablespoons dill (finely chopped)
- 2 tablespoons thick yogurt
- 1 tablespoon extra-virgin olive oil
- 1 tablespoon freshly grated horseradish
- 2 teaspoons white-wine or apple cider vinegar
- Salt and pepper to taste

Method:

1. Cook the potatoes in salted water until tender
2. Whisk the oil, yogurt, vinegar, dill and horseradish together in a small bowl and season to taste

3. Drain the potatoes, leaving them in the colander for a few minutes to steam
4. Cut larger potatoes in half so they are all roughly the same size
5. Toss in the dressing while still hot
6. Add the red onion and mix
7. Season the steak and cook to your preference, leaving to cool before thinly slicing
8. Plate up the potato salad, top with beef and garnish with fresh dill fronds

Potato and Apple Latkes

These delicious, Eastern European pancakes are great with cured or smoked fish, making a great starter. This recipe serves four to six people.

Pancake Ingredients:

- 18oz/500g potatoes (peeled)
- 1oz/30g plain flour
- 1 onion
- 1 crisp apple such as Braeburn (cored but not peeled)
- 1 egg (lightly beaten)
- 2 tablespoons chives (finely chopped)
- Salt and pepper
- Oil for frying

Horseradish Cream Ingredients:

- 5¼ fl oz/150ml crème fraîche
- 2 tablespoons freshly grated horseradish
- 1 teaspoon lemon juice or apple cider vinegar
- 1 teaspoon Dijon mustard
- ½ teaspoon caster sugar

To Serve:

- 1 apple (cut into thin slivers)
- Pickled herring, rollmops or equivalent

Method:

1. Preheat your oven to 350F/180C and put a baking tray in the oven
2. Line a colander with a clean tea towel and put it in your sink
3. Grate the onion, potatoes and apple
4. Put them in the colander and squeeze out as much liquid as you can
5. Transfer to a bowl, add the flour, chives, egg and lemon juice and season to taste
6. Stir well until thoroughly combined
7. Heat ½" of oil in a large pan on a medium to high heat
8. Shape large tablespoons of the pancake mixture into pancakes about 2" across
9. Drop them into the oil, avoiding overcrowding, and cook for 4 minutes per side until golden brown
10. Keep the cooked pancakes warm on the tray in the oven until they are all cooked
11. Mix the sauce ingredients together until smooth
12. Serve the latkes with slices of the fish and apple topped with a dollop of the horseradish cream

Grated Horseradish with Beef

Hyssop

Hyssop, *Hyssopus officinalis*, is a perennial or evergreen shrub with aromatic leaves and tubular blue flowers with two lips. It is best known from Psalm 51 in the Bible where it is used as a cleansing herb, "Purge me with Hyssop and I shall be clean".

At a Glance Facts

~~Annual~~ / ~~Biennial~~ / **Perennial**	
Position:	Full sun to partial shade
Soil:	Moist, well-drained
Hardiness	Fully hardy
USDA Zones:	3-10
Sow:	Summer
Harvest:	Before the flowers bloom

Hyssop grows up to two feet tall and is native to southern Europe, found in the Balkans, Turkey and the Mediterranean countries. The leaves are dark green, narrow, with a strong, bitter taste, and slightly minty smell.

Hyssop has a long history of medicinal use by humans, with Hypocrates recommending it to treat bronchitis. Since then, its use has extended to coughs, colds, fevers, pulmonary disease and herpes. It is commonly used for physical cleansing, not only of the body but of spaces too. In Beyerl's Compendium of Herbal Magick he states, "There is probably no herbe better suited for the physical cleansing and washing of one's temple, ritual tools or even ritual robes."

Bees love this herb to the point beekeepers used to rub hyssop leaves on hives to make the bees stay. The flowers also attract butterflies and hummingbirds.

Do not confuse hyssop with *Agastache fornieulu*, or anise hyssop, common in the United States but unrelated to *Hyssopus officinalis*. Anise hyssop has purple flowers and pointed leaves, tasting of anise and used as a substitute for anise in cooking.

Growing Instructions

Hyssop likes to grow in well drained, fertile soil that is either neutral on the pH scale or slightly alkaline. It prefers positioning in full sun, though will grow in partial shade. The plants are short lived for a perennial and need replacing every few years for a good, healthy crop.

Grow from seed, sown in the spring, or softwood cuttings taken in the summer. Seedlings are spaced at 15-18" apart. In spring or fall, propagate hyssop by root division or heel cuttings.

Do not plant it near radishes as the plants do not grow well together, but it does make a good companion for grapes and cabbages, where it deters cabbage moths.

Plant Care

Hyssop does not require a lot of maintenance or care. Water regularly during dry weather and prune back in late winter or early spring to encourage fresh growth.

Preserve hyssop leaves by drying. Harvest in August, before the flowers open. Pick leaves that are on green parts of the plant, not the woody stems. Harvest on a dry day and dry quickly, out of bright sunlight and with good air circulation to preserve as much of their active ingredients as possible. A sunny room with a temperature of between 70-90F/20-32C is ideal, or an airing cupboard with the door left open.

It takes around six days for the leaves to dry fully. If left longer, the leaves discolor and the flavor is lost. Store in a cool, dry place in an airtight container and hyssop leaves will keep for 12-18 months.

Culinary Uses

Use hyssop in small quantities in cooking, at least initially. The leaves are bitter with a slight mint or camphor taste that can be a little overpowering. As you get used to hyssop, you can use more. Both the leaves and the flowers have uses in cooking, but never together. The stronger flavored leaves overpower the more delicate tasting flowers and their flavor is lost.

Use the leaves, dried or fresh, in stews, soups and herbal teas. Fresh leaves work well with soft cheese, sandwiches, dips, pasta and butters while the flowers are a wonderful addition to a green salad.

Generally, you use hyssop by itself, but it combines well with other herbs such as chervil, chives, parsley, bay and sage. Adding hyssop and sage to a fatty fish or meat dish can make it easier to digest.

Bitters, digestives and liquors such as Absinthe, Chartreuse and Benedictine all make use of hyssop, but it is not so popular in cooking because it can be overpowering. However, a couple of hyssop leaves can make a compote or stewed prunes much more interesting to eat! Try adding a teaspoon of ground, dried hyssop leaves to a peach cobbler and you will find the taste to be significantly improved.

A small pinch of hyssop flavors lentil and mushroom dishes as well as soups. Sausages and pâtés taste fantastic when seasoned with hyssop. This herb also works well with fish. In Panama, fish farmers feed hyssop leaves to live fish so they take on its flavor.

Health Uses

Use hyssop in the same way as sage is for many complaints such as poor digestion, to get rid of worms and as a gargle for sore throats. Use this herb to help relieve coughs or any congestion of the airways. Combine it with horehound to treat asthma, bronchitis, coughs and consumption.

As this herb encourages the production of mucous while stimulating expectoration, it is excellent at treating upper respiratory congestions. It can irritate mucous membranes so is often used after the infection has peaked.

Use the leaves as a poultice to heal minor burns, sores and bruises. Make a wash by boiling two teaspoons of dried hyssop in boiling water and steeping for twenty minutes that treats insect stings, body lice, bites and herpes simplex.

Beauty Uses

Hyssop is good for treating skin complaints, but is not widely used in the beauty industry. Common hyssop is often confused in beauty with water hyssop (*Bacopa monnieri*), which is no relation of *Hyssopus officinalis.*

Make a hyssop tea/wash and use it as a face cleanser. It helps to reduce the appearance of pores, making your skin appear smoother and softer. It is great for oily skin, helping to not only deep clean pores, but also balancing skin oil levels. In addition, as a natural cleanser, it is excellent for people with sensitive skin and can reduce the sensitivity.

Pests, Problems & Diseases

Hyssop is generally disease and pest free, though can be affected by leafhoppers.

Recommended Varieties

Common hyssop is usually found in garden stores, though there are some other interesting cultivars, including the aforementioned anise hyssop:

- Common Hyssop (*Hyssopnus officianlis*) – growing up to 2 feet tall, usually with purple flowers but white and pink flowering varieties exist. The leaves bear a resemblance to those of the rosemary plant and it is excellent for attracting pollinating insects, butterflies and hummingbirds. Common hyssop grows in USDA zones 3 to 10.
- Rock Hyssop (*Hyssopnus officianlis subsp. arisatus*) – a much lower growing cultivar with purple flowers, popular in rock gardens and as

a path edging. This variety grows in USDA zones 3 to 9.

- Anise Hyssop (*Agastache foe-niculum*) – not a direct relation to common hyssop, but a member of the mint family. It looks similar to lavender in its flowers, color and size, though smells and tastes of anise. This cultivar grows in USDA zones 6 to 10.
- Korean Hyssop (*Agastache rugose*) – known as Korean mint, this is similar to anise hyssop, though slightly hardier, growing in USDA zones 5 to 10. It grows from two to five feet tall, depending on cultivar.
- Giant Hyssops – a number of *Agastache* species are referred to as giant hyssops, including *Agastache nepetoides*, which has yellow flower spikes, grows in USDA zones 2 to 8 and has no scent. There are many other giant varieties with colors ranging from purple to blue to pink and more. Generally, giant hyssops are two or three feet tall and hardy in USDA zones 6 to 9.
- Hot Hyssops – also known as South Western or Mexican hyssops, they originate in warmer climates and have more fiery colors than the muted blues and purples of common hyssop. These hyssops are very popular with hummingbirds. Sunset hyssop (*Agastache rupestric*) grows to about four feet tall, has a licorice scent and bright orange flowers, hardy from USDA zones 4 to 9. Orange Hummingbird Mint (*Agastache aurantiaca*) is hardy for zones 6 to 10 and has peach or orange flowers.

Recipes

Blue Hyssop Lemonade

The hyssop in this lemonade gives it a delicious flavor. Try swapping the hyssop for another herb like mint, time, tarragon or basil.

Instructions:

- 8 cups water
- ⅓ cup honey
- Juice of 6 lemons
- 4 tablespoons common hyssop (chopped)

Method:

1. Boil the water in a large, lidded pan
2. Add the honey and hyssop
3. Cover, turn the heat off and steep for 15 minutes
4. Strain the herbs and discard
5. Mix with the lemon juice and refrigerate for at least 2 hours

Chamomile Tea
This is a great tea to drink after a meal to help digestion.

Ingredients:

- 1¾ pints/1 liter freshly boiled water
- 2 chamomile tea bags
- 2 tablespoons fresh mint leaves
- 1 tablespoon hyssop leaves

Method

1. Put the tea bags and herbs into a tea pot and add the water
2. Steep for a minimum of 5 minutes
3. Serve with mint or hyssop leaves garnishing the cups

Glazed Hyssop Carrots
This is a great way to serve carrots and make them even nicer! You can try this with a mixture of parsnips and carrots.

Ingredients:

- 17½oz /500g young or Chanterelle carrots (scraped and thinly sliced)
- 1 cup chicken/vegetable stock
- 1 tablespoon unsalted butter
- 1 tablespoon honey
- 1 tablespoon fresh hyssop leaves (finely chopped)
- Salt and pepper to taste

Method:

1. Put all the ingredients except the hyssop into a saucepan and stir well
2. Bring to a simmer on a medium heat
3. Reduce the heat to low, cover and cook until the carrots are tender and the liquid syrupy (around 20 minutes) taking care it does not burn
4. Remove from heat, toss with the hyssop and serve

Baked Peppers
These make for a great lunch or light meal and are delicious with fresh bread, salad or fries. The bitterness of the hyssop offsets the sweetness of the peppers and tomatoes very well.

Ingredients:

- 16 cherry tomatoes (halved)
- 8 anchovy fillets (drained/rinsed and roughly chopped)
- 4 red bell peppers (halved lengthways and seeds/pith removed
- 3 garlic cloves (peeled and finely sliced)
- 2 sprigs hyssop leaves (finely chopped)
- Extra-virgin olive oil
- Salt

Method:

1. Preheat your oven to 400F/200C
2. Lay the peppers, cut side up on a greased baking dish
3. Put a few garlic slices in each bell pepper half
4. To each pepper half, add a pinch of hyssop leaves, a tablespoon of oil and a pinch of salt
5. Evenly divide the tomatoes between the pepper halves
6. Bake in your oven until the peppers are full of juice and start to collapse
7. Stir in a teaspoon of anchovies to each pepper
8. Bake for 10 minutes, then serve

Hyssop Face Mask

This is a simple to make face mask that harnesses the properties of hyssop to cleanse and purify your skin.

Ingredients:

- 2 tablespoons full fat milk (substitute for almond or coconut milk)
- 2 teaspoons dried hyssop
- 1 teaspoon French green clay (or any other clay)

Method:

1. Use a pestle and mortar to grind the hyssop into a powder
2. Heat the milk in a small pan until almost boiling
3. Stir in the hyssop
4. Remove from the heat and steep for a minimum of 5 minutes – leave it longer for a stronger face mask
5. Add the clay, stirring it in quickly so the mixture just coats the spoon but is still runny
6. Apply to a clean face, leave to dry for 10-15 minutes then rinse off with warm water
7. Pat your face dry and moisturize

Lavender

Common lavender, *Lavandula angustifolia*, is a very easy to grow evergreen shrub that has masses of delightfully scented flowers poking up from silvery grey/grey leaves.

At a Glance Facts

~~Annual~~ / ~~Biennial~~ / **Perennial**	
Position:	Full sun
Soil:	Well-drained
Hardiness	Hardy
USDA Zones:	5-9
Sow:	Spring to summer
Harvest:	Summer to early fall

Lavender is drought tolerant and grows in borders or containers.

This herb is documented as being used by humans for over 2,500 years and is a favorite herb of many people. The Ancient Egyptians prized lavender for its perfume and used it in their mummification rituals. The Phoenicians and Arabian tribes also used lavender as a perfume. The name lavender comes from the Latin word 'lavo', which means 'to wash' as both the Romans and Greeks bathed in lavender scented water.

Lavender is thought to originate in Greece and, around 600BC, travelled from the Greek Hyeres Islands to France. Today, lavender grows across much of Europe, notably found in Italy, Spain, England and France.

In the early 1600s, lavender travelled across the Atlantic Ocean, making its way to the New World. Meanwhile, the English developed their own strain of lavender that came to be known as 'English' lavender. Queen Elizabeth I of England particularly prized lavender, using it as a perfume and a conserve. According to British lore, the Queen commanded that her royal table should never be without a lavender conserve and instructed her gardeners to ensure she had a year round supply of fresh lavender.

Lavender is still a popular scent in cosmetics, having increased in popularity in England under the reign of Queen Victoria who had lavender in every room of her palace. Her royal household used lavender for everything from washing floors to freshening the air and keeping the royal linens smelling fresh.

In World War I, soldiers' wounds were bathed in lavender and today the French graze lambs in lavender fields so the meat is tender and fresh.

Lavender is a very popular herb, best known for its scent, but is beautiful in your garden. It is a great addition to a sensory garden and is very attractive to bees and pollinating insects. It is a wonderful in any garden and you can harvest and dry the flowers every year to make scented poesies to put in your linen drawers!

Growing Instructions

Plant lavender between April and May in any type of soil. It thrives in poor soils, though likes a free-draining soil. It is an ideal plant for an alkaline or chalky soil but prefers a position in full sun. In heavy soils such as clay, lavender does not live too long, getting very woody at the base. If you have a heavy soil, dig in gravel and organic matter to improve drainage. Growing on a mound helps to stop the roots getting too wet and you are recommended to grow a lavender hedge on a ridge for the same reason.

Gardeners rarely grow lavender from seed. Take hardwood cuttings after flowering in the fall or softwood/semi-ripe cuttings from young plants early in the summer. Dry seed heads and sow, though remember the seeds will not grow true and the flower colors will vary.

Space plants three feet apart if growing individually, or one foot apart if growing a hedge. Lavender is suited for containers, but ensure the compost is free-draining and regularly watered during the summer. Half-hardy and tender varieties are better in containers so they can be moved inside during winter.

Plant Care

Prune lavender every year otherwise it becomes leggy and woody, with fewer flowers. Use secateurs to remove the flower stalks and an inch of this year's growth, leaving some green behind. Prune in late summer, after flowering. Remove and replace neglected, woody plants, as Lavender does not grow easily from the woody growth. Be careful when pruning not to cut back into old wood as the plant may struggle to recover.

To harvest lavender, cut the long flower spikes just as the flowers start to open. Bunch the flowers up and leave to dry in the sun, which takes four or five days. Alternatively, hang indoors in a warm, dry location or spread on a sheet to dry. Store in glass or ceramic containers with tight fitting lids to keep the oils in the flowers

You can divide young plants; older plants do not handle this well. Move lavender in early spring, before it starts growing, leaving plenty of soil on the roots.

Culinary Uses

Lavender has some culinary uses, though is not very popular in American or British cuisine. If you are using dried lavender flowers, use a third of the amount of fresh flowers to avoid overpowering the dish. Adding too much lavender to a dish makes it very perfume like and bitter, so best to start with a little and add more as required.

Lavender flowers add a lovely color to any salad and in bread making, substituted for rosemary. Put the flowers in sugar and leave, sealed tightly, for two or three weeks to create a lavender sugar for use in baking.

Health Uses

Lavender has quite a few health uses, but is best known for its relaxing and calming ability. Lavender essential oil is known to improve sleep quality. Just a few drops on your pillow at night will help you have a much better night's sleep.

Avoid putting lavender oil directly on to your skin as it can cause irritation in some people. Lavender oil is best mixed with a carrier such as a base oil, e.g. almond oil, or a cream before use.

Lavender essential oil is also very good at alleviating the symptoms associated with PMT. Put some in a diffuser and in about ten minutes it will boost your mood.

The calming abilities of lavender also help reduce anxiety. Inhaling lavender essential oil every day for two weeks has been clinically proven to reduce anxiety. Some dental surgeries have lavender oil diffusers in their reception because it helps to reduce patients' anxiety.

Lavender oil has an analgesic and anti-inflammatory effect, so is good for relieving mild to moderate pain. Use it as a massage oil or in a diffuser to help with neck or back pain, period pain or osteoarthritic pain.

Migraines are an unpleasant type of headache, reduced by inhaling lavender essential oil or rubbing it, in a base oil or cream, on the temples and nape of the neck. Mix it with peppermint oil for an extra cooling effect.

Head lice are another problem that lavender oil is effective at dealing with, particularly when mixed with tea tree oil and coconut oil. Massage the mixture into your hair and leave it for a couple of hours. Then shampoo, rinse and apply conditioner, then use a nit comb to remove both the nits and their eggs. Repeat every couple of days for two weeks and they should be gone.

Add lavender oil to an aloe vera gel to ease sunburn and skin irritation. It is very calming and soothing.

Beauty Uses

Lavender is very good for your skin as it has strong antiseptic properties. It is popular as a scent in many products such as soaps, skin creams and more.

Mix 15 drops of lavender oil with 15 drops of rose oil in 5 teaspoons of witch hazel and 5 tablespoons of water to make a great cleanser and toner for mature or dry skin. Apply in the morning and evening, and then moisturize your skin.

Make a simple skin moisturizer by mixing three drops of lavender essential oil with a teaspoon of wheat germ oil. Apply twice a day for softer, healthier skin.

Mix four drops of lavender essential oil with a tablespoon of tea tree oil and a teaspoon of a carrier oil or neutral cream for an effective acne treatment. Apply the mixture before you go to bed and leave it overnight. Wash it off next morning using a mild facewash. Repeat this daily and you will notice an improvement in your skin within a few weeks.

To treat sunburn, mix 10 drops of lavender oil with 5 teaspoons of aloe vera gel. Apply once or twice a day for instant relief. In a few days, you will see a big improvement in your skin.

Lavender has quite a few beauty uses and is particularly good as a scent. I collect and dry lavender flowers with my daughter, put them into sown pouches and leave them in drawers to freshen clothing. Mostly, though, people prize lavender for its ability to calm and relax.

Pests, Problems & Diseases

Lavender is generally an easy plant to grow. The biggest problem gardeners have is when it becomes leggy and flowering diminishes. Regular pruning, as detailed above, will ensure your lavender looks fantastic all the time.

Avoid planting lavender in heavy or wet soils as it does not like them and the roots will rot. Lavender does suffer with some insect problems such as the rosemary beetle and Liguian leafhopper. In damp conditions, lavender can suffer from grey molds.

Recommended Varieties

There are over 45 different species of lavender, and over 450 different varieties, so you really are spoilt for choice. Which variety you choose will depend on where you are growing it. Most people grow English or French lavender, as these are good for the oil and flowers.

Here are some of the most commonly grown lavenders with some of their uses.

- *Lavendula angustifolia* 'Ashdown Forest' – growing to 20" x 30", this cultivar produces pale lavender flowers in early summer and is ideal for hedging
- *L. angustifolia* 'Hidcote' – a very popular cultivar with bushy, grey-green foliage and dark, violet colored flowers appearing from late June. Grows to 24" high and about 30" wide and makes a great hedge
- *L. angustifolia* 'Royal Purple' – long, deep purple colored flowers appearing in early June above grey-green foliage. A good hedging plant, grows to 18" tall and spreads to around 32" wide
- *L. angustifolia* 'Nana Alba' – a very compact plant with light green leaves and plenty of white flowers appearing in late June. Height and spread is around 12", good for the front of borders or low hedges
- *L. angustifolia* 'Little Lottie' – grey-green foliage and pale pink flowers appearing from late June. Grows to around 15" tall and about 26" wide and is great for low hedges or the front of borders
- *L. angustifolia* 'Garden Beauty' – yellow, variegated leaves appear in spring, fading to a cream color in summer and then green during winter. Produces lavender colored flowers from mid-June and grows to around 20" tall and about 28" wide
- *L. x chaytoriae* 'Sawyers' – silvery-grey foliage producing tall, bushy lilac flowers from early July. Grows up to 28" tall and has a wide

spread of around 48"

- *L. angustifolia* 'Miss Katherine' – green foliage and pink to pale purple flowers appearing in early summer. Grows up to 24" tall and around 32" wide
- *L. x intermedia* 'Edelweiss' – bushy, grey-green foliage and plenty of white flowers from late July onward. Grows up to 30" tall and spreads to about 36" wide
- *Lavandula stoechas* French Lavender – great for containers, has a long summer flowering period, but are only half hardy

Recipes

Cottage Cheese Bread

This is a great recipe, producing one large loaf of bread. It is quite quick to make and the herbs give it a delicious taste.

Ingredients:

- 3 cups plus 3 tablespoons bread flour
- 1 cup low fat cottage cheese
- ¼ cup honey
- ¼ cup warm water (110F/43C)
- 2 eggs (at room temperature)
- 2 tablespoons extra-virgin olive oil
- 1 tablespoon fresh thyme leaves (finely chopped)
- ½ tablespoon fresh basil leaves (finely chopped)
- 3 teaspoons instant active dry yeast
- 1 teaspoon lavender flowers (finely chopped)
- ¼ teaspoon baking soda

Method:

1. If you have a bread machine, add all the ingredients to the pan in your bread machine and process according to the manufacturer's instructions. You can cook the bread in the bread machine or remove the dough and cook it in the oven
2. Otherwise, process all the ingredients in a stand mixer with a dough hook to form an elastic ball. Add more water, a little at the time if you think the dough is looking too dry or more flour if you feel it is too moist
3. Knead the dough on a floured surface for around 15 minutes until elastic
4. Place in a glass bowl, cover with plastic wrap and rest for 10 to 15 minutes

5. Fold the dough a few times, then return to the bowl, cover and leave in a warm place for 30-50 minutes until it has doubled in size
6. Preheat your oven to 400F/200C
7. Shape the bread into a round loaf or place in a bread tin
8. Score the top of the loaf with a sharp knife, making three diagonal slashes that are ½" deep
9. Cook in your oven for 20-25 minutes until nicely browned and the internal temperature is between 200-210F/93-99C
10. Cool on a wire rack

Lavender Jelly

This is a really tasty jelly that was very popular in England in Victorian times. It is great served with ice cream or any pudding, though makes a good accompaniment to meats, particularly poultry and lamb; try serving it at your next Thanksgiving celebration! It also works well when paired with brie cheese. This will make around 5½ pints of jelly.

Ingredients:

- 4 cups white (granulated) sugar
- 3½ cups water
- ½ cup dried lavender flowers
- ¼ cup lemon juice
- 3oz liquid pectin or 1¾oz packet of powdered pectin

Method:

1. Sterilize some jars and prepare your canner for use, make sure the jars are hot when you put the jelly in later
2. Bring the water to the boil in a large pan
3. Remove from the heat and stir in the lavender flowers
4. Leave for 20 minutes to steep
5. Strain into a second pan, discarding the flowers
6. Add the lemon juice and pectin, stirring until the pectin has dissolved
7. Return to the heat, and boil on a high heat
8. Add the sugar and stir well until dissolved
9. Allow to boil on a hard rolling boil for 2 minutes for a soft set or 4 minutes for a medium set
10. Test the setting point
11. When at the desired consistency, transfer to the jars, leaving ½" headspace, seal and process in your canner for 10 minutes
12. Can and store until required

Lavender Sorbet

This is a lovely dessert that has a delicate flavor. It is very refreshing after a meal and its unusual flavor will impress your dinner guests. English lavender is the best variety to use, with dried flowers having a stronger taste. This recipe takes about 15 minutes to make 10-12 servings, plus freezing time. The vodka is optional, but it helps the sorbet to remain soft, as it does not freeze fully. Although you can use any alcohol, vodka works well as it has no taste to detract from the lavender.

Ingredients:

- 2 cups water
- 1 cup white (granulated) sugar
- 2½ tablespoons lemon juice
- 2 tablespoons vodka
- 1 tablespoon dried lavender flowers (food grade)

Method:

1. Heat the sugar and water, stirring regularly, in a pan on a medium heat
2. Add the lavender flowers and stir well
3. Bring to the boil, stirring often, then reduce the heat to low and simmer for 5 minutes
4. Remove from the heat, cover and leave to stand for 10 minutes
5. Strain the mixture into a large bowl
6. Add the vodka and lemon juice and stir until combined
7. If you own an ice cream maker, transfer everything to your ice cream maker and process according to the manufacturer's instructions
8. If not, pour the mixture into a container, cover and put into your freezer
9. When it is part frozen, remove it from the freezer, mash it with a fork and then freeze again
10. When completely frozen, remove from the freezer and process until smooth in your food processor
11. Return to the container, cover and freeze

Lemon Balm

Lemon balm, *Melissa officinalis*, is a popular member of the mint family with a strong lemony smell and taste.

At a Glance Facts

~~Annual~~ / ~~Biennial~~ / **Perennial**	
Position:	Full sun to partial shade
Soil:	Well-drained
Hardiness	Fully hardy
USDA Zones:	4-9
Sow:	Spring or fall
Harvest:	Any time

This bushy perennial plant is highly invasive, growing from runners like mint where it will soon take over any garden. The leaves are broad, oval shaped with scalloped edges and a very strong lemon smell to them. The flowers are leafy spikes and pale purple or creamy-white in color.

Lemon balm is naturalized across much of Europe and America, growing from seeds or by division. It will spread from its roots and many people grow it in containers to prevent it from becoming invasive.

Known as Cure-All, for its medicinal uses, Sweet Mary or the Honey Plant, this herb originated in the Mediterranean. This calming herb has been cultivated for over two thousand years for its medicinal and culinary properties.

Bees love lemon balm and are strongly associated with it. The Romans called the plant '*apiastrum*' from the Latin word '*apias*', meaning bee. The scientific name '*melissa*', is the Greek word for honeybee. In the Middle Ages, bee keepers rubbed lemon balm leaves on bee hives to increase the honey production. The Ancient Greek, Pliny, noted that bees often formed colonies near to lemon balm plants.

The plant not only attracts bees and pollinating insects, but is also popular with butterflies and hummingbirds. This plant is often mistakenly referred to as bee balm, which is a separate plant of the species *Monarda.*

Lemon balm tea has a long history of use as a rejuvenating tonic. King Charles V of France drank lemon balm daily as he believed it would bring him long life and good health. Unfortunately, he died at the age of 42 due to an abscess on his arm from an attempted poisoning. However, in the 13th century, the Prince of Glamorgan also drank lemon balm tea daily and lived to the ripe old age of 108! A gentleman by the name of John Hussey of Sydenham also claimed lemon balm prolonged life and after regularly drinking the tea, he lived to be 116!

In the 17th century, the Carmelite nuns produced their famous Carmelite Water, known as Eau de Melisse de Carmes from lemon balm and other herbs (including cilantro, lemon zest and angelica root). This treated nervous disorders and is still available today in Germany as Klosterfrau Melissengeist.

Growing Instructions

You do not have to try hard to grow lemon balm as it will literally grow anywhere. Most people buy pre-grown plants, though you can grow it from seed, from cuttings or by division. Mature plants need 12-15" between them for good air circulation and ease of access.

Lemon balm will grow in virtually any soil, though prefers a pH range of 6.0 to 7.5, but will grow in soil with a pH of anywhere from 5.6 to 9.0.

Start the seeds 6-8 weeks before the last frost, planting on top of a good quality compost with a light covering of soil. They germinate in 12 to 21 days, requiring moist soil throughout the germination period. Do not allow the soil to dry out between waterings and do not overwater.

Plant out in full sun or a shady spot, though lemon balm does prefer protection from the heat of the midday sun in hotter climates. This herb prefers a fertile, moist soil, but is generally tolerant of most soil types. For larger, more succulent leaves, grow in partial shade rather than full sun.

Plant Care

Harvest regularly throughout the growing season to encourage the production of new leaves. Cut back after flowering to prevent it seeding itself and to promote leaf growth. Variegated cultivars need cutting back in early summer to encourage the continued production of colored growth.

Lift and divide large clumps of lemon balm in the fall to rejuvenate mature plants.

Container grown plants need lifting up on pot feet in winter to allow excess moisture to drain away.

Culinary Uses

Lemon balm is usually made into a herbal tea, though do not leave it to steep too long otherwise it becomes bitter.

The leaves are very good with fish and chicken, working well with vegetables and even in salads. They are used in liquors such as Chartreuse and Benedictine. Add lemon balm to butter to make a lemon herb butter or added to vinegars or oils to give them a lemon flavor.

As a herb, lemon balm pairs well with mint, dill, parsley, basil and chives. When dried, it loses some of its flavor. Chop lemon balm leaves and mix with mayo, then use to make a potato salad.

The flavor of lemon balm works very well with fresh peas, potatoes and broad beans. Add a few leaves to the pan in the last few minutes of cooking to impart a lemony flavor.

Health Uses

Herbalists have a lot of respect for lemon balm for its healing ability, being attributed the ability to extend life and keep people healthy. Commonly used as a digestive aid and to calm nerves, it also treats headaches, stomach cramps, and urinary tract infections.

Lemon balm is a carminative herb, which means it eases abdominal cramping and aids the digestive process. Containing oils called 'terpenes', it relaxes muscles and eases excess gas.

Other key components of lemon balm are 'choloretics' and 'colagogues', both of which helps with gall and liver problems. The former encourages the liver to create more bile, which is used to digest fats whereas the latter helps to move the bile out of the gall bladder. Drink lemon balm tea just after meals for the best digestive relief.

Rosmarinic acid, found in lemon balm, is an enzyme that increases the levels of gamma amino-butyric acid (GABA) in the brain. This neurotransmitter is used by the brain to remain balanced and not get over excited or stressed. It also helps regulate sleep cycles and has a sedative effective. This acid also reduces free radicals that protect nerve cells in the brain from deteriorating. Lemon balm also contains other powerful antioxidants, including 'eugenol', which stops free radicals from getting to brain cells.

Although lemon balm is generally safe to use, in high doses it can have a mild sedative effect. It can interact with some medications, particularly thyroid or chemotherapy medication. Talk to your physician if you are planning on using lemon balm to ensure there are no negative interactions with any drugs you are taking.

Beauty Uses

Lemon balm essential oil is one of the most expensive oils on the market. The oil is steam distilled, with the most oil coming from the upper parts of the plant. The cost is high because oil yields are low; two pounds of lemon balm will only produce about half a millilitre of essential oil! Suppliers will mix lemon balm oil with cheaper oils such as lemongrass or citronella to reduce the cost. Beware of these if you are using the oil for medicinal or beauty purposes.

Lemon balm treats skin conditions, particularly the herpes virus, so is a good ingredient in cold sore cream. It has strong antibacterial and anti-inflammatory properties and is good for other skin complaints including acne and sunburn.

Lemon balm is good for your skin because it contains two compounds, 'caffeic' and 'ferulic' acid, which penetrate the top layers of the skin and protect it against ultra-violet damage. The high levels of flavonoids (strong antioxidants) and tannins contribute to its beneficial effects on your skin.

Use the essential oil, an infused oil or chopped leaves in neutral base creams or gels to make your own skin creams. Use on sunburnt or irritated skin, or apply to your face to fight acne.

Pests, Problems & Diseases

Lemon balm does not suffer from many diseases. It can be affected by leafhoppers, whitefly, or spider mites, but correct plant spacing, watering and keeping the surrounding area free from weeds will help reduce these problems.

Plants that are too close together or in too damp an area can suffer from powdery mildew.

The main problem with lemon balm is its invasiveness. It very quickly takes over a garden and needs maintaining to prevent it from growing out of control. Growing in containers can help keep lemon balm under control, though it can creep out on runners from the holes in the bottom of the container!

Recommended Varieties

There are a couple of cultivars available, though most people grow *Melissa officinalis.*

- 'All Gold' – has gold colored leaves, retaining the lemon scent
- 'Aurea' – has gold and green variegated, lemon scented leaves
- 'Compacta' - a dwarf cultivar that grows to 6"/15cm tall

Recipes

Lemon Balm Cookies
These are very sweet cookies, but the slightly sour taste of the lemon balm offsets the sweetness nicely. It takes about 15 minutes to prepare this dish, and then it requires 3 hours in the refrigerator but only takes 8 to 10 minutes to cook.

Ingredients:

- 2⅓ cups all-purpose (plain) flour
- 1 cup butter (softened)
- ⅔ cup white (granulated) sugar
- 1 egg
- 2 tablespoons lemon balm leaves (minced)
- 1 teaspoon salt
- 1 teaspoon lemon juice
- Whole lemon balm leaves to garnish

Method:

1. Mix the minced lemon balm with the lemon juice in a small bowl, pressing the mixture down with the back of a spoon
2. In your mixer bowl, cream the butter and sugar together until it becomes light and fluffy
3. Beat in the egg and lemon balm plus its juices
4. Gradually beat in the flour and salt
5. Roll into a cylinder in wax paper
6. Cover and refrigerate until firm, about 3 hours
7. Preheat your oven to 350F/175C
8. Cut the cookie dough into ⅛ inch thick slices
9. Cook on a cookie sheet for 8 to 10 minutes, until edges brown

Lemon Balm Bread

I love herbal breads, the flavors are always so good and everyone finds them very interesting. This is a great bread suitable for freezing and perfect for impressing friends and family! Unlike most breads, this one is not left to rise, so is ready in under an hour.

Ingredients:

- 1¾ cups all-purpose flour (sifted)
- ⅔ cup white (granulated) sugar
- ¼ cup lemon balm leaves (finely chopped)
- 2 large eggs
- 1 stick unsalted butter
- 4 teaspoons lemon juice
- 1 teaspoon baking powder
- Pinch of salt
- Grated zest of 1 lemon

Glaze Ingredients:

- ½ cup hot water
- ¼ cup white (granulated) sugar
- ¼ cup lemon balm leaves (finely chopped)
- Juice of 1 lemon

Method:

1. Preheat your oven to 350F/175C
2. Cream the butter in a mixer together with the chopped lemon balm leaves
3. Add the sugar and beat well
4. Add the rest of the ingredients and beat until thoroughly combined
5. Pour the mix into greased and floured bread tins
6. Bake for between 30-45 minutes, until well done, then remove, leaving in the bread pans
7. Mix the glaze ingredients together in a small bowl
8. Pour the glaze over the hot bread and leave for 4 to 6 hours
9. Remove from the pan and refrigerate until required

Lemon Balm Pesto
This is a great alternative to basil pesto and is delicious with pasta, fish or chicken. Best of all, it only takes a few minutes to make!

Ingredients:

- 2 cups fresh lemon balm leaves
- ½ cup extra-virgin olive oil

3 garlic cloves

Method:

1. Blend all the ingredients in your food processor, drizzling in the oil until the desired consistency is reached

Lemony Tea
This is a great tea that is very lemony and full of flavor.

Ingredients:

- ¼ cup lemon balm leaves
- ¼ cup lemon verbena leaves
- 2 tablespoons lemon grass leaves
- 2 tablespoons lemon thyme leaves
- 1 tablespoon lavender flowers

Method:

1. Mix the ingredients together and store in an airtight container
2. Use 1 to 2 teaspoons of the mixture per cup of boiling water when making tea

Rosy Herb Tea
A very simple tea that has a delicate flavor. Sweeten to taste when serving.

Ingredients:

- ½ cup red rose petals (food grade if buying, ensure no sprays used if from your garden)
- 2 tablespoons lemon balm leaves (fresh or dried)
- 1 tablespoon rosemary (fresh or dried)

Method:

1. Mix the herbs together well and store in an airtight container until required
2. Use a teaspoon of the mixture per cup of boiling water
3. Strain after 5-7 minutes and sweeten to taste

Lemon Balm Vinaigrette Dressing

This is a lovely dressing for salads with a great hint of lemon.

Instructions:

- 3 tablespoons extra-virgin olive oil
- 2 tablespoons red/white wine vinegar (whichever you prefer)
- 6-8 lemon balm leaves
- Large pinch of salt
- Ground black pepper to taste

Method:

1. Stack the lemon balm leaves, roll them up and then cut them into thin strips, then chop finely
2. Mix all the ingredients together in a bowl
3. Refrigerate in a sealed container until required

Lemon Balm Lemonade

This nice lemonade harnesses the health properties of lemon balm.

Ingredients:

- 4 lemons
- 2½ cups water
- ⅔ cup boiling water
- ½ cup white (granulated) sugar
- ½ cup fresh lemon balm leaves

Method:

1. Scrub the lemons and peel the rind, avoiding the pith
2. Put the lemon balm, lemon rind and the sugar into a heat proof pitcher or bowl
3. Pour the boiling water into the pitcher
4. Stir well, crushing the lemon balm against the side of the pitcher to release their flavor
5. Leave to infuse for 15 minutes, then strain and cool
6. Cut the lemons in half, squeezing out the juice into a bowl
7. Strain the juice into a large pitcher, adding some sprigs of fresh lemon balm
8. Top up with water and ice, as required
9. Refrigerate until required

Lemon Balm Lip Balm

This is an excellent lip balm to treat cold sores. You will need some lemon balm infused oil. Adjust the amount of beeswax depending on how firm you like your lip balm. When applying this, use cotton buds and be careful not to contaminate your lip balm with the cold sore virus.

Ingredients:

- 4 tablespoons lemon balm infused oil
- 2 tablespoons beeswax
- 1 tablespoon plus 1 teaspoon coconut oil
- 1 tablespoon shea butter
- ½ tablespoon tamanu oil
- ½ tablespoon castor oil
- 25 drops peppermint essential oil
- 15 drops tea tree oil

Method:

1. Mix all the ingredients together, warming the coconut oil and beeswax to melt it
2. While still warm, pour into small tins or jars with lids
3. Leave open until full cooled, then seal tightly and store in a cool, dark place

Lemon Grass

Lemon Grass, *Cymbopogon citratus*, is an aromatic, perennial grass with lance shaped, blue/green leaves, which are full of oils that have a whole host of medical and cosmetic uses as well as being tasty when cooked.

At a Glance Facts

~~Annual~~ / ~~Biennial~~ / **Perennial**	
Position:	Full sun
Soil:	Moist, well-drained
Hardiness	No
USDA Zones:	9-10
Sow:	Spring
Harvest:	Any time

The leaves grow up to three feet long and loose, branched sprays of green to pink/brown flowers appear in late summer and early fall. There are around 55 species of lemongrass, but only the West and East Indian varieties are used in cooking.

Originating in Sri Lanka and South India, lemongrass now grows all around the world. Although it is not frost tolerant, it can be grown as an annual in cooler areas, though will not usually flower. Overwinter it indoors in a sunny position. The stalks are popular in Asian cooking and used to make a healing tea.

For over 2000 years, people have been using lemongrass as a medicine for fevers both as a herb and as a tea. Today, it is popular in Asian cooking and its oil is popular in everything from drinks to food and fragrances.

Growing Instructions

Unless you live in a tropical or semi-tropical area, lemongrass needs growing under glass. It prefers full sun, a loamy compost and moderate humidity.

Sow seeds in early spring; they require a temperature of 55-64F/13-18C to germinate. In late spring, propagate by division. The fresh stalks sold in supermarkets will often root if planted out.

Sow the seeds thinly on the surface of small pots, pressing them down so they are just under the soil. Place the pots in a saucer of water to water from underneath. Use a heated propagator to improve the germination rate.

Once the seedlings are large enough to handle they need transplanting. Put three seedlings in a small pot filled with a good quality compost and put in a sunny, frost-free location.

When roots start to come through the bottom of the pot, transplant the lemongrass plants to a larger pot. Repeat until you are using an 8"/20cm pot. At this point, put the pots outside in a sunny, sheltered location providing it is warm enough. Bring them indoors at night if there is any risk of frost.

Keep the plants moist during the growing season. In late summer, move your plants back indoors in a bright, cool position. Reduce watering; making sure the compost is just about moist. A temperature of around 40F/5C is ideal for lemongrass plants.

If you live in USDA zones 9 to 10, then lemongrass will grow in the ground. Start the seedlings as above and plant out in early summer at the stage where you are transferring your plants to an 8" pot.

Plant Care

Feed lemongrass regularly throughout the growing season with a dilute, balanced feed.

In fall, when the foliage begins to turn brown, cut the leaves back to 4"/10cm long. Stop feeding over winter, starting again in spring when new growth appears.

Stems bought in shops will grow when planted directly into compost. Place in a sunny location and roots will quickly appear. As before, when the roots appear through the bottom of the container, transplant to a new, larger container.

Harvest lemongrass all year round, cutting complete stems, or cutting leaves down to 4" long. Store stems in your refrigerator until required. However, lemongrass is best used fresh, popular in curries, sauces and with meat or fish.

Culinary Uses

Lemongrass has a taste very similar to lemon zest and is popular in a wide variety of dishes from curries to stir-fries to soups, stews and pickles. It is also very popular as a herbal tea. Herbal tea blends often use lemongrass for its lemon flavor with a popular pairing being green tea. Lemongrass is popular in a variety of cocktails too, such as the Soho cocktail.

Asian cuisine, particularly Thai, uses a lot of lemongrass. It can be a bit woody or fibrous, so is often finely minced. If you use larger pieces in a dish, remove them before serving, as you would with bay leaves.

This herb pairs very well with both chicken and seafood, but also works with red meats such as lamb, pork and beef. Thai chicken noodle soup or Thai carrot soup make for great soups to exhibit the flavor of lemongrass. Tom Yum soup is one of the best known lemongrass dishes. Traditional satay sauce uses a lemongrass marinade before the meat is grilled, then dipped in the peanut sauce.

Lemongrass is a great herb to use in food. It is excellent in sauces, such as a white wine and lemongrass sauce that works well with mussels or combine with ginger for a great fish sauce.

Health Uses

Lemongrass has a number of health benefits, yet little scientific research has been performed to substantiate these claims. Doctors know lemongrass tea is high in antioxidants and fights free radicals, reducing inflammation in the body.

Lemongrass tea helps to reduce anxiety, having a calming effect. Research shows that even smelling lemongrass helps to lower anxiety levels, https://www.mskcc.org/cancer-care/integrative-medicine/herbs/lemongrass.

Early research indicates that lemongrass extracts lowers cholesterol levels in animals, though the results are dose dependent. Introducing some lemongrass into your diet could have a beneficial effect on your cholesterol levels, https://www.ncbi.nlm.nih.gov/pmc/articles/PMC3217679/.

It appears lemongrass has some ability to fight infection. Studies show this herb reduces the incidences of infections such as thrush. https://www.mskcc.org/cancer-care/integrative-medicine/herbs/lemongrass

Chewing on fresh lemongrass appears to have a beneficial effect on your dental health. It inhibits bacterial growth, which is linked to causing cavities. https://www.sciencedirect.com/science/article/pii/S0308814608002756.

Drinking lemongrass tea also appears to increase the red blood cell count according to a 2015 study. Although the research showed an increase in red blood cells, scientists are still identifying how his increase incurs. https://www.liebertpub.com/doi/abs/10.1089/jmf.2013.0184.

Drinking lemongrass tea helps to reduce bloating due to its diuretic properties. According to research, lemongrass tea is one of the best diuretics available! https://www.jrnjournal.org/article/S1051-2276(14)00157-5/abstract

Beauty Uses

Lemongrass contains plenty of nutrients good for your skin and hair, including vitamins A and C. It is also high in many minerals that are very good for your body too. The astringent properties of this herb helps to keep your pores closed too. Be careful using the essential oil as it can irritate some people's skin.

As an astringent, lemongrass helps to control oily skin. Mix ½ cup of distilled water with a teaspoon of witch hazel and three drop of lemongrass essential oil to make an excellent spray for your skin.

With its lemony scent and natural antibiotic action, lemongrass makes for a great deodorant. It kills the bacteria that creates body odor and helps to prevent excess sweating. Mix ¼ cup witch hazel with ½ cup distilled water and add 4 drops each of lavender, lemongrass and geranium essential oils to make a great deodorant spray.

Adding a few drops of lemongrass essential oil to your shampoo or conditioner will help your skin look silky and shiny.

There are many other uses for lemongrass relating to skin and hair. It is good for controlling dandruff and fungal infections, reducing the signs of acne and blackheads and much more. You can make your own infused oil or use the fresh leaves in poultice form rather than buy the essential oil.

Pests, Problems & Diseases

Lemongrass is generally disease and pest free.

Recommended Varieties

Cymbopogon citratus is the most commonly found lemongrass variety with blue green leaves. *Cymbopogon flexuosus* is an East Indian strain that is good for cooking with both a strong smell and flavor.

Recipes

Lemongrass Chili Chicken

This is a Thai dish with a thick, aromatic sauce, generally served with steamed rice. It takes up to an hour to prepare and cook, making two servings.

Ingredients:

- 12oz/350g chicken (cut into bite-sized chunks)
- 3½fl oz/100ml chicken stock
- 2 garlic cloves (finely chopped)
- 2 lemongrass stalks (finely chopped)
- 1 red chilli (deseeded and finely chopped)
- ½ small head of broccoli (cut into small florets)
- 1 tablespoon superfine (caster) sugar
- 1 tablespoon sunflower oil
- 1 tablespoon Thai fish sauce
- Handful of fresh mint, cilantro and/or basil leaves to garnish

Method:

1. Mix the fish sauce, garlic, lemongrass and chilli together in a bowl
2. Put the chicken in a separate bowl and add half the lemongrass mix
3. Stir well, cover and refrigerate for 20 minutes
4. Heat the oil in a wok on a high heat
5. Add the remaining lemongrass mixture and fry for 1 minute, until the fragrance is released
6. Add the chicken mixture, frying for 4-5 minutes until the chicken pieces have an even color
7. Add the broccoli and fry for a further minute
8. Pour the chicken stock into the wok, then stir in the sugar
9. Reduce the heat and simmer for a few minutes until the stock has reduced to the consistency of a thick sauce
10. Serve immediately with steamed rich, garnished with herbs

Chicken and Lemongrass Fried Rice

This is a great, quick meal to make, taking less than 15 minutes to prepare and cook. A healthy, tasty meal that serves 4 people.

Ingredients:

- 14oz/400g chicken breast (thinly sliced)
- 11¼oz/320g bell peppers (thinly sliced – use pre-cut peppers for speed)
- 8¾oz/250g cooked long-grain rice (use a microwaved pouch for speed)
- 1oz/30g cashew nuts (toasted and roughly chopped)
- 3 garlic cloves (finely chopped)
- 1" piece of fresh ginger (peeled and finely chopped)
- 1 lemongrass stalk (finely chopped)
- 1 red chili (deseeded and finely chopped)
- 2 tablespoons soy sauce
- 1 tablespoon mirin
- 1 tablespoon sesame oil
- 1 tablespoon oyster sauce
- ½ tablespoon vegetable oil
- Handful of torn cilantro leaves (to garnish)
- 1 lime (cut into wedges, to serve)

Method:

1. Heat the oil in a wok on a high heat
2. Cook the chicken for 5 minutes, stirring occasionally until cooked through, then transfer to a plate
3. In the same wok, fry the chili, lemongrass, garlic and ginger for 1 minute to release the fragrance
4. Add the peppers and cook, stirring often, for 3 minutes
5. Add the rice and cook for a further minute, stirring to prevent clumps forming
6. Add the chicken, soy sauce, oyster sauce, mirin and sesame oil and cook for 1 minute
7. Divide between 4 bowls, garnish the cilantro and cashew nuts, serving with a lime wedge on the side

Lemon Verbena

Lemon verbena, *Aloysia citrodora*, is a deciduous shrub, growing up to 8 feet/2.5m tall with lance shaped leaves with a strong, lemon smell. It produces small white or pale lilac colored flowers.

At a Glance Facts

Annual / ~~Biennial~~ / Perennial	
Position:	Full sun to partial shade
Soil:	Well-drained
Hardiness	Half hardy
USDA Zones:	8-10
Sow:	Spring
Harvest:	Any time

This herb originated in the South America, found from Bolivia and Uruguay down to Argentina, Peru and Chile. Explorers brought this plant back to Europe in the 18th century where the perfume industry made use of its oil until lemon balm and lemongrass become more popular. Also known as verbena or the lemon bee bush, this herb is prized for its culinary and medicinal uses.

Perfume companies still use lemon verbena in their products, with Givenchy using this herb in their 'Very Irresistible' fragrance. This is a versatile herb that can be grown in your garden; though in cooler areas treat it as an annual unless you can bring it inside during winter. This is an ideal plant for a sensory garden as just brushing against the leaves releases the lemony scent. Out of all the lemon scented plants, this is by far the strongest smelling.

Growing Instructions

Lemon verbena likes a well-drained soil in full sun. In heavy, waterlogged or clay soils, the roots can rot. It is a half-hardy plant, meaning it can survive some frosts, but cannot survive hard frosts or extended periods of cold. Mulching in fall to protect the roots can help this plant survive in cooler areas. In areas with cold winters, it will need bringing indoors or to be treated as an annual.

Although you can grow this herb from seed, it is difficult to germinate and slow to grow. Most gardeners will buy ready grown plants or propagate this herb from softwood cuttings.

This is not the easiest herb to grow and can be a bit of a diva in your garden. When stressed, it drops its leaves, but they will grow back again. Overwinter lemon verbena by stopping watering it in late fall so the plant becomes dormant and then bring it indoors. In northern areas, it is often easier to start with fresh plants each year.

When growing outdoors, space the plants one foot apart, leaving at least 1½ feet between rows. When growing in containers, use one that is at least 12" in diameter so the plant has plenty of space to grow.

Plant Care

Fertilize every two weeks during the growing season, particularly when growing in containers. Feeding is not required over winter.

Harvest as and when required. Dry the leaves in small bunches or spread out on trays and then store the fully dried leaves in airtight containers.

When growing in containers, sink the container into the ground during summer to prevent it from drying out or overheating.

When temperatures drop below 40F/4C, lemon verbena will drop its leaves and become dormant. When moved indoors, lemon verbena will often drop its leaves too, so it can be easier to allow the plant to become dormant outside and then move it inside. While in the dormant (leafless) state, do not overwater as this is the easiest way to kill this herb!

Culinary Uses

The strong lemon scent of this plant means it has a wide range of culinary uses. It is popular as a flavoring in fruity drinks or dressings and goes well in soups, marinades, jams and desserts. Unlike many other herbs, lemon verbena does not lose its flavor when cooked. It pairs well with most fruits, vanilla and sits nicely in seafood dishes. Feel free to use it in any recipe instead of lemon zest.

Blend lemon verbena with mint and you have a wonderful herbal tea. The chopped leaves bring out the flavor of many fish or poultry dishes and it is an excellent addition to any meat stuffing or rice dish.

Eat young leaves like spinach, either by itself, added to a dish or fresh in a salad. Older leaves become tougher, so treat them like bay leaves in dishes and remove before serving. Alternatively, finely mince them if you prefer to leave them in. Use the leaves to make infused oils or flavored vinegars.

Infused oils are very easy to make. Heat a couple of cups of extra-virgin olive oil (or your preferred oil) in a pan until almost smoking then remove from the heat. Add a large handful of crushed lemon verbena leaves, cover and leave for 2-3 hours to steep. Strain and store in a sealed container. Use this oil on fish or grilled vegetables.

Health Uses

Lemon verbena has many medicinal uses too, being a calmative, sedative and an aid to digestion. Traditionally, herbalists use it to treat candida, but it also has antispasmodic and antimicrobial properties. It is high in flavonoids, particularly leteolin, which is a powerful free radical scavenger

Drunk as a tea, lemon verbena has soothing qualities that calms the stomach, reduces bloating and stops cramping. It helps to regulate your appetite and balance out your metabolism.

With high levels of antioxidants, lemon verbena boosts your immune system and increases white blood cells. Research, https://link.springer.com/article/10.1007/s00421-010-1684-3, indicates this herb is very good at reducing oxidative stress levels and keeping you healthy.

As an anti-inflammatory, lemon verbena reduces joint pain and speeds recovery of injuries to your joints. This is particularly useful for anyone with arthritis and joint pain. Research, indicates this is due to the high levels of antioxidants in this herb:
https://www.sciencedirect.com/science/article/pii/S0009308409003545.

For anyone who exercises, lemon verbena is an excellent pre-workout drink. Research, https://link.springer.com/chapter/10.1007/978-3-319-07320-0_11, shows that the high levels of antioxidants decreases muscle damage from working out, but without slowing muscle mass development and stamina improvement.

Another use for lemon verbena is as a diaphoretic, meaning it increases sweating. Traditional medicine uses this herb to break fevers and increase healing time for inflammatory illnesses.

Research has shown that the antioxidants found in lemon verbena affects the body's hormonal balance. While it does not have a major effect, it is calming when drunk as a tea. It is useful for anyone who suffers from stress or nervous afflictions as it also calms the mind.

Lemon verbena is a herb with a lot of positive properties, but some people do have a mild allergic reaction in the form of dermatitis. If you have any type of kidney disorder, the active ingredients in this herb can make your condition worse, so avoid this herb. All in all, lemon verbena is a very useful herb medicinally and research is showing some promising uses for it.

Beauty Uses

With its high antioxidant levels, lemon verbena has plenty of beauty uses from breaking down cellulite to toning and relaxing your skin. Commercially, this herb is a common ingredient in natural soaps where it leaves your skin feeling soft, balanced and toned.

Used in a soap, as an infusion or as a poultice, lemon verbena firms the skin, reducing the visible signs of aging due to its high levels of antioxidants. Use this herb to clean the skin, kill harmful bacteria that causes spots and reduce the appearance of blemishes and mild scarring. Use this herb as a face wash to cleanse your skin, nourish it and leave it feeling soft and smooth.

Use lemon verbena oil on cotton wool balls to wash your face. It gets rid of dirt, bacteria and excess sebum, which causes acne and spots. The great thing about this herb is that it cleans your skin without leaving it feeling dry.

With its strong lemon scent, this herb has been popular in perfume, soaps, potpourri and more. The herb acts as a natural deodorant and is popular in beauty salons as a skin cleanser. There are plenty of beauty uses for lemon verbena and it works very well when combined with other, less aromatic herbs.

Pests, Problems & Diseases

You will have very few problems growing lemon verbena. Whiteflies and spider mites can sometimes be a problem with this herb. Some gardeners will not grow lemon verbena because they feel it attracts these pests.

Recommended Varieties

No cultivars are readily available.

Recipes

Lemon Verbena Soap

This citrus soap is very easy to make and a great way for your skin to benefit from the therapeutic and beauty properties of this herb. It is a popular soap on craft markets and makes a great gift when wrapped in cellophane.

Ingredients:

- 12 tablespoons unscented soap (finely grated)
- 2 tablespoons glycerine (warmed)
- 2 tablespoons lemon verbena leaves (finely chopped)
- 1 tablespoon clear honey
- Few drops food coloring (optional)

Method:

1. Mix the lemon verbena with the warmed glycerine and leave for two hours to infuse
2. Melt the soap in the top of a double boiler on a low heat

3. Remove from the heat when melted
4. Mix in the lemon verbena solution, stirring well until thoroughly combined
5. Add the honey and any food coloring, then stir until the color is even throughout the mixture
6. Pour into pre-greased soap molds
7. Leave to set, then remove, wrap and store until required

Lemon and Mint Tea

A very simple tea that only takes a few minutes to prepare. Combining the flavor of mint and lemon verbena, it is a refreshing and calming drink.

Ingredients:

- 2 cups of boiling water
- 20 fresh mint leaves (washed – no stems)
- 15 lemon verbena leaves (washed – adjust to taste)

Method:

1. Put the herbs into a tea pot
2. Pour in the boiling water
3. Cover, and steep for 3-5 minutes, depending on taste
4. Strain into cups and drink

Lemon Verbena Jelly

This is a very nice jelly that is refreshing and tasty. The combination of apple and lemon verbena makes for a very delicious and versatile jelly that will keep for a couple of years.

Ingredients:

- $3\frac{1}{4}$lbs/1.5kg cooking apples
- $2\frac{1}{4}$lbs-$3\frac{1}{4}$lbs/1-1.5kg white (granulated) sugar
- $1\frac{3}{4}$ pints/1 liter water
- 10 bushy fresh sprigs of lemon verbena
- Juice of 1 lemon
- Jelly bag
- Jam funnel
- Preserving jars with lids

Method:

1. Roughly chop the apples without peeling or coring them
2. Place them in a large pan together with the water

3. Bring to the boil, then reduce the heat and simmer for 30-40 minutes until the apples are very soft (easily crushable against the side of the pan)
4. Use the jelly bag to strain the apple mixture into a large bowl or jug with a capacity of at least 4 pints. Leave this overnight to allow the juice to drip out, do not squeeze the bag
5. Measure the amount of juice
6. For each 1 pint/600ml of juice add 1lb/450g of sugar
7. Put the juice and sugar into a large pan and bring to the boil slowly, stirring often to dissolve the sugar
8. Sterilize and warm the jars
9. Add the lemon verbena to the pan together with the lemon juice
10. Boil for 30-40 minutes, skimming off the scum
11. When the jelly has reduced, test the setting point and remove from the heat when ready
12. Remove the lemon verbena using a wooden spoon
13. Jar, seal the lids, cool and store, refrigerating once opened

Lovage

Lovage, *Levisticum officinale*, is a hairless perennial growing up to 6½ feet/2m tall with dark green leaves and yellow green flowers. The plant itself smells similar to celery and the seeds are also very aromatic.

At a Glance Facts

~~Annual~~ / ~~Biennial~~ / **Perennial**	
Position:	Full sun to partial shade
Soil:	Loam, moist, well-drained
Hardiness	Yes, down to -4F/-20C
USDA Zones:	3-9
Sow:	March to May
Harvest:	Summer

The young leaves are great in salads, stews and soups or dried and used in a herbal tea. Blanch the shoots and eat as a vegetable. Cook the roots as you would any other root vegetable or use raw in salads. This plant not only makes for good eating, but looks great as an ornamental plant, happy in full sun or partial shade.

Lovage is a member of the same family as carrots and parsley. It originated in Southern Europe and the more mountainous areas around the Mediterranean.

This has a long history of human use; the ancient Greeks chewed the leaves to relieve gas and ease digestive problems. At one point, lovage seeds rivalled those of black pepper for cost as they were so valued.

Lovage came to America with the European settlers and established itself in New England. They candied the roots and chewed on the seeds to keep them alert, particularly during long church services!

There are two other wild lovage varieties. Sea or Scottish lovage grows wild along the North Atlantic coast of America and in northern Britain. Black lovage, or Alexander's, grows around the Mediterranean and in Britain.

This herb is also known as sea parsley, due to the strong celery flavor it imparts to dishes. The leaves and stems can even be candied like Angelica. Drying the leaves brings out the flavor, making it more intense.

Growing Instructions

Plant the seeds in spring, sowing into a good quality seed compost and covering thinly with perlite. Do not sow too many seeds per pot as it grows very large. Place the seeds on a sunny window or in a heated propagator. Once the seedlings are large enough to handle, prick them out and transplant to one plant per pot.

Once they have established a strong root system, plant out in late spring or early summer. Ensure the soil is deep, rich and moist and position the plants in full sun or partial shade.

Plant Care

Lovage needs cutting back to ground level in the fall when it starts to die back, mainly to prevent it from self-seeding. It is a prolific self seeder and will very quickly take over any area it is growing in.

In the middle of summer, trim the plant to encourage the production of fresh shoots.

In early spring, large lovage clumps can be divided and replanted to gain extra plants.

Pick the leaves before the plant flowers for the best flavor. Blanch young shoots, like you do with celery, by earthing up around the young stems or wrapping light proof paper around the stems. This gives the shoot a better flavor.

Culinary Uses

Lovage used to be a very popular herb and salad vegetable because of its similarity in taste to celery. As celery became more popular, lovage fell out of favor.

All parts of the lovage plant can be used. The young leaves are chopped and used in any dish as a substitute for celery, though it has a much stronger flavor than celery. The leaves work very well in stews, soups, salads, egg salad, potato salad and in frittatas.

Use the seeds to make cordials or put in salads or mashed potatoes. Crush the seeds and use in biscuits, pastries, breads or with cheese.

Chop the stems and stalks to use in stews and sauces or crystalize them for cake decorating instead of angelica.

Peel the roots before use as the skin is bitter and then use as a vegetable or pickle.

Lovage leaves work very well when used for cooking lentils. Sweat some leaves in a pan with some onions and then cook the lentils slowly with the lovage. Lovage and sorrel make for a very tasty pesto rather than the traditional basil. The leaves are also great in pasta or as a pizza topping! Try leek and lovage soup or even just a lovage soup.

This herb is very versatile in the kitchen as all parts of it can be used. The celery taste is strong and it has a wide variety of uses. With good ornamental looks and so many uses, it is one to grow in your garden.

Health Uses

Lovage has a long tradition of therapeutic use. One of the most common forms of use was in a tea made from the leaves and stalk. This was used to treat everything from sore throats to jaundice to arthritis. As a strong diuretic, herbalists used lovage to treat kidney stones and increase the flow of urine.

The roots were made into salves used to treat skin problems and added to bath water to ease joint or skin problems. Chew on the seeds to ease gas and digestion problems. In the past, lovage leaves were fried in oil and applied as a poultice to treat boils.

Today, lovage is not commonly used therapeutically. It was popular in the past and perhaps it is a herb that should be revisited as it has some very intriguing properties.

Beauty Uses

Lovage has both antioxidant and anti-inflammatory properties meaning it is excellent for treating acne, blackheads and skin conditions such as psoriasis. Eating this herb will provide some relief to these conditions, but applying the leaves topically as a poultice or making a cream from them will provide a more effective remedy.

There is no current research into lovage, probably because it is a herb that is not particularly popular these days. Historically, it was popular to reverse cellular damage and reduce the signs of ageing due to its levels of antioxidants. It increases the flow of blood to the surface of the skin, which helps to make your skin look better and firmer.

Pests, Problems & Diseases

There are generally few problems with lovage. New growth can suffer from aphids and occasionally you will find leaf mining flies bothering your plants. Apart from this, lovage is a problem free plant to grow.

Recommended Varieties

No cultivars are available for general purchase.

Recipes

Potato and Lovage Soup

This is a great soup where the lovage brings out the flavor of the potato. Use fresh or dried lovage leaves depend on what you have to hand. Feel free to add carrots or other vegetables to this soup mix, just remember to adjust the amount of liquid appropriately. Make this soup as thick as you like by blending some or all of the cooked soup.

Ingredients:

- 2 cups chicken/vegetable broth
- 1 cup milk or heavy cream
- 3 potatoes (chopped)
- 2 medium onions (finely chopped)
- 1oz butter
- 4 tablespoons lovage leaves (finely chopped)
- 3 tablespoons all-purpose flour
- Salt and pepper to taste

Method:

1. Cook the onions in the melted butter until tender, about 5 minutes, then add the lovage
2. Whisk in the flour and cook for a further minute, stirring constantly, on a medium heat
3. Add the broth gradually, stirring it in
4. Add the potatoes, cover and simmer for around 15 minutes until the potatoes are tender
5. Add the milk, then season to taste
6. Bring to a gentle simmer, stirring often, being very careful not to boil the mixture otherwise the milk will curdle
7. When well combined, serve

Lovage Potato Salad

Potatoes go very well with lovage. This dish works very well with new potatoes and takes 30-45 minutes to cook, making 2 servings.

Ingredients:

- 1lb 2oz/500g new potatoes (boil until tender and cut into chunks)
- 3½fl oz/100ml extra-virgin olive oil
- 3½fl oz/100ml sunflower oil
- 7-8 cornichons (finely chopped)
- 3 anchovies in oil (drained and chopped)

- 2 egg yolks
- 1 garlic clove (chopped)
- ½ small red onion (chopped)
- 2 tablespoons capers (drained
- 2 tablespoons Dijon mustard
- Juice of 1 lemon
- 1 teaspoon white wine vinegar
- Salt and pepper
- Small handful each of fresh dill, lovage and tarragon (chopped)

Method:

1. Put the mustard, lemon juice, egg yolks and white wine vinegar into your blender and blend well
2. In a jug, mix the oils together
3. Drizzle the oils into the blender slowly, mixing continuously until the mixture takes on a mayonnaise type consistency
4. Pour the mixture into a separate bowl
5. Add the rest of the ingredients, mix well and season to taste

Lungwort

Common lungwort, *Pulmonaria officinalis*, is a semi-green evergreen growing up to one foot tall. It has broad leaves with white-green spots and clusters of flowers that open pink and change to blue, appearing early in spring.

At a Glance Facts

~~Annual~~ / ~~Biennial~~ / **Perennial**	
Position:	Partial shade
Soil:	Moist, well-drained
Hardiness	Yes, down to -4F/-20C
USDA Zones:	4-8
Sow:	Spring
Harvest:	Summer, after flowering

Its name originates from herbalists believing the leaves looked like a lung, so the plant would treat lung disorders. Although science has disproved this belief, the name has stuck to this herb. It has many other names including Jerusalem cowslip, spotted dog, soldiers and sailors, and Bethlehem sage.

Nowadays, people grow lungworts mainly as ornamental plants for their fuzzy leaves, which have white spots on them as if someone has splashed them with bleach.

Although modern science has disproved the lung treatment properties of this herb, in the 14th century herbalists mixed it with wormwood to treat the bubonic plague. Even though its medical abilities have been discredited, modern herbalists still mainly it for respiratory conditions.

Growing Instructions

Lungwort is a popular ornamental plant with some cultivars having different colored leaves and flowers. This plant prefers partial shade and is one of the few plants that can survive under black walnut trees (walnuts release a toxin into the soil around them to prevent other plants from growing).

Lungwort prefers a moist soil, but can grow in a drier location if it has enough shade. It is a good plant to grow under trees as it likes soil with lots of organic matter in.

Common lungwort grows well from seed when planted out in spring after the risk of frost has passed. Ornamental cultivars do not grow true from seed, and are propagated by division in early spring or fall.

Plant Care

Divide established plants in early spring or fall. Dig up your plant, cut it into pieces ensuring each piece has a good-sized piece of root and several leaves. Replant where required and water well. Lungwort will wilt after division, so needs regular watering but not over-watering.

Water established plants every 7 to 10 days to keep them moist. Feed with a balanced fertilizer every spring.

When flowering is complete, harvest or remove old leaves, drying for medicinal use or composting if you have enough of them.

Culinary Uses

Although the leaves are edible, the fact they are hairy puts many people off them. When cooked, the hairs disappear, but the leaves have a very definite flavor that not everyone finds pleasant. Lungwort can be substituted for spinach in some cases, but when cooked, the leaves can become a bit slimy.

Use lungwort leaves as a thickening agent or substitute for okra in West African cooking.

Health Uses

Herbalists use lungwort to treat breathing conditions, stomach and kidney problems and urinary tract infections. Some herbalists use lungwort as an astringent on the skin and as a poultice to treat wounds.

Anyone suffering from a cold or breathing difficulties will find that lungwort tea is very helpful to them. Drinking lungwort tea will provide some relief when made using the dried leaves. The leaves have a bitter taste, so most people sweeten the tea to make it more palatable.

This herb is used to treat a wide variety of respiratory complaints from whooping cough to asthma and bronchitis. Traditionally, people used lungwort for tuberculosis, catarrh and coughing too.

As little research has been performed on this herb, these claims are tough to substantiate. According to historical and anecdotal evidence, lungwort is good for treating most respiratory disorders. It helps to remove mucus from the lungs and the tea also helps smokers reduce the amount of tar in their lungs.

With high levels of phenolic compounds, lungwort is full of antioxidants. Its positive effects are thought to be down to these compounds. Of course, taking lungwort tea also means you receive all the other benefits of anything high in antioxidants.

Lungwort tea helps to settle your stomach, relieving indigestion and reducing diarrhea. With mild diuretic properties, it helps relieve discomfort from water retention. Traditionally, herbalists used lungwort to treat cystitis

Beauty Uses

Being high in antioxidants, lungwort is good for making your skin stronger, younger and reducing the visible signs of aging. Apply the leaves to your skin over a cut or minor wound and a chemical compound called 'allantoin' in the leaves will help heal tissue damage and speed healing.

Use a poultice or a cooled tea to treat a wide variety of skin complaints including blisters, burns, ulcers and eczema. It has astringent and anti-inflammatory properties that are beneficial for your skin.

Pests, Problems & Diseases

Lungwort is generally pest free. In dry or crowded conditions, this herb can suffer from powdery mildew. Should you encounter this issue, lift and divide your plants to provide better air circulation.

Recommended Varieties

Although traditionally common lungwort is grown, many attractive cultivars are available that are excellent ornamental plants for your garden. Some of the most popular include:

1. *Pulmonaria* 'Ice Ballet' – apple green leaves with lots of white spots. Pure white flowers appear in spring. This cultivar grows to a height of about one foot and spreads to about two feet wide, making for an excellent ground cover plant.
2. *Pulmonaria* 'Opal' – a ground covering variety with bright silver spots on the leaves. The early spring flowers are a beautiful pale blue.
3. *Pulmonaria* 'Blake's Silver' – silver foliage with a green rim and leaf base. The flowers appear in March and point outwards rather than down. The rich pink flowers soften to a more pastel shade of pink with a hint of blue on the edges. As the season progresses, they change to a soft blue with a pink eye. A very pretty cultivar that stands out in any garden.
4. *Pulmonaria* 'Majeste' – another silver leaf variety with flowers starting off pink and fading to a purple color.
5. *Pulmonaria* 'Blue Ensign' – a vigorous cultivar with deep blue flowers appearing in early spring. The leaves are a deep green color and virtually spot free.

Recipes

Lungwort is not particularly popular in the kitchen and for healing it is mainly used as a tea.

Lungwort Tea

Lungwort tea can be a little bitter and is best sweetened with honey.

Ingredients:

- 1 tablespoon dried lungwort leaves
- 1 cup boiling water

Method:

1. Put the herbs in the cup and fill with water
2. Steep for 10 minutes
3. Strain, sweeten and drink

Marjoram

Sweet marjoram, *Origanum majorana*, is a half hardy flowering herb, loved by bees and popular in Italian and Greek cuisine. Closely related to oregano, marjoram is used fresh, unlike oregano that is generally dried. The flavor of marjoram is much more delicate than that of oregano.

At a Glance Facts

~~Annual~~ / ~~Biennial~~ / **Perennial**	
Position:	Full sun to partial shade
Soil:	Well-drained
Hardiness	Yes, down to -4F/-20C
USDA Zones:	6-11
Sow:	February to May
Harvest:	June to September

Marjoram originated in Asia and spread to Europe where it was cultivated around the Mediterranean. The ancient Greeks used marjoram in cooking, medicinally and ritually. The Greeks and Romans considered Marjoram a symbol of love and happiness. During the marriage ceremony, couples were crowned with a sweet marjoram wreath to ensure their marriage was full of love and happy. Both of these cultures also thought that marjoram growing on a grave blessed the occupant with peace and happiness in the afterlife.

Today gardeners grow marjoram mainly because it attracts bees. It is great to have in your garden because it attracts a lot of pollinating insects. I have several large plants around my garden and they are always alive with bees when in flower.

Growing Instructions

Grow from seed or buy ready grown plants from supermarkets or garden centers. Start seeds indoors from February to May. Plant in small pots filled with a good quality seed compost. Sow the seeds on the surface and cover with a thin layer of sieved compost. Water carefully and then leave somewhere warm to germinate. The seeds will germinate in 8 to 14 days.

Once the seedlings are large enough to handle, transplant so there are three per 3" pot.

When the risk of frost has passed, or in early summer, plant out in a sunny, sheltered location in well-drained soil. Alternatively, plant out into a larger container.

Marjoram typically grows to two or three feet (60-90cm) tall. Leave 15-18"/38-45cm between plants.

Propagate marjoram by root division, softwood cuttings or semi-hardwood cuttings.

Plant Care

Water regularly, but do not overwater, particularly in containers, as the roots can rot, though when grown in the ground marjoram is relatively drought tolerant. In winter, lift containers off the ground to prevent the contents getting too wet.

Once the flowers fade in summer, trim the plant and give it a good feed with a balanced, liquid fertilizer. Any dead stems need cutting back to the base.

Pick the leaves before the flowers open for the best flavor, though leaves can be harvested throughout the year but will be slightly more bitter once the flowers have opened. Use fresh, dry or freeze for later use. Dry by hanging cuttings upside down in a dark, dry, well-ventilated location.

Culinary Uses

Marjoram works very well with meats; whether roasted or cooked in a stew. However, it is also a great addition to many vegetarian dishes, despite being known as 'the meat herb'.

Add fresh leaves to salads or egg dishes or chop and use with cold meats, soups or poultry dishes. As an aromatic herb, it works very well with roast meats, beef burgers and spaghetti bolognaise. Add at the end of cooking to ensure your dish retains the full flavor of marjoram.

When dried, the flavor of marjoram increases, unlike many other herbs. It combines very well with sage and thyme, both of which work well with most meat dishes.

As it is milder than oregano, you can use quite a lot of it in a dish before it becomes overpowering.

Health Uses

Marjoram is rich in minerals such as calcium, phosphorus and magnesium as well as vitamins A and C. For centuries, humans have used marjoram to treat a variety of conditions, for pain relief and as an antiseptic. Recent research shows much of the folklore about marjoram is rooted in truth and it is a powerful medicinal herb,
https://www.ncbi.nlm.nih.gov/pmc/articles/PMC5871212/.

Singers drink marjoram tea to keep their voices in good condition. A steam inhalation of marjoram clears the sinuses and eases a sore throat.

Marjoram has antiviral and antibacterial properties, so protects you against common illnesses like the cold. It improves digestion and helps with constipation. It appears to lower blood pressure and helps your blood to circulate as well as reduce the build-up of bad cholesterol.

As a diaphoretic, it induces sweating so is helpful in removing toxins from your system. It is also a mild diuretic, so will help cleanse your kidneys and remove excess water from too.

Be aware marjoram is a member of the mint family, so do not use if you are allergic to sage, oregano, mint, lavender, basil or hyssop.

Beauty Uses

Marjoram has a number of beauty uses and is found in many commercial skin cleansing products as it helps make skin smooth and prevent wrinkles. It also helps reduce inflammation, skin rashes and acne.

With high levels of antioxidants, marjoram is beneficial for your skin and helps balance your skin tone, brightening a dull complexion and whitening skin. It helps to prevent facial wrinkles and as a cleanser or wash, is excellent at combatting acne.

Marjoram oil is very good for your hair. It is an excellent cleanser for your hair as an oil or strong infusion, and treats a dry scalp and dandruff. Many people claim it rejuvenates and strengthens hair from the roots. Use marjoram oil as a final rinse, and then allow your hair to dry naturally for maximum benefit. Dilute 10-15 drops of marjoram essential oil in some lukewarm water and use this to rinse your hair.

Use marjoram essential oil in your daily facial care regime. Add a drop of the oil to some face cream or lotion just before applying it to your face. Research shows that regular application is more effective than higher doses. For body care, use 4 or 5 drops of oil per 5ml of body lotion, applying as normal.

Pests, Problems & Diseases

Marjoram does not tend to suffer from diseases. Aphids, which will live on new growth, can affect it; pick these off by hand. Glasshouse red spider mites may be a problem as they thrive in hot, dry environments. Mist the plants regularly to prevent these mites from establishing themselves.

Recommended Varieties

There are a number of sweet marjoram cultivars:

- Golden Marjoram (*Origanum vulgare* 'Aereum') – named after the color of its leaves, it bears pink flowers in summer
- *Origanum vulgare* 'Nanum' – a dwarf cultivar with small, oval, green leaves and white flowers
- *Origanum x applii* – with strong, pungent leaves, this cultivar is not frost hardy, so protect over winter
- Pot Marjoram (*Origanum onites*) –has dark green, hairy leaves with pink flowers.

Recipes

Italian Seasoning

This simple to make Italian style seasoning combines a number of herbs you can grow in your garden. Store in an airtight container or freeze until required if using fresh herbs. Increase the quantity of ingredients to make a larger batch. You can use fresh or dried herbs here, though dried will store better.

Ingredients:

- 2 tablespoons each of basil, oregano, marjoram and thyme
- 1 tablespoon rosemary

Method:

1. Blend for 60-90 seconds in your food processor until finely chopped

Roasted Marjoram Sweet Potatoes

A lovely way to serve sweet potatoes with the marjoram really bringing out their flavor. Garnish with fresh parsley, marjoram and grated Parmesan cheese.

Ingredients:

- 3lb sweet potatoes (peeled and cut into ¾" cubes)
- 1 tablespoon extra-virgin olive oil
- 1 tablespoon fresh marjoram (finely chopped)
- 4 teaspoons garlic cloves (minced)
- Sprigs of fresh marjoram

Method:

1. Preheat your oven to 450F/230C
2. Place the sweet potatoes, marjoram and oil in a large bowl and toss until the potatoes are well coated
3. Spread the sweet potatoes in a single layer on one or two baking sheets
4. Place a sprig of fresh marjoram on the sweet potatoes, one sprig per baking sheet
5. Put one baking sheet on the top rack of your oven and the other on the bottom rack
6. Roast for 10 minutes then switch places, stirring the sweet potatoes
7. Roast for 5 more minutes, stir and roast for an additional 5 minutes until the sweet potatoes are tender and start to brown evenly
8. Sprinkle 2 teaspoons of garlic on each baking sheet and toss so it is evenly distributed
9. Roast for a further 5 minutes until brown and crisp
10. Serve, seasoning with salt and pepper (if required) and garnished with Parmesan cheese, parsley and marjoram

Marjoram Tea

An easy way to benefit from the healing properties of marjoram.

Ingredients:

- 1 teaspoon honey
- ¼ teaspoon dried marjoram
- 1 cup boiling water

Method:

1. Put the leaves in a cup and cover with the boiling water
2. Steep for 3 minutes until fragrant
3. Strain the leaves, add honey and drink

Marjoram Green Beans

A very simple vegetable dish that has a distinct flavor from the marjoram.

Ingredients:

- 1½lbs fresh green beans (topped and tailed and cut into 1" pieces)
- ¾ cup water
- 3 tablespoons butter
- ½ teaspoon salt
- ¼ teaspoon ground black pepper
- ¼ teaspoon dried marjoram

Method:

1. Put the water and beans in a large saucepan and boil
2. Reduce the heat, cover and cook until crisp but tender (8-10 minutes)
3. Drain and return to the pan
4. Add the butter, salt, pepper and marjoram and stir well until the butter has melted

Sweet Marjoram Lamb

A great way to serve lamb that shows off the potential of marjoram when served with meat. Serve sliced on a bed of salad or with your choice of vegetables.

Ingredients:

- 4 lamp steaks (trimmed – your choice of cut)
- 2 tablespoons extra-virgin olive oil
- 1 tablespoon fresh sweet marjoram (chopped)
- ½ tablespoon lemon juice

Method:

1. Preheat your oven to 375F/190C
2. Mix the oil, lemon juice and marjoram together in a small bowl
3. Rub into the lamb
4. Place the lamb on a plate, cover and refrigerate for 15-20 minutes for the marinade flavors to infuse
5. Put a roasting dish big enough to hold all 4 lamb steaks in the oven to heat
6. Heat a frying pan on a medium to high heat and brown the lamb all over
7. Transfer the lamb to the roasting dish and place in the oven
8. Cook until the meat is cooked to your preference
9. Remove from the oven and serve with vegetables or leave to rest for 10 minutes, slice and serve on a bed of salad

Mint

Mint or *Mentha*, is a popular herb grown for its leaves that make great tea, a popular mint sauce (commonly served with roast lamb) and a wide variety of dishes. There are many different varieties of mint, all with different aromas; some of which are not so good in the kitchen.

At a Glance Facts

~~Annual~~ / ~~Biennial~~ / **Perennial**	
Position:	Full sun to partial shade
Soil:	Rich, moist
Hardiness	Full to tender, depending on cultivar
USDA Zones:	3-11
Sow:	March to May
Harvest:	May to October

Humans have cultivated mint for so long that it no longer exists in the wild. In the Bible (Matthew XXIII, 23) the Pharisees used mint as a tithe, together with cumin and anise, indicating the value placed on this herb.

According to Ancient Greek Myth, Pluto's wife (Proserpine) turned a hated rival into a mint plant. The Latin '*Mentha*' and Greek 'Minthe', meaning mint, are both associated with metamorphosed beauty. The Ancient Greeks used mint to scent their arms.

The Romans introduced mint into England, and then the Pilgrim Fathers brought mint to America. In the 14th Century, an early toothpaste formulation used mint to help whiten teeth. According to Culpepper (a famous herbalist who lived from 1616 to 1654), mint was never to be given to a wounded man as it prevents wounds from healing, yet Culpepper used mint to treat around 40 different ailments. According to superstition, mint must not be cut by iron, though the reasoning behind this superstition is unclear.

Mint is a lovely herb to grow in your garden and has a multitude of uses. Be aware that most cultivars are extremely invasive and will take over your garden. Growing mint in containers is a good way to prevent this, though watch the roots do not escape through the holes in the bottom of the pot.

Growing Instructions

You can grow mint from seed, but most people will buy young plants that are available in supermarkets and garden centers throughout the year. It is a very vigorous plant and good to grow in containers near your home so you can quickly pick some of the fresh herb.

Mint does not mind growing in a shady area, though it will grow in full sun but needs regular watering, particularly if in a container.

Cuttings or root division easily propagates mint. Plant seeds indoors 8-10 weeks before the last frost, keeping the soil moist until the seeds germinate 10-15 days later. Seed grown mint is usually ready to harvest with 2-3 months.

Grow mint in a rich, moist soil, ideally one that is slightly acidic.

Plant Care

Outdoor mint will die back in the winter, but is harvestable any time from late spring to the middle of fall. Regular harvesting helps to keep the plant compact with plenty of fresh growth.

Mint is an easy-going plant that is surprisingly difficult to kill off; ask anyone who has mint running rampant in your garden and they will tell you exactly how difficult it is to get rid of this plant! Regular watering is essential, particularly during hot, dry weather.

In late summer, when the plant has finished flowering, cut the flower shoots back to 2"/5cm above ground level.

Do not grow different varieties of mint close together, as they can lose their scent and flavor, blending in to all smelt and taste the same.

Divide container grown mint every couple of years to prevent it become pot bound and congested.

Store the fresh leaves for winter use by chopping, adding to an ice cube tray then filling with water and freezing. This keeps the flavor of fresh mint for use in the winter months when the herb has died back.

Culinary Uses

Popular in a wide variety of cuisines, mint gives zest and flavor to any dish. The common mint found in supermarkets is usually spearmint, though there are many other cultivars such as peppermint, ginger mint, apple mint and more.

As a tea, spearmint and peppermint settle stomachs and are refreshing. Use mint in alcoholic drinks such as a mojito or Mint Julep, or just added to water to make it more interesting.

Middle Eastern cuisines relies heavily on mint with it being a key component in dishes such as tabbouleh.

The flavor of mint compliments many meats, most notably lamb and poultry. The English serve roast lamb with mint sauce, which is very easy to make at home. Add fresh mint to peas, new potatoes or green beans when boiling to give them a delicious flavor.

Mint is very popular as a flavoring in many commercial products, though is probably best known for its appearance in toothpaste and mouthwashes due to its anti-microbial properties. It can be added to lots of different dishes, but is very popular as a herbal tea by itself or mixed with other herbs, including green tea.

Health Uses

Mint is high in a number of vital vitamins, including A, C and B2, plus essential minerals such as copper, iron, calcium and manganese.

Mint has numerous health benefits, being used by humans for thousands of years. It contains rosmarinic acid, a powerful antioxidant and anti-inflammatory, that relieves seasonal allergy symptoms such as hay fever. Regularly drinking mint tea during hay fever season can help reduce the symptoms from your allergy.

As a natural source of menthol, mint tea is excellent when suffering from a cold. It relieves sore throats and breaks up phlegm and mucus.

Mint has a long history of easing digestive issues. The tea calms an upset stomach and reduces the discomfort from indigestion. Peppermint helps to reduce gas and provide relief from flatulence.

Research shows that peppermint oil reduces the pain people with irritable bowel syndrome (IBS) experienced.

Scientists have spent a lot of time studying mint, which is why it is found in so many commercial products. Use it at home in cooking or as a tea to benefit from the healing effects of this herb.

Beauty Uses

Delicious in a meal, mint also has many beauty uses. An infusion or poultice of fresh mint leaves applied to your skin has a refreshing and soothing effect. It leaves your skin looking bright and reduces the appearance of any blemishes. As well as this, mint hydrates and tones your skin as it tightens and cleans your pores. With a high antioxidant content, mint also reduces the visible signs of aging, minimizing wrinkles and fine lines on your face.

Mint contains salicylic acid and has strong antibacterial properties, plus contains vitamin A. All of this combines to make a very effective acne treatment. A poultice or infusion will clean your pores, reduce the oiliness of your skin and dry up any acne. As it is a good skin cleaner, it also reduces the appearance of blackheads, unclogging pores and eventually getting rid of them.

As an anti-inflammatory, mint is excellent for soothing skin complaints such as rashes, itchiness and insect bites.

Mint is excellent for treating your skin and leaves you smelling great afterwards! Use the fresh herb as an infusion to wash your skin or apply for longer as a poultice. Mix mint leaves in with a facemask to benefit from the beauty properties of this herb.

Pests, Problems & Diseases

Mint is generally a hardy plant, though rust can affect it. Symptoms include yellow, black or orange spots or blisters appearing on leaves and the stems become pale and distorted. If you spot these symptoms, dig up and destroy infected plants. Check new plants carefully for signs of disease before buying.

Aphids and spittlebugs (froghoppers) are another problem, particularly on new growth. Pick these off by hand and destroy them or spray with water. Spittlebugs rarely cause lasting damage to plants and are more unsightly and off-putting than anything else.

Another potential problem are the shiny green mint beetles, which like to eat the leaves of the mint plant. In small numbers, they cause little damage, but larger infestations cause serious damage. These are relatively large so are easy to pick off by hand and destroy.

Recommended Varieties

There are over 600 mint cultivars, all with different flavors, shapes and sizes. Some are better for use in the kitchen or as a tea than others. These are some of the most popular and commonly grown varieties of mint. Supermarkets will usually sell garden mint, and garden centers will usually stock some of the other varieties. For the more unusual cultivars, an online supplier or specialist nursery will be required.

- Garden Mint (*Menta spicata*) – growing to about two feet tall, this is the most commonly grown mint variety with pointed, green leaves with serrated edges and purple flowers appearing in summer. Plant in moist, well-drained soil in full sun or partial shade. Use this cultivar to make mint sauce, mint tea and add to boiled new potatoes and peas.
- Apple Mint (*Mentha suaveolens*) – growing up to three feet tall, this cultivar has large, round, hairy leaves and produces mauve flowers in summer. It likes the same conditions as garden mint and the leaves are used in the same was, though have a hint of apple to them.
- Atlas Mountains Mint (*Mentha suaveolens subsp. timija*) – growing up to two feet tall, this has grey/green hairy leaves and produces mauve flowers in late summer to early fall. It prefers poor soil that is well-drained. Use the leaves in cooking, salads and chutney.
- Banana Mint (*Mentha spicata* 'Banana') – a tender perennial, growing up to two feet tall. With small leaves smelling like bananas, this cultivar produces mauve flowers in summer that attract bees and butterflies. Grows in similar conditions to garden mint and used in fruit salads and drinks.
- Basil Mint (*Mentha x piperita Citrata Basil*) – growing up to 1½ feet tall, this hardy, perennial mint has shiny dark green/purple leaves that are oval in shape. The scent is a mix of basil and peppermint. The mauve flowers appear in late summer to early fall and this cultivar requires similar growing conditions to garden mint. This variety works well in salads, with fish or chicken and medicinally, to relieve indigestion and chest infections.
- Berries and Cream Mint (*Mentha ssp.* Berries and Cream) – growing up to two feet tall, this cultivar has dark green leaves and produces lilac flowers during the summer months. The scent is definitely mint, but with a hint of red berries, making it good for cooking or in drinks.
- Bowles Mint (*Menta alopecuroides*) – a spreading perennial with strong smelling, oval leaves. During the summer, it has spikes of tubular, whorled pink flowers. Use the leaves in salads, for cooking or to make tea.
- Buddleia Mint (*Mentha longifloia Buddleia*) – grows up to 2½ feet tall, this hardy perennial has grey/green leaves and purple flowers from late summer to early fall that attract hoverflies and butterflies. This cultivar is not used in the kitchen and is grown as an ornamental or

used in flower arranging.

- Chocolate Peppermint (*Mentha x piperite Citrata Chocolate*) – growing to just a foot tall, this spreading plant has soft leaves with brown markings. The foliage has a definite peppermint scent, but with a hint of dark chocolate. It produces pink flowers during the summer months that attract bees and butterflies. Use the leaves in drinks.
- Corsican Mint (*Mentha requienni*) – a ground cover variety, growing to just a couple of inches tall. It has tiny leaves and a strong scent, producing small purple flowers in the summer. Not typically used in the kitchen, it is sometimes added to stews, sauces and salads.
- Curly Mint (*Menta spicata* 'crispa') – growing up to three feet tall, this vigorous mint attracts bees and butterflies to its pale lilac flowers throughout the summer months. The bright green leaves are curly and have the typical mint scent, used in salads or for cooking.
- Eua de Cologne Mint (*Mentha x piperite Citrata*) – growing up to 1½ feet tall, this cultivar is very vigorous with bronze-green leaves with a warm, spicy smell. The mauve flowers appear during summer. Use the leaves in scent water (particularly baths) or for flavoring.
- English Mint Lamb (*Mentha spicata* English Lamb) – growing up to two feet tall, this cultivar has an excellent scent and flavor. Use the leaves as you would garden mint.
- Black Peppermint (*Mentha x piperite*) – growing to around two feet tall, this has pale, purple/pink flowers during summer and a strong peppermint flavor. Use the leaves for herbal tea or chop them onto sweet desserts.
- Pineapple Mint (*Mentha suaveolens Variegata*) – a popular cultivar growing up to two feet tall. The green and white variegated leaves have a pineapple scent, but this cultivar rarely flowers. The leaves are particularly nice on a fruit salad.

Recipes

British Mint Sauce

This is a lovely sauce, usually served with lamb, but good with most meats. This recipe is easy to make, taking about 10 minutes. Do not use malt or dark vinegar with this recipe as it kills the mint flavor, instead use a white wine vinegar. Use any variety of mint, but common garden mint is by far the best for this recipe.

Ingredients:

- Large handful of fresh mint leaves
- 5 tablespoons boiling water

- 3 tablespoons white wine vinegar
- 1½ tablespoons white (granulated) sugar

Method:

1. Remove the mint leaves from the stalks, checking for insects and discarding the stalks
2. Wash the mint and roughly chop
3. Put in a heatproof jug and add the sugar
4. Pour in the boiling water, stirring gently to dissolve the sugar
5. Cover with plastic wrap and leave to cool
6. When cool, add the vinegar and stir well
7. Taste test the sauce, adding more water if it is too strong and more mint if too weak
8. Cover again and leave for 1-3 hours for the flavors to combine
9. Serve immediately or store in a sealed container in your refrigerator

Mint Tea

A popular way to consume mint. Sweeten with honey if you prefer and mix in other herbs to make your own, unique tea.

Ingredients:

- Handful of fresh mint
- Honey (to taste)

Method:

1. Crush the mint leaves between your hands to release their flavor
2. Place the leaves in a cafetiere or teapot
3. Fill the pot with boiling water and steep for 3-4 minutes until the water becomes pale yellow or green
4. Strain, sweeten and drink

Skin Whitening Face Pack

A simple face pack that takes a couple of minutes to make and is applied for 20 minutes, before rinsing off with cold water. This face pack hydrates your skin, lightens any blemishes and calms inflammation

Ingredients:

- 10-12 mint leaves
- ½" slice cucumber
- ½ tablespoon honey

Method:

1. Grind or blend the ingredients together to make a smooth mixture
2. Apply to your face
3. Leave for 20 minutes then rinse off with cool water

Glowing Skin Face Pack

Another simple face pack that will leave you with lovely, glowing skin. It takes a couple of minutes to make and is applied for half an hour. The banana contains vital vitamins and minerals to hydrate and nourish your skin. Combined with mint, it boosts collagen production, reduces scarring, fights spots and leaves your skin looking radiant.

Ingredients:

- 10-12 mint leaves
- 2 tablespoons mashed banana

Method:

1. Grind or blend the ingredients together to form a smooth mixture
2. Apply like a normal face pack, leaving for 15-30 minutes before rinsing

Acne Busting Face Pack

A great face pack for fighting acne. The mint leaves contain salicylic acid which treats acne while the lemon juice improves the healing process of your skin and fades scars.

Ingredients:

- 10-12 mint leaves
- 1 tablespoon lemon juice

Method:

1. Grind or blend the ingredients together
2. Apply to areas affected by acne
3. Leave for 15 minutes before rinsing off

Refreshing Skin Scrub

An excellent scrub for anyone with sensitive or dry skin. Gentle on your face, this scrub cleans your pores and removes dead skin cells while leaving your skin looking radiant.

Ingredients:

- 1 tablespoon oats
- 2 teaspoons milk
- 1 teaspoon honey
- 10-12 mint leaves
- ½" slice of cucumber

Method:

1. Mash the mint leaves and grate the cucumber
2. Mix all the ingredients together to make a coarse mixture
3. Apply to your face and leave for 7 minutes
4. Scrub your face in circular motions to remove dead skin cells for 2-3 minutes
5. Rinse with cool water and repeat 2 or 3 times a week

Nettle

Common stinging nettle, *Urtica dioica*, is a wild weed that quickly takes over any area it grows in, crowding out other plants. Growing 4 to 6 feet tall, this weed is instantly recognizable, but despite its invasive nature and nasty sting, has many beneficial properties and uses.

At a Glance Facts

~~Annual~~ / ~~Biennial~~ / **Perennial**	
Position:	Full sun to partial shade
Soil:	Rich, moist
Hardiness	Hardy
USDA Zones:	3-10
Sow:	Spring
Harvest:	Young leaves throughout the year

Nettles have stinging hairs on them that can be painful, so need picking with sturdy gloves on. Wear long sleeves too and ideally tuck your sleeves into your gloves as it is very easy to get stung. The severity of the sting does vary between people, with some people suffering more than others when stung by nettles. This plant grows wild across Europe and North America, commonly found in hedgerows and by the side of the road. It spreads from seed and from an underground network of rhizomes that grow very long and are extremely difficult to remove.

Nettles have a long association with humans, with many myths and legends building up around this plant. The Norse associated nettles with both Thor (god of Thunder) and Loki (trickster god), who had a magical fishing net made from nettles. In ancient Celtic lore, thick patches of nettles indicated fairies lived nearby. To the Celts, the nettle sting protected against sorcery, black magic and fair mischief.

For a long time, nettles rivalled both flax and hemp (later cotton) as a fiber used for threads and yarn. Nettle thread was used to make everything from sailcloth to table linen in the 17th and 18th century. However, with the rise of the industrial revolution and the mechanization of manufacturing processes, other fibers proved more cost effective. In some areas of Scotland, the locals still use nettles to make cloth!

Nettle oil was used in the same way paraffin oil is today. The juice and curdled milk was used in cheese production, particularly for Cheshire Cheese in England. The juice had many other uses, including sealing leaky barrels, driving frogs away from beehives and keeping flies away from the food larder. Gardeners prize nettle compost for its high concentrations of minerals.

When the Romans invaded Britain, they discovered the damp weather did not agree with their joints and many suffered from rheumatism. Roman soldiers beat their legs with nettles to warm up and reduce the stiffness from rheumatism.

In Anglo-Saxon times, nettle was known as 'wergula', a sacred herb. It was brewed into a beer that helped treat rheumatism and people still make nettle beer today (it is ready to drink in about a week). With a high vitamin C content, nettles were a valuable tonic in spring, boosting the health of a population who had lived on grain and salted meat through winter. Today, nettle tea or soup is an ideal treatment for anaemia due to its high iron levels which are easily absorbed by the body. The Tibetan sage Milarepa (AD 1051-1135) supposedly lived on nettle soup for so many years that he turned green!

Growing Instructions

There are many varieties of nettle, from the common stinging nettle to the harmless dead nettle. Stinging nettles are very distantly related to mint and has inherited its ability to take over an area. They are good to grow to keep deer or other animals out of a garden.

Sow seeds 4 and 6 weeks before the last frost date. Plant 1-3 seeds per 3" pot and cover with ¼" soil. Keep moist and the seeds should germinate in about 14 days. You can direct sow outdoors after the last frost.

Nettles need about a foot between plants when cultivated, but most people plant nettles in a corner of their garden that is not in use to try to prevent them from spreading. It usually fails. Personally, I do not encourage them into the garden as they are easily found in the wild and young children are far too easily stung when playing in your garden. I highly recommend nettle tea as a health tonic and nettle compost is amazing for your plants, used by many championship growers.

Plant Care

Keep the soil damp until you finish harvesting the nettles. Once the harvest is complete, cut the plant back by a third, leaving the cut sections on the ground to break down. Remove any seed heads that form to prevent the plant spreading. This encourages more leaf production and a better crop in the second year.

In fall, when the leaves turn yellow, cut the nettles down to 4” tall, again leaving the fallen growth on the ground.

Mulch with manure and wood ash to encourage strong, bushy growth.

Keep an eye out for stragglers, growing outside of your designated nettle patch from the underground rhizomes. Remove these, together with the roots and compost, though dry them in the sun for a few days before composting to prevent them from rooting.

Keep children and pets away from nettles as the stings can be painful. Some people are allergic to nettle stings, so be careful if you have any other allergies. An anti-histamine cream will ease the symptoms of nettle stings.

When grown from seed, nettles are ready to harvest in about 90 days. Harvest young, tender leaves when the plants are about a foot high in early spring. Pick the top two or three pairs of leaves from each plant. Although you can continue to pick leaves throughout the summer, the stalks and stems become more fibrous. The young, top leaves are still usable. Immersing in boiling water or cooking destroys the hairs that cause the sting, making nettles safe to eat or drink.

Culinary Uses

The best nettles to eat are young, tender nettles from plants shorter than a foot tall. As the leaves mature, they become more fibrous and chewy.

Once picked, allow the leaves to wilt, which reduces and even eliminates the stinging hairs. Hot water will also destroy the sting.

Cook nettle leaves like spinach, remembering they will reduce to about a quarter of the fresh amount. Cooking destroys the formic acid contained within the leaves. Do not eat nettle leaves raw.

With high levels of vitamins A and C, as well as iron, nettles are very beneficial for you. Use nettles to make pesto, beer or the juice from the leaves as a rennet for cheese production. The stems are very strong and the fibers are used to make cloth.

Traditionally, nettles are eaten in the spring once the first shoots appear. The Scottish ate Nettle Kail (a soup) on Shrove Tuesday to welcome spring. Before our modern era, nettles were one of the first vegetables available in the spring and vital for people's health after a winter diet of meat and grain. If you have never eaten nettles or drank nettle tea, then it is definitely worth a try, but remember to sweeten the tea, as it can be a little bitter.

Health Uses

Stinging nettles have a long history of medicinal use, having been used for thousands of years. The ancient Egyptians treated lower back pain and arthritis with it.

Although the fresh herb stings and is hard to handle, the processed or cooked herb has many health benefits.

Nettles contain a surprising amount of nutrients including several B vitamins as well as vitamins A, C and K. It contains iron, calcium, phosphorus, potassium, sodium and magnesium as well as all of the essential amino acids. It contains many beneficial fats and is extremely high in antioxidants (https://www.ncbi.nlm.nih.gov/pubmed/19149749). Studies show that nettles are an excellent source of many essential nutrients for the human body – https://www.sciencedirect.com/science/article/pii/S2210803312000978.

Nettles have a strong anti-inflammatory effect, so are excellent for helping your body heal itself and fight infections. Studies showed that stinging nettles reduced inflammatory hormones, https://www.ncbi.nlm.nih.gov/pubmed/9923611 and http://www.ncbi.nlm.nih.gov/pubmed/8740085. Consuming stinging nettle products or applying a cream made from stinging nettles proved effective at relieving inflammatory conditions such as arthritis. In a study of 27 people, a stinging nettle cream significantly reduced pain from arthritis when compared to a placebo – https://www.ncbi.nlm.nih.gov/pubmed/10911825.

Early research is very positive, but not considered sufficient for medical recommendation. Another study showed that taking a tablet containing stinging nettle extract also significantly reduced arthritis pain, allowing participants to reduce their daily dosage of anti-inflammatory pain relief tablets - https://www.ncbi.nlm.nih.gov/pubmed/20015358.

Other research shows stinging nettle extract helps treat both short and long term urination problems caused by benign prostatic hyperplasia (BPH) or enlarged prostate gland. Around half of men aged over 51 suffer from this and studies show nettle extract to be effective without any negative side effects, https://www.ncbi.nlm.nih.gov/pubmed/16635963 and https://www.ncbi.nlm.nih.gov/pubmed/18038253. Research has not indicated how this compares to conventional treatment.

Hay fever is a problem for many people across the world, and research shows stinging nettle extracts inhibit inflammation that triggers these seasonal allergies (https://www.ncbi.nlm.nih.gov/pubmed/19140159) by blocking histamine receptors and stopping your body's immune cells releasing the chemicals that trigger an allergic reaction. Human studies show that this extract is not much more effective than a placebo, https://www.ncbi.nlm.nih.gov/pubmed/2192379, but further research is still required.

Approximately a third of American adults suffers with high blood pressure, which puts you at risk of stroke and heart disease. Traditionally, herbalists used stinging nettles to treat high blood pressure, https://www.ncbi.nlm.nih.gov/pubmed/27585814. Test-tube and animal studies show stinging nettles stimulate the production of nitric oxide, which acts as a vasodilator that relaxes the muscles of your blood vessels, widening them. Studies show promising results in using stinging nettles to lower blood pressure levels, https://www.ncbi.nlm.nih.gov/pubmed/17170603 and https://www.ncbi.nlm.nih.gov/pubmed/12020933, but further human studies are required to fully understand how this works.

Other research indicates that stinging nettles can help with controlling blood sugar, but further research is required before this treatment is available. Nettles appear to contain compounds that act in a similar manner to insulin, https://www.ncbi.nlm.nih.gov/pubmed/20013820. A study of 46 people over three months found that taking 500mg of stinging nettle extract three times a day significantly lowered the participant's blood sugar levels when compared to the control group taking a placebo, https://www.ncbi.nlm.nih.gov/pubmed/24273930/.

Plenty of research is underway into the medicinal effects of stinging nettles, much of which is based on traditional lore. Stinging nettle extract reduces excessive bleeding, particularly after surgery https://www.ncbi.nlm.nih.gov/pubmed/23724529. It also protects your liver from damage from both toxins and heavy metals, which are common in our modern society, https://www.ncbi.nlm.nih.gov/pubmed/27047060.

Because of the strong effects of stinging nettles, do not take it without consulting a doctor if you are taking blood thinners, diuretics, lithium, diabetic medication or blood pressure medication. Be aware that some people can suffer serious, life threatening allergic reactions to nettle stings.

Beauty Uses

Stinging nettles have quite a few beauty uses; though make sure you have taken away their sting before using them!

Dried nettle leaves are excellent for treating skin blemishes, acne and as a tonic for oily, acne prone skin. With strong astringent properties, nettle leaves tighten skin and are good as a poultice (with the stings removed) for skin problems such as eczema, chicken pox and insect bites. With anti-inflammatory properties, the leaves are also good for treating burn scars and easing burns.

Use a poultice of nettles on eczema affected skin, but also drink two or three cups of nettle tea a day. This helps to remove toxins from your body and reduce the appearance of your eczema.

A nettle infusion or nettle oil is good for treating hair loss, dandruff and stimulating hair growth. Drinking nettle tea and massaging your scalp with nettle oil helps combat hair loss and encourage hair growth. Infuse coconut oil with dried nettle leaves or juice from fresh, crushed nettle leaves and massage into your scalp to treat dandruff.

Pests, Problems & Diseases

Nettles do not suffer from pests or diseases.

Recommended Varieties

There are between 30 and 45 different plants in the genus *Urtica* and family *Urticaceae.* Many of these grow wild as weeds and are rarely encouraged into formal gardens, but welcomed into wild gardens.

- Wood Nettle (*Laportea Canadensis*) – native to the Eastern United States, this plant is used as a food and medicine
- Dwarf Nettle (*Urtica urens*) – a smaller version of the common nettle with smaller, dark leaves
- Roman Nettle (*Uritca pilulifera*) – quite rare and has balls of flowers and seeds
- Fen Nettle (*Urtica dioica subsp. galeopsifolia*) – looks exactly like a stinging nettle but has no sting
- Dead Nettles – these are not related to stinging nettles at all and are members of the mint (*Lamiaceae*) family. These are ornamental and grow in the wild. You can suck the base of the white flowers to get a small taste of nectar and bees are attracted to this plant. Some varieties of dead nettle have pink or purple flowers.

Recipes

Nettle Tea

This is one of the best ways to benefit from the health properties of nettles. Make the tea from fresh, young nettles for the best taste, but many people still find nettle tea a little bitter so sweeten it with some honey or your favorite sweetener. Serve hot or as an iced tea.

Ingredients:

- 4 cups of water
- 1 cup of young nettle leaves
- Sweetener to taste

Method:

1. Remove as much stem as possible from the nettles (feel free to do this after the next step to avoid the sting)
2. Put the nettles in a bowl and wash them with warm to hot water to remove insects and stinging hairs
3. Drain the nettles and put into a large saucepan
4. Add the 4 cups of water and bring to the boil
5. Simmer for 15 minutes, taste and sweeten as required
6. Serve hot or cool and serve with ice for an iced tea

Sautéed Stinging Nettles

This is a great way to serve stinging nettles, like serving any other green vegetable. As always, young leaves are the best to eat.

Ingredients:

- 1lb fresh stinging nettles
- 2 tablespoons extra-virgin olive oil (or other cooking oil)

Method:

1. Clean the stinging nettles by immersing them in water and swishing them around (wearing gloves). Remove from the water, shake and drain. Alternatively, blanche in boiling, slightly salted water for 10-20 seconds and then plunge them into a bowl of ice water to cool them quickly
2. Squeeze excess water from the nettles and put to one side
3. Heat the oil in a large pan
4. Add the nettles and cook for 2-4 minutes, stirring frequently, until the nettles are tender. Keep the heat high to evaporate off excess liquid
5. Season with salt and serve

Nettle Risotto

This is a lovely dish, making two servings, that uses the sharp, citrus flavor of sorrel to complement the earthy taste of nettles. Some shops sell sorrel, but it is easy to grow at home.

Ingredients:

- 6oz/175g risotto rice
- 3½oz/100g young nettle tops
- 1¾oz/50g parmesan cheese (finely grated) plus extra to serve
- 1¾oz/50g sorrel leaves (finely shredded)
- 1oz/30g butter
- 1½pints/900ml chicken/vegetable stock
- 1 onion (finely chopped)

Method:

1. Wash the nettles, removing any stalks
2. Bring a pan of salted water to the boil, add the nettles and return to the boil
3. Blanch for 2-3 minutes, then drain and cool
4. When cool enough to handle, squeeze the water out of the nettles and finely chop
5. Heat the stock until close to boiling, reduce the heat and keep warm
6. In a large pan, melt the butter on a medium to low heat
7. Add the onion and cool for around 8-10 minutes until translucent and soft, but not browned
8. Add the rice, stir well to coat the grains and then add one third of the hot stock
9. Bring to a gentle simmer, stirring often and cook until most of the stock has been absorbed

10. Add the nettles and some more stock, adding additional stock when the liquid in the pan has been absorbed
11. Continue adding stock for 18-20 minutes until the texture is loose and creamy and the rice is cooked to your preference (not all the stock may be required)
12. Stir in the sorrel and season to taste
13. Put little bits of butter over the risotto and sprinkle with grated cheese
14. Cover, leave for 5 minutes and stir in
15. Serve immediately

Nettle Soup

This is a simple recipe for making nettle soup. It is very forgiving, so use what you have to hand and season to your own preference. Add more potatoes to thicken the soup.

Ingredients:

- 1 large onion (finely chopped)
- 2 pints vegetable/chicken stock
- 2 large potatoes (chopped)
- 1 large carrot (chopped)
- Salt, pepper and herbs to taste
- 2oz butter
- 4 handfuls young nettle tops (washed and stalks removed)

Method:

1. Melt the butter in a large pan and cook the onion for 8-10 minutes until softened
2. Add the stock and season to taste
3. Add the potatoes and carrots
4. Simmer until the vegetables are almost tender
5. Add the nettles, stir well and simmer for 10 minutes
6. Add cream, if desired, and check seasoning
7. Puree and serve

Nettle Bread

This is a really good recipe for a tasty bread with stinging nettles that makes six large sandwich rolls. It is worth making and is surprisingly nice!

Ingredients:

- 17½oz/500g strong white flour
- ¾pint/350ml luke warm water
- 6 large nettle leaves (for the top –scalded)
- 1 egg (beaten)
- Large handful of young nettle tops (scalded in boiling water and chopped)
- 2 tablespoons extra-virgin olive oil
- 1 tablespoon honey
- 1 teaspoon salt
- 1 teaspoon easy bake yeast

Method:

1. Sieve the flour and salt together in a large bowl, add the yeast and stir well
2. Add the honey, oil and water, stirring again
3. Add the chopped nettles and mix well to create a soft dough
4. Turn the dough out onto a floured surface and knead for 10 minutes until smooth and elastic
5. Drizzle some oil into a bowl, add the dough, cover and leave to rise for 2 hours somewhere warm until doubled in size
6. Divide the dough into 6 balls and put on a greased baking tray
7. Cover with kitchen paper or a tea towel and leave for 45 minutes to rise
8. Brush with the egg, place a nettle on top of each dough ball and brush again with the egg
9. Preheat your oven to 430F/220C
10. Bake for 35 minutes until golden; the bread rolls are ready when they sound hollow when you tap their bottom
11. Remove from the oven and cool on a wire rack

Nettle Pancakes

These are a great treat to make in spring. Fill these pancakes with sweet or savory fillings. A great use for an invasive weed!

Ingredients:

- 1¾oz/50g white (plain) flour
- 1¾oz/50g spelt flour
- 1¾oz/50g butter (melted)
- 1¾oz/50g fresh young nettles (scalded, stems removed and chopped)
- 1 pint/500ml milk
- 2 eggs

Method:

1. Sift both flours into a bowl
2. Beat in the eggs, milk and butter
3. Add the nettles and stir very well
4. Heat some butter or oil in a frying pan until smoking hot
5. Add the batter mixture to make pancakes as thick or thin as you like them
6. Cook on both sides until golden brown and cooked through
7. Serve hot with your choice of filling

Oregano

Oregano, *Origanum vulgare*, is a close relative of marjoram with strong and pungent leaves. This perennial herb is important in Mediterranean, particularly Greek and Italian, cooking as well as being popular in Mexican cuisine. Oregano is more frequently used dry rather than fresh.

At a Glance Facts

~~Annual~~ / ~~Biennial~~ / **Perennial**	
Position:	Full sun to partial shade
Soil:	Well-drained
Hardiness	Yes, down to -4F/-20C
USDA Zones:	5-10
Sow:	February to May
Harvest:	May to October

Oregano grows wild in Greece with many mountains literally covered with the plant! The name of the plant translates from Greek as 'joy of the mountain', showing how much the Greeks like this plant being on their hills. Greek mythology tells us that the goddess Aphrodite created the scent of oregano as a symbol of joy and happiness.

The Romans also adopted oregano, and through their expansion and the later exploration by Europeans, spread it across Europe, China, northern Africa and into the Americas.

Oregano has a long history of healing use and modern research indicates it has powerful antioxidants, cancer fighting properties and more. The best oregano oil, with the highest levels of these beneficial compounds is the Greek oil.

Growing Instructions

Grow from seed or buy ready-grown plants from your supermarket or local garden center.

Sow seeds indoors from February to May. Fill a small pot with compost, scatter several seeds on the surface and cover with a thin layer of sieved compost. Water, then place on a sunny windowsill or in a heated propagator to germinate.

Once the seedlings are big enough to handle, prick out to three seedlings per 3"/8cm container.

Water regularly, but avoid overwatering as the roots can rot. Plant outside in a sunny, sheltered spot after the risk of frost has passed or transplant into a larger pot to mature.

Plant Care

Trim the plants in the summer, after the flowers fade. Container grown plants then require a feed with a balanced liquid fertilizer.

In winter, cut dead stems back to the ground. Lift pots off the ground to allow excess water to drain.

For a supply of leaves through winter, lift the plants in the fall, pot them up and put them in a bright position under cover.

For the best flavor, pick the leaves before the flower buds open. Dried oregano has a stronger flavor than fresh.

Culinary Uses

Oregano is wild marjoram, but has a stronger flavor than culinary marjoram, so has different uses in the kitchen. In cooking, consider it as a separate herb. Substitute marjoram for oregano, but as it has a milder flavor, use twice as much marjoram. The dried herb has a much stronger taste than the fresh herb. As a rough guide, when a recipe calls for a tablespoon of fresh oregano, use a teaspoon of the dried herb.

Oregano has a very distinct smell and both the tiny leaves and the pink/purple flowers are edible, with the flowers popular in salads.

Cooks use oregano to flavor a wide range of dishes from the tomato sauce on pizzas, to spaghetti bolognaise, chilli and more.

When harvesting oregano for use, wash the herb thoroughly and then remove the leaves from the woody stalks. If using oregano in a bouquet garni, there is no need to do this.

Oregano complements a number of other herbs such as onion, garlic, thyme, basil and parsley. Using olive oil with oregano really brings out its flavor.

Like many herbs, oregano loses its flavor when cooked, so always add it towards the end of cooking. Add a little at a time to a dish, tasting after each addition as too much oregano can make your meal bitter.

Health Uses

Oregano is a very useful herb with high levels of antioxidants, https://www.ncbi.nlm.nih.gov/pubmed/8933203, that fight cell damage caused by free radicals.

Oregano contains high levels of the antioxidants carvacrol and thymol. Research is underway into using these to combat a wide variety of illnesses, including cancer, and initial results are promising. In a test-tube study, researchers used oregano extract to treat colon cancer cells and discovered that it not only stopped the cancer cells from growing, but also helped to kill off the malignant cells, https://www.ncbi.nlm.nih.gov/pubmed/19373612. Another study, https://www.ncbi.nlm.nih.gov/pubmed/26214321, showed how carvacrol suppressed both the spread and growth of colon cancer cells. Although these tests are promising, a lot more research is required for the discovery of an effective treatment.

Compounds in oregano have antibacterial properties and a study showed these to be effective in treating 23 different types of commonly found bacteria, https://www.ncbi.nlm.nih.gov/pubmed/19783523. A separate study, https://www.ncbi.nlm.nih.gov/pmc/articles/PMC4400296/, found that oregano oil was very effective as an antimicrobial. Further research is still required to understand how to apply these findings to treating humans.

As well as its antibacterial properties, some studies have indicated oregano has antiviral properties too. A study, https://www.ncbi.nlm.nih.gov/pubmed/24779581, found that carvacrol inactivated the notorious norovirus within an hour of treatment! Another test-tube study, https://www.ncbi.nlm.nih.gov/pubmed/22890541, showed that within one hour, carvacrol and thymol inactivated 90% of the herpes simplex virus. Again, the initial research is promising but further development is required before use on humans.

There is a lot of promising research into oregano and hopefully over the next decade or so, this should result in a new set of drugs for human use. In the meantime, you can benefit from oregano by included it in your meals.

Beauty Uses

With its high levels of antioxidants, oregano has a whole host of skin benefits. With antifungal and antiseptic properties, it is widely used in medicated skin care products and is excellent for treating spots and acne.

Treat fungal infections with an application of oregano oil, or mix it with a neutral base cream. Use it for most fungal infections including athlete's foot and toenail fungus as well as for easing eczema and psoriasis. Apply every day for two weeks and you will see positive results.

Oregano helps to reduce the visible signs of aging such as fine facial lines. Mix the essential oil into a face cream or mask, or make a poultice of fresh leaves. It will tighten and firm your skin as well as combat spots, acne and blocked pores!

Whether you decide to use the fresh herb or the essential oil is up to you, but including it in your beauty regime will help leave your skin looking younger and glowing.

Pests, Problems & Diseases

Oregano tends not to suffer from many pests or diseases. Aphids sometimes affect new growth. When growing under glass or indoors, red spider mites can infect your plants, so mist them regularly to keep the growing environment humid.

Recommended Varieties

There are several cultivars of oregano, but the confusion comes from the number of plants called oregano that are not even the same species. As well as the edible cultivars, there are a number of ornamental varieties grown for their foliage or flowers.

- Compact Oregano (*Origanum vulgare 'Compactum'*) – a dwarf variety with pink flowers
- Golden Oregano (*Origanum vulgare 'Aurem Crispum'*) – a showy variety with crinkled golden leaves and the usual pink flowers
- Greek Oregano (*Origanum vulgare hirtum*) – a pungent oregano hardy in USDA zones 5 to 11. This cultivar has white flowers and fuzzy green leaves. It is also known as *Origanum heracleoticum* and *Origanum vulgare prismaticum*
- Mexican Oregano (*Poliomintha maderensis*) – not a member of the *Origanum* family, but referred to as oregano. Hardy only in zones 9b to 11, it has pretty, ornamental flowers. Often used in Mexican cooking along with *Lippia graveolens* and *Plectranthus amboinicus* which are also, confusingly, referred to as Mexican oregano!
- Italian Oregano (*Origanum x majoricum*) – a hybrid of sweet marjoram and common oregano, hardy in USDA zones 6 to 9. With delicate, light green leave and off white flowers, this herb combines the pungency of Greek oregano with the mild flavor that makes sweet marjoram so popular. This hybrid is sterile so is grown from cuttings or by division.
- Hopflower Oregano (*Origanum libanoticum*) – an ornamental variety, hardy to USDA zone 4b with lavender colored flowers and a trailing growth habit.

Recipes

Before using oregano oil on your skin, do a patch test to check for allergies as this oil can cause itchiness in some people.

Oregano Oil Face Mask

This simple face mask harnesses the power of oregano to reduce the signs of aging and clear spots or acne.

Ingredients:

- ¼ cup aloe vera gel
- 1 tablespoon cucumber juice
- 3 drops oregano essential oil

Method:

1. Mix the ingredients together, use a blender if necessary
2. Apply to your skin
3. Leave for 5 minutes then rinse with cold water

Oregano Skin Toner

This skin toner is excellent for anyone suffering with acne or oily skin. As an added advantage, this will also tighten the skin on your face. This will store for a week when refrigerated.

Ingredients:

- 3 cups water
- 3 tablespoons dried oregano leaves

Method:

1. Boil the leaves in the water for 10 minutes
2. Remove from the heat and cool
3. Strain into an airtight container and refrigerate when cool
4. Apply to affected areas of your face using cotton wool

Roast Oregano Chicken

An easy recipe that shows off the taste of oregano on chicken breasts. Serve with roast potatoes and your favorite vegetables. This makes enough for 6 people and takes about 40 minutes to make.

Ingredients:

- 6 chicken breast fillets (skinless and boneless)
- 1¾oz/50g butter (melted)
- 4 tablespoons lemon juice
- 2 tablespoons soy sauce
- 2 tablespoons Worcestershire sauce
- 2 teaspoons dried oregano
- 1 teaspoon garlic granules

Method:

1. Preheat your oven to 375F/190C
2. In a small bowl, mix together everything except the chicken breasts until thoroughly combined
3. Put the chicken into a high sided baking dish
4. Pour the oregano mixture over the chicken, making sure it is well covered
5. Bake for 15 minutes then baste and bake for a further 15 minutes until cooked through
6. Serve immediately or cool and slice to use on a salad

Chimichurri Sauce

This classic Argentinian sauce is great on steak or used as a marinade on chicken, particularly before barbecuing. It is quick to make, but needs a few hours or, ideally, overnight, for the flavors to combine, so best make it the day before.

Ingredients:

- ¾ cup/180ml extra-virgin olive oil
- 4 tablespoons white wine vinegar
- 2 tablespoons fresh oregano (chopped)
- 2 tablespoons green bell pepper (chopped)
- 2 tablespoons fresh basil (torn)
- 1 tablespoon scallions (spring onion) (chopped)
- Salt and pepper to taste

Method:

1. Blend all of the ingredients in your food processor until mostly smooth, but still a little chunky
2. Pour into a bowl, cover and refrigerate for 3 hours or overnight to allow the flavors to mature
3. Serve over steaks or marinade meat in it before grilling it

Parsley

Parsley, *Petroselinum crispum*, is a biennial herb usually grown as an annual. Best known as a garnish, it has many more uses including in sauces, butters, dressings and more.

At a Glance Facts

~~Annual~~ / **Biennial** / ~~Perennial~~	
Position:	Full sun to partial shade
Soil:	Moist, loam, well-drained
Hardiness	Yes, down to -4F/-20C
USDA Zones:	4-9
Sow:	March to June
Harvest:	June to August

Culinary wise, there are two common varieties. Curly leaf parsley looks great as a garnish as its leaves are very attractive, though its milder taste means it is less frequently used in cooking.. However, cooks more frequently use the stronger tasting flat leaved parsley, which looks very similar to cilantro.

Parsley has a long history of human use, with many claiming it to be the world's most popular herb. Native to the Mediterranean area, parsley grows all over the world. A relative of celery, parsley derives its name from the Ancient Greek word '*petroselinon*', meaning 'rock celery'.

Surprisingly, parsley was popular as a medicinal plant before it made an appearance in the kitchen. The Ancient Greeks considered this herb sacred, using it to decorate tombs, for funeral wreaths and give it to winners of athletic competitions. The Greeks even garnished dead people with parsley because it helped to reduce the smell! Greek mythology says the first parsley grew from the blood of Archemorus, the son of Death, who was eaten by snakes. In their grief, the Greeks founded the Nemean Games to honor him and presented the winners with parsley crowns.

The English believed it was bad luck to transplant parsley as to do so would cause offense to the guardian of the plants. Giving away parsley root was considered bad luck and cutting parsley would ensure you were crossed in love! According to British legend, only witches were able to germinate parsley seeds, giving you an idea how difficult it is to grow this plant from seed!

According to folklore, parsley has to travel to hell and back seven (or nine according to some sources) times before it will germinate. They say you should sow nine times the seeds as you actually need, as the devil will keep the rest for himself!

Despite the rather grim folklore attached to parsley, it remains a popular culinary herb in a wide variety of cuisines, particularly Greek and Mediterranean.

Growing Instructions

Sow parsley outdoors from the start of spring through to the beginning of summer. It requires well-drained soil in a sunny or partially shaded position. Sow the seeds in ½" deep trenches, cover with soil and the water. When large enough to handle, thin to 6"/15cm between plants and the same distance between rows.

Parsley will happily grow in containers. Sow seeds thinly across the surface of a 10"/25cm pot filled with good quality seed compost. Cover with ½" of compost and water in. Leave in a cool spot to germinate, ensuring it does not dry out. It can take up to six weeks for the seeds to germinate, which is perhaps the origin of the legend about parsley travelling to hell and back. Once the seedlings are large enough to handle, thin, leaving around ¾" between plants.

Plant Care

Keep your plants well watered, particularly when growing in containers and during hot, dry spells. During the growing season, feed with a balanced liquid fertilizer every few weeks.

During the flowering season, remove the flower heads so you can harvest the herb for longer. Cut individual leaves or stems from near the base using scissors. Parsley is best used fresh, but can be dried or frozen for use out of season.

Flat Leaf Parsley

Once flowering has finished, cut the plant back. If any shoots start to turn yellow, remove them from your plant and compost them.

Culinary Uses

Use the curly leaf parsley as a garnish. With a milder flavor, it is not popular in cooking. The flat-leaf or Italian parsley, has a much strong flavorer that it retains even when cooked. Parsley works well with many different dishes from fish to potatoes to eggs and more. Curly leaf parsley looks fresh for longer and is easy to mince, but is harder to wash as dirt and bugs hide in the curls.

Parsley is probably the most widely used culinary herb across the world. It is favored by many people for its ability to absorb odors, particularly that of garlic. Rub your hands with it after handling garlic or chew a small sprig after eating garlic and it acts as a natural deodorizer.

The most common use for curly leaf parsley is as a garnish, though the French deep-fry it and serve it with meat. Many herb mixes include parsley such as bouquet garni, used to flavor stocks, stews and soups, and fines herbs, popular in French cuisine where parsley is combined with chives, tarragon and chervil.

Middle Eastern cuisine makes extensive use of parsley to make falafels, tabbouleh and chickpea dishes. Chickpea fritters, a popular dish in the Middle East, have a green outer shell colored by parsley.

The British make a parsley sauce to serve with fish dishes, broad beans and cold ham. They also garnish potato salad with parsley, though chives are another popular choice.

Many dishes call for parsley as an ingredient. Unless it is for a garnish, this usually means you should use flat-leaf parsley. It is good in many Mediterranean dishes from lasagne to spaghetti bolognaise. It works well in Shepherd's Pie where the parsley flavors the potato on top. This versatile herb is worth having in your kitchen.

Curly Leaf Parsley

Health Uses

Parsley has high levels of vitamins, making it a very good addition to your diet. A serving of parsley has twice the amount of iron as spinach and three times more vitamin C than an orange! Parsley is one of the best sources of vitamin K, containing 574% of the daily recommended amount. Vitamin K improves bone health as it helps your body to absorb calcium and excrete any excess. Early research indicates vitamin K may play a role in the prevention and treatment of neurological diseases like Alzheimer's disease.

Parsley acts as a diuretic, helping to dissolve and expel gallstones as well as stop them from forming. This effect means it is useful when on a diet to get rid of excess water and bloating. Parsley root protects your liver and moderates blood sugar levels.

Anyone who suffers from allergies should add parsley to their diet. It inhibits the secretion of histamine and can reduce the symptoms of allergies, including hives. If you have hay fever, then eating parsley during hay fever season can help reduce its impact on you.

Early research shows parsley contains cancer fighting compounds such as the flavonol myricetin and apigenin. Studies have shown the latter to reduce the size of tumors in an aggressive form of breast cancer. More research needs to be done to create drugs for human use, but the initial results are exciting.

Beauty Uses

Parsley is high in antioxidants as well as minerals, all of which are very beneficial to your skin. The high levels of vitamin C found in parsley stimulates the production of collagen, which keeps your skin looking young. Commercial anti-aging creams use vitamin C because it is effective, and parsley is a cheaper, more natural source of this valuable anti-aging compound. The vitamin K found in parsley improves the elasticity of your skin and reduces redness, making it look much better.

Making an infusion of parsley and then rinsing your face daily is an excellent way to benefit from this skin altering effect. Of course, adding parsley to your diet also helps, though some people like to add parsley to their morning juices! If you are a juice person, then this is a great way to get the many benefits of parsley.

Making a face mask from parsley will help nourish your skin, treat acne and reduce dark spots or discoloration. Parsley has an antibacterial effect on your skin, which kills the bacteria that causes spots and acne. Eating or washing your face with parsley balances inflamed or oily skin, helping to ease skin eruptions and speed healing. Parsley contains high levels of zinc too, which has a positive effect on reducing and eliminating acne.

A parsley infusion makes an excellent hair tonic when massaged directly into the scalp. It stimulates hair growth, makes your hair shiny and helps to bring out your natural hair color. The antioxidant apigenin, contained in parsley, stimulates hair follicles, which promotes hair growth.

With the high level of vitamins and minerals, parsley is also very good for your eyes. Its high levels of beta-carotene and the carotenoids lutein and zeaxanthin, parsley provides protection against eye diseases and age related degeneration.

Pests, Problems & Diseases

Parsley does have its fair share of problems and pests. It is susceptible to carrot fly due to its close relation to the carrot and aphids are attracted to it. Covering parsley will keep both pests off. Growing onions, garlic or other strongly scented plants near to parsley will help keep carrot fly away as it hunts by scent and these strong smells confuse it. Pick aphids off by hand or use a homemade garlic based spray to get rid of them.

Aphids spread a virus called 'carrot motley dwarf' that turns the leaves yellow or pink and stunts the growth. The foliage dies off so your harvest is negatively affected. Either remove and destroy infected plants or control aphids when you first spot them.

Recommended Varieties

There are over thirty different varieties of parsley, though only a handful are cultivated at home. These are the most commonly grown varieties:

- Common Parsley (*Petroselinum crispum*) – grows curly leaves on stems of between 8" and 14" long. Prefers a well-drained soil that is moist and will grow in dense clumps. Used in the kitchen as a garnish.
- Italian Parsley (*Petroselinum neapolitanum*) – a flat-leaf parsley growing up to 24-36" tall. Likes a rich, moist soil and does not like drying out. Has a stronger, sweeter flavor than the previous cultivar. The leaves are used in a wide variety of dishes both fresh and dried.
- Hamburg Parsley (*Petroselnium tuberosum*) – grown for the fleshy roots that are similar to parsnip and taste like a nutty celery/parsley cross. Growing to 24" tall and about 12" wide, the leaves look like ferns and are used like the Italian and common parsley.
- Japanese Parsley (*Cryptotaenia japonica*) – looks similar to flat-leaf parsley but originates in the Far East, notably Japan and China. This is an evergreen perennial, hardy in USDA zones 5 to 11. It grows to about three feet tall with a two foot spread. Although common in Asian cooking, the leaves are slightly bitter, making it less popular in Western cooking. Use the stems as you would celery and the leaves like normal parsley. Protect this cultivar from hot afternoon sun as it has a tendency for the leaves to scorch.

Recipes

Pommes Persillade

This is very simply potatoes with a persillade, i.e. a mixture of garlic and parsley. This is commonly served with lamb, though works as a side dish for most meals.

Ingredients:

- 2 medium potatoes (peeled and cubed)
- 2 garlic cloves (minced)
- ¼ cup flat-leaf parsley (finely chopped)
- 2 tablespoons extra-virgin olive oil
- 1 tablespoon butter
- Salt and pepper

Method:

1. Mix the parsley and garlic together in a small bowl
2. Heat the oil in a frying pan on a high heat
3. Cook the potato cubes until they are soft on the inside and a crispy light brown on the outside
4. Add the butter and cook for 3-5 minutes until the potatoes are virtually cooked
5. 1 minute before serving, add the garlic and parsley, tossing the potatoes well to ensure they are evenly coated
6. Season to taste, remove from heat and serve immediately

Parsley Fish Cakes

Parsley goes well with fish and potato, which is great for this recipe! Make these fish cakes with any fish you like, though salmon, cod and haddock are particularly good. It takes about 1 hour 40 minutes to make this recipe and it will serve four people.

Ingredients:

- 1lb/450g potatoes (mashed – ensuring no lumps)
- 1lb/450g skinned fish fillets
- 4oz/115g fresh breadcrumbs
- 1 egg (beaten)
- 4 tablespoons oil (for frying – any oil will do)
- 2 tablespoons fresh parsley (chopped)
- 1 tablespoon all-purpose (plain) flour
- Zest of 1 lemon (grated)
- Salt and pepper

Method:

1. Simmer the fish in a covered pan of water for 5 minutes
2. Drain the fish, transfer to a plate and cool
3. When cooled, break the fish into flakes or small pieces, using a fork and remove any bones
4. In a large bowl, mix together the fish, potato, parsley and lemon zest, then season to taste
5. Use your hands to shape the mixture into fish cakes; make 4 large or 6 to 8 small
6. Put the flour, breadcrumbs and eggs in separate, shallow bowls (for dredging)
7. Coat each fish cake with flour, then dip into the egg and roll in breadcrumbs, ensuring they are thoroughly covered
8. Put on a plate and refrigerate for 30-60 minutes or until required

9. Heat the oil in a frying pan
10. Fry the fish cakes for 5-7 minutes on each side, until the breadcrumbs are golden brown and the cakes cooked throughout
11. Serve immediately

Tabbouleh

Tabbouleh is the national dish of Lebanon in North Africa. It is a delicious salad with an interesting combination of flavors made from bulgur wheat and featuring fresh parsley. Serve with grilled, barbecued or roasted vegetables or meats. This recipe takes around 1 hour and 15 minutes to make and serves 4 people. Eat using small lettuce leaves as scoops or pitta bread.

Ingredients:

- 3oz/75g bulgur (cracked) wheat
- 2oz/50g fresh flat-leaf parsley (chopped)
- 2oz/50g fresh mint leaves (chopped)
- 3fl oz/85ml extra-virgin olive oil
- 6 scallions (spring onions) (chopped)
- 2 medium tomatoes (chopped)
- Juice of 2 lemons
- Salt and pepper

Method:

1. Put the wheat into a bowl and cover with lemon juice, leaving to stand for 1 hour, stirring occasionally
2. Add the herbs and scallions, mixing well
3. Pour in the olive oil, season to taste and stir well
4. Transfer to a serving dish, put the diced tomatoes on top and enjoy

Parsley and Lemon Face Mask

This is a refreshing and revitalizing face mask that will tighten your skin and keep it looking great. Be aware that the lemon juice may sting if you have open acne sores or spots, in which case wash it off straight away. Do not worry if the parsley still has bits of leaves and stalk in, you will still benefit from it.

Ingredients:

- 1 medium head of curly parsley (soak in warm water to clean first)
- 2 teaspoons honey (Manuka honey is ideal)
- 1 teaspoon fresh lemon juice (reduce or remove if you have sensitive skin)

Method:

1. Chop the parsley, then crush in a mortar and pestle until it is almost a paste
2. Add the honey and lemon juice and mash well
3. Apply to a clean face, leave for 10-15 minutes then remove with cool water and pat dry

Rosemary

Rosemary, *Rosmarinus officinalis*, is a bushy shrub with a very distinctive smell. With small, long leaves and pale violet or blue flowers, this is a popular plant to grow in a herb garden or border. It is instantly recognizable, particularly from the scent when the leaves are rubbed together. This herb grows quite large and need regular pruning to maintain its shape and stop it from becoming leggy.

At a Glance Facts

~~Annual~~ / ~~Biennial~~ / **Perennial**	
Position:	Full sun
Soil:	Moist, well-drained
Hardiness	Yes to 23F/-5C to 14F/-10C
USDA Zones:	1-10
Sow:	March to May
Harvest:	May to October

Native to the coastal areas of the Mediterranean, including North Africa, legend tells us rosemary grows 'where one can hear the sea'. Its Latin name derives from '*ros*' meaning 'dew' and '*marinus*' meaning 'sea', giving it a nickname of 'dew of the sea', perhaps referring to the small, sea blue flowers found on many cultivars. In the Middle Ages, rosemary was called 'Guardrobe'.

Rosemary is steeped in myth and legend from its long association with people. Both the Romans and Ancient Greeks usually grew rosemary in the gardens, as they believed it protected them from evil spirits and it would only grow in the gardens of righteous souls! The oldest written reference to rosemary occurs in cuneiform tablets dating back to around 5000BC.

The Romans brought rosemary to Britain, where many hundreds of years later, settlers took the plant to North America. Rosemary improves circulation and strengthens blood vessels, helping with memory and boosting your energy levels. Sniffing rosemary oil or sprigs of rosemary when tired boosts alertness and is used before exams to help stimulate your memory and ensure you are fully alert.

Rosemary has a lovely scent and is a great culinary and healing herb. It is excellent in sensory gardens and when pruned regularly, maintains a good looking plant.

Growing Instructions

Although rosemary does grow from seed, the results are often poor and germination is slow and unreliable. Buy part grown plants or take cuttings from established plants and root.

Rosemary grows equally well in the ground or in containers, though choose large containers (12-24") as this plant does grow quite big. Plant in the ground in a sheltered position in well-drained soil and full sun. Rosemary does not like its roots being wet in winter. In hotter environments, you can place rosemary in partial shade.

Most rosemary cultivars are hardy to zone 9 (20F/-7C) and extreme cold weather will kill the plant. If you grow rosemary in containers and live in a colder area, move them indoors or to a warmer spot during the winter months.

Plant Care

Rosemary is relatively drought tolerant, though requires regularly watering during dry weather, particularly if grown in containers. Feed container grown plants with a balanced liquid feed once flowering has finished. Ensure container grown plants have plenty of room between them to allow the air to circulate to prevent mold forming. Lift containers off the ground using pot feet during winter to prevent the roots from getting too wet.

Harvest fresh shoots as required and use immediately or dry. Fresh rosemary will store in a plastic bag in your refrigerator for up to a week,

Rosemary can grow out of control and get very leggy. When the flowers start to fade, cut back the stems. Pinching off the growing tips during the growing season will help create bushy plants. Hard pruning can be done in spring to allow for new growth to mature.

Culinary Uses

Rosemary has many culinary uses and has a delightful taste. It works well in dishes such as stews, soups or casserole and pairs well with most meats, but particularly with poultry, lamb and oily fish. Rosemary also pairs well with vegetables with one of my favorite pairings being new potatoes roasted in a couple of tablespoons of apple cider vinegar and sprinkled with rosemary. Try it … it is fantastic!

Add whole sprigs of rosemary to stews and meat dishes to give flavor. These can be removed before serving as the stems can be a bit woody. Alternatively, strip the leaves from the stems and add the leaves to your meals.

Rosemary is a key component in Mediterranean cooking where it is frequently paired with pork, chicken and lamb. As it has a strong flavor, be careful not to use too much rosemary as it is easy to overwhelm a dish.

Rosemary dries very well due to the high levels of oil in the leaves. Fresh and dried rosemary have similar tastes, though sometimes the dried version has a stronger flavor.

Health Uses

Rosemary has many potential health benefits due to its high levels of antioxidants and anti-inflammatory compounds.

Europeans use rosemary to treat indigestion and in Germany it is an officially approved treatment. Although this is a traditional use, so far, no medical evidence is available to substantiate this claim - https://www.medicalnewstoday.com/articles/163484.php.

One of my favorite uses of rosemary is to improve concentration, wake you up and help your memory. Sniffing rosemary oil or a fresh sprig of rosemary helps to clear the mind and help you feel more alert. Whenever I used to sit exams, I always had a bottle of rosemary essential oil to sniff to help keep my mind in focus - https://www.ncbi.nlm.nih.gov/pmc/articles/PMC3736918/.

Due to its antioxidant levels, particularly its content of carnosic acid, Rosemary is good for the brain, helping to protect against brain damage and speed recovery in stroke victims – https://www.ncbi.nlm.nih.gov/pubmed/28243285. Initial studies into rosemary preventing brain aging diseases such as Alzheimer's show plenty of promise, but further research is still required to produce viable drugs - https://www.ncbi.nlm.nih.gov/pubmed/26092628.

Early research into rosemary shows it to be a promising component of future cancer drugs. Crude ethanolic rosemary extract (RO) slowed the spread of both leukemia and breast carcinoma cells in humans - https://www.ncbi.nlm.nih.gov/pubmed/17487414. A separate study shows rosemary to be effect against both tumors and inflammation - https://www.ncbi.nlm.nih.gov/pubmed/17827696.

Other research showed that adding rosemary extract to ground beef meant fewer cancer causing agents developed during cooking, http://onlinelibrary.wiley.com/doi/10.1111/j.1750-3841.2006.00149.x/abstract. This could mean rosemary can prevent or at least reduce carcinogens forming when cooking meat.

Carnosic acid, the antioxidant found in rosemary has major benefits for your eye health according to one study – https://www.eurekalert.org/pub_releases/2012-11/smri-cfi112712.php. It appears to protect the eye, particularly the outer retina from age-related degeneration, which is the most common eye disease affecting Americans -

https://www.medicalnewstoday.com/articles/152105.php.

In general, rosemary has no side effects, but it can make some people ill when taken in large doses. When taken in the amounts used in cooking, it is rare for it to have a negative effect. Pregnant women are advised not to take too much rosemary as high doses can cause a miscarriage.

If you are taking any blood-thinning or blood pressure medication, diuretics or lithium, you should not take rosemary. Rosemary can have a diuretic effect that will cause the lithium to build up to toxic levels very quickly.

Beauty Uses

Rosemary has many beauty benefits too and is often taken as a herbal tea. As a tea, rosemary helps weight loss, aids digestion, reduces your risk of cancer and boosts your memory!

The phytochemical components of rosemary tea inhibit lipase, which is an enzyme that breaks fat down, creating lipids. Lipase is inactive so the fat does not break down, meaning you feel fuller and do not want to eat as much.

Rosemary tea can be both drank and applied directly to the skin. As well as its antioxidant properties, it has antimicrobial properties too. Use rosemary tea topically to cure fungal or bacterial infections, blisters and even acne! Plus, its high levels of antioxidants also mean it tightens your skin, reduces the signs of aging and leaves your skin looking fresh and glowing.

The same rosemary tea helps improve blood circulation in your scalp, which boosts hair growth. Rinse your hair regularly with a rosemary tea to reduce the signs of baldness, stop your hair falling out or losing its color and reduce dandruff. It will treat any scalp fungal infections too.

Pests, Problems & Diseases

Late frosts can damage or even kill rosemary. If a hard frost is forecast, cover your rosemary with horticultural fleece to protect it.

Scale insects can infect rosemary plants. Pick these off by hand or use biological controls.

Rosemary beetles will strip the plant of leaves very quickly. These small, oval beetles with metallic purple and green stripes are attractive to look at, but their larvae are the problem. Check your plants regularly for signs if infection and remove any beetles by hand.

Aphids can infect new growth, but apart from that, rosemary is pretty hardy and does not have many pests, diseases or problems.

Recommended Varieties

There are two main types of rosemary; upright and low, ground cover. Within these two categories there are many different cultivars varying in size, shape and leaves. It can get a bit confusing as sometimes the same cultivar is sold under multiple names. However, most people grow *Rosmarinus officinalis* as it is the herb used by herbalists and in the kitchen.

- *Rosmarinus officinalis* – the upright, culinary rosemary with needle-like gray/green leaves. The flowers are pale blue, appearing in small clusters at the ends of the branches. This cultivar is an evergreen and grows from three to five feet tall.
- *Rosmarinus officinalis* 'Majorica Pink' – originating in the Spanish, Balearic Islands, it is similar to *R. officinalis* but has pink flowers. This cultivar is worth growing with *R. officinalis* as the two different flower colors really stand out.
- *Rosmarinus officinalis* 'Tuscan Blue' – growing up to six feet tall, this cultivar originates in Tuscany, Italy. The flowers are a dark blue and the leaves very aromatic. Although this cultivar can be grown in short-season areas, it prefers a warmer climate.
- *Rosmarinus officinalis* 'Miss Jessopp's Upright' – grows from five to eight feet tall with slate blue flowers. The leaves are dark gray/green and very aromatic. This cultivar was bred to be hardy to zone 8 and originated in Miss Jessopp's nursey in Santa Barbara, California from a cutting taken at Sissinghurst Castle.
- *Rosmarinus officinalis* 'Arp' – one of the hardiest rosemary cultivars, overwintering in USDA zone 6. This cultivar grows from three to

five feet tall and has very pale blue, almost white, flowers. This plant is very sensitive to water logged soil, so requires good drainage.

- *Rosmarinus officinalis* 'Prostratus' – a low growing cultivar, growing between one and two feet tall but spreading up to eight feet wide. The glossy, dark green leaves have a distinct pine fragrance. The flowers are a light blue color.
- *Rosmarinus officinalis* 'Lockwood de Forest' – similar to the previous cultivar but with lighter colored leaves and darker blue flowers.
- *Rosmarinus officinalis angustifolius* – originating in Corsica and not considered a culinary variety. This cultivar smells like a pine tree and grows like one too. It grows from two to four feet tall with very needle like leaves and dark blue flowers. It is hardy to USDA zone 9 or 25F/-4C.

Recipes

Rosemary Garlic Butter

This butter is great in pasta, on a steak, mashed into a baked potato or spread on bread for home-made garlic bread. It is easy to make and very delicious.

Ingredients:

- 4oz butter (room temperature)
- 2 garlic cloves (minced and mashed)
- 1 teaspoon salt
- 1 teaspoon lemon juice (fresh)
- ½ teaspoon fresh rosemary leaves (finely chopped)

Method:

1. Mix the garlic, lemon juice and salt together in a small bowl
2. Add the rosemary leaves and stir until thoroughly combined
3. Add the butter and mash until well blended
4. Place the butter on wax paper and shape into a log or patty
5. Wrap, then refrigerate until required

Rosemary Tea

This is a simple way to make rosemary tea. Sweeten to taste or mix with lemon balm for a refreshing, healing drink.

Ingredients:

- 1 cup boiling water
- 1 teaspoon rosemary leaves
- 1 teaspoon honey/sugar/sweetener (optional)

Method:

1. Steep the rosemary in the water for around 5 minutes
2. Sweeten to taste and enjoy

Rosemary Hair Rinse

A great hair rinse that leaves your hair looking great, reducing dandruff and improving hair growth too. Use a couple of times a week.

Ingredients:

- 2 teaspoons fresh rosemary leaves
- 2 cups of water

Method:

1. Bring the water to the boil
2. Add the rosemary
3. Reduce the heat to a simmer and cover the pan
4. Switch the heat off after 5 minutes and leave to cool
5. Strain the liquid into a squeezy bottle
6. Rinse your hair after shampooing and leave to 2-3 minutes before washing out

Rosemary Sweet Potato Fries

This simple recipe takes about half an hour to make and will serve four people. Instead of sweet potatoes, try this with potatoes, beetroot, carrots or parsnips to make for an interesting dish.

Ingredients:

- 3 large sweet potatoes (peeled and cut into ¼" strips)
- 1 garlic clove (minced)
- 3 tablespoons extra-virgin olive oil
- 1 tablespoon fresh rosemary (minced)
- 1 teaspoon cornstarch
- ¾ teaspoon salt
- Small pinch of black pepper

Method:

1. Preheat your oven to 425F/220C
2. Put the all of the ingredients into a re-sealable plastic bag
3. Shake well until the potatoes are thoroughly coated
4. Oil two baking pans

5. Arrange the potatoes in a single layer and bake for approximately 30 minutes until tender and light brown, turning occasionally

Butternut Squash Lasagna

This is a lovely take on the lasagna that serves eight people. It will take about an hour and a half to make, but is well worth the time.

Ingredients:

- 9 uncooked lasagna noodles
- 6 garlic cloves (minced)
- 3lb butternut squash (peeled and cut crosswise into ¼" slices)
- 4 cups fat free milk
- 1⅓ cups Parmesan cheese (shredded)
- 6 tablespoons all-purpose (plain) flour
- 2 tablespoons extra-virgin olive oil
- 1 tablespoon fresh rosemary (minced)
- 1 teaspoon salt (divided)

Method:

1. Preheat your oven to 425F/220C
2. Cook the noodles according to their instructions and drain
3. In a large bowl, mix the oil, squash and ½ teaspoon of salt, tossing well so it is thoroughly coated
4. Spray a baking pan (15x10x1") with oil and spread the butternut squash over the pan
5. Cook until tender, about 10-15 minutes
6. Remove from the oven and turn the oven down to 375F/190C
7. Put the rest of the salt and the flour into a large saucepan and slowly whisk in the milk
8. Bring to the boil, stirring constantly
9. Cook for 1-2 minutes, stirring all the time, until thickened
10. Add the garlic and rosemary, stir well and remove from the heat
11. Spray a 13x9" baking dish with cooking spray
12. Spread 1 cup of the sauce over the bottom of your baking dish
13. Layer three lasagna noodles, a third of the cheese, a third of the squash and 1 cup of sauce
14. Repeat twice, then sprinkle the top with the leftover cheese
15. Cover and bake for 40 minutes
16. Remove the cover, bake for a further 10 minutes until the top is lightly browned
17. Stand for 10 minutes, then serve

Herby Roasted Vegetables

These are delicious and go well with most dishes, but are popular with your Sunday roast. This recipe makes 10 servings and takes approximately 50 minutes to make and cook.

Ingredients:

- 2 medium carrots (halved lengthwise and cut into 2" pieces)
- 1 large potato (peeled and cut into 1" cubes)
- 1 medium turnip (peeled and cut into 1" cubes)
- 1 medium sweet potato (peeled and cut into 1" cubes)
- 1 medium parsnip (peeled, halved lengthwise and cut into 2" pieces)
- ½lb kohlrabi (peeled and cut into 1" cubes)
- 6 large shallots (halved)
- 6 thyme sprigs
- 6 rosemary sprigs
- 3 tablespoons extra-virgin olive oil
- 2 teaspoons freshly ground pepper
- 1 teaspoon salt

Method:

1. Pre-heat your oven to 425F/220C
2. Boil the vegetables (except the shallots) in water for 6 to 8 minutes until crisp but tender, then drain
3. Transfer the vegetables to a large bowl and add the shallots
4. Mix the salt, pepper and oil in a small bowl
5. Drizzle this over the vegetables and toss well
6. Grease two large baking pans and divide the vegetables between the two
7. Arrange herb sprigs around the vegetables
8. Bake, uncovered, until tender, stirring occasionally – about 20-25 minutes

Rue

Common rue, *Ruta graveolens*, is a beautiful, aromatic herb that despite its many uses has fallen out of favor in modern times. Wear gloves when you handle this herb as it can cause a bad skin reaction and has a bitter taste that our modern palettes do not appreciate.

At a Glance Facts

~~Annual~~ / ~~Biennial~~ / **Perennial**	
Position:	Full sun to partial shade
Soil:	Light, well-drained
Hardiness	Hardy
USDA Zones:	4-9
Sow:	March to May
Harvest:	June to September

Rue is very hardy, thrives on neglect and, once established, is very drought resistant. It is a good herb to grow in areas where nothing else will grow.

Known as the 'herb of grace', the early Roman Catholic Church used rue together with holy water to wash away sins. The Romans brought rue to England, where they called it Ruta, later shortened to rue. Although the name is the same as the word rue, meaning sorrow and regret, the actual name derives from Latin '*graveolens*' meaning 'having a strong or offensive smell'. This herb has a musty smell that not everyone enjoys.

Despite the bitter flavor, the oil and leaves, both fresh and dried, have many uses in foods and perfumes. The Romans cooked with the seeds and in the Middle Ages rue was believed to repel insects, serpents and scorpions so the leaves were scattered around a house. In England, courtrooms spread rue around the room to prevent the judge contracting 'jail fever'. As late as the middle of the 19th century, wearing a sprig of rue around the neck was believed to protect against disease.

Today, rue is used in some foods and drinks, though only in very small amounts due to its bitterness. It can upset your stomach too. It is, however, still very popular in Ethiopian cuisine.

Growing Instructions

Sow rue seeds on the surface of the soil as they need light to germinate. Germination time is anything from one to four weeks. The seeds require a temperature of at least 68F/20C to germinate outside. If starting the seeds indoors, ensure they are in a sunny location for successful germination and transplant when they are big enough to handle.

Rue thrives in poor soil, but does prefer soil that drains well and a position in full sun. Acting as a natural insect repellent, rue is a good companion to many plants as it protects them from pests. Rue is a good companion for figs, raspberries and roses, but inhibits the growth of mint, sage and basil.

Plant Care

Although cold hardy, mulch rue in winter to protect it from severe temperatures.

Harvest the buds before it seeds, as they are the best part of the plant to cook with. Once the plant seeds, the herb becomes much bitterer.

Be careful when pruning and harvesting as the essential oils in rue can cause photodermatitis, resulting in a blistering rash like you get from poison ivy. Many people harvest rue either at sunset or on cloudy days when there is less light.

Culinary Uses

The bitter taste of rue means it has not been popular in Western cooking for several hundred years. However, Ethiopian cooking does still use rue. The Italians make a brandy, 'Candolini Grappa Ruta', from rue, even with a piece of leaf floating in the bottle. This brandy is definitely an acquired taste, with a lot people finding it too bitter.

To get the flavor of rue without the bitterness, simmer some leaves in hot water for no more than a minute and then strain. Its bitter flavor means it works well with acidic, sour foods such tomato sauces or dishes with olives. The acidic flavor tones down the bitterness of rue, making it more palatable.

The Ethiopians use the leaf and seed of rue in their traditional coffee, which is apparently extremely nice and worth a try.

Beauty Uses

Rue is very rarely directly applied to the skin as it is considered toxic, akin to poison ivy, though its oil is found as a fragrance in some soaps and cosmetics.

This herb does have anti-fungal properties and health spas sometimes use it the oil for therapeutic facial steams. The antioxidant properties of rue help to reduce the signs of aging, keeping your skin looking younger.

Traditionally, herbalists used rue to treat itchy skin or fungal infections such as athlete's foot. The oil is also very effective at treating head lice. However, due to its toxicity, it should be used very carefully, if at all.

Health Uses

Rue is not recommended to be ingested directly as it is poisonous. Traditionally, it was used in small quantities to treat a variety of ailments, but today herbalists use less risky herbs.

Rue should not be taken by anyone with stomach, kidney, liver or intestinal problems as it can make them worse. Pregnant women should avoid rue as it can cause abortion and have a very negative effect on the mother.

Rue is not a herb to self-medicate. If you decide rue is something you need to take, consult with a doctor or herbalist first

Pests, Problems & Diseases

Rue repels insects, so suffers from few problems. It is generally disease resistant and problem free.

Recommended Varieties

There are no cultivars of rue. The herb you buy and grow today, is a direct descendent of the original herbs grown in the Mediterranean thousands of years ago.

Recipes

Be very careful when harvesting this herb as getting the sap on your skin causes symptoms similar to poison ivy contact. If you are using this fresh, patch test it first on your skin. Harvest in low light conditions to reduce the risk of skin damage, wearing gloves and a long sleeve top.

Due to the risks involved with ingesting this herb or using it on your skin, no recipes will be provided.

Saffron

Saffron, *Crocus sativus*, is the most expensive spice in the world, usually being more expensive than gold, weight for weight! Saffron comes from a crocus, which is a bulb planted in the soil. Each plant will produce two or three flowers, each of which produce three pieces of saffron.

At a Glance Facts

~~Annual~~ / ~~Biennial~~ / **Perennial**	
Position:	Full sun
Soil:	Well-drained
Hardiness	Yes, down to -4F/-20C
USDA Zones:	6-9
Sow:	June to September
Harvest:	Fall

Although you can grow your own saffron, you will need a lot of plants to make enough to use in more than one dish! Many people substitute safflower or turmeric instead of saffron, with the latter often referred to as 'the poor man's saffron'.

Saffron originated in the Eastern Mediterranean, around Persia and the surrounding area. The earliest written record comes from 2,300BC where Sargon of Akkad referred to his city of Azupiranu as 'Saffron City'. Greek frescos dating from 1,500BC show saffron and an Egyptian papyrus from 1,600BC talks about the medical function of saffron. The Arabs took saffron out of Persia to Spain and India, and then the Romans spread it further afield.

Harvesting and processing saffron is a long job that has to be done by hand, which is part of what makes it so expensive. There is no mechanical way to harvest saffron; the pistils must be removed very carefully by hand. During the drying process, they lose about 80% of its volume. To produce a single kilogram of dried saffron takes around 200,000 flowers and 500 hours of manual work! Fortunately, you do not need large quantities of this herb; four or five strands are enough for a meal such as a risotto that serves four people.

Growing Instructions

Plant saffron corms in the ground or in containers. They do not need transplanting. Plant 4-6"/10-15cm deep leaving 4"/10cm between corms. Plant from June through to September in weed free soil. Loosen the soil with a hand fork before planting.

Locate the saffron bed in an area that gets lots of sun in the fall, when the crocuses are flowering. Avoid a heavy clay soil as this will cause the corms to rot. Digging in some fertilizer such as compost or manure, before planting can help loosen the soil and provide a better quality soil for your saffron to grow in.

Water after planting, but then this plant should require little or no extra water throughout the rest of the year. If there is a drought in September, then watering once or twice will help the plants get through it.

Over time, the corms multiply. In three years, one corm will multiply to around five.

Plant Care

The flowers usually appear in October, but local weather conditions may affect this. In your first year, the flowers may appear a little later. In good conditions, the flowers can last up to a month before you need to harvest them, but poor weather can cause the flowers to die back quicker.

There are two methods of harvesting saffron. If you have lots of flowers, cut each flower off and then remove the three red filaments (pistils) with tweezers while sat comfortably at a table. If you do not have a lot of flowers, leave the flowers in place and remove the saffron strands by hand, again using tweezers or a small pair of scissors.

Before use, the filaments are dried. Place on a sieve or paper towels in a single layer in a well ventilated location until dry. Once dry, the pistils are very light and easily broken. It will take up to a week for the saffron to fully dry. Store in an airtight container in a dark place and leave for at least a month before using. Saffron will store and be good to use for two years.

To make one gram of saffron will take around 150 flowers. In the first year, you can expect about two thirds of the corms to produce a single flower and then in the following two years, each corm will produce two flowers.

Culinary Uses

When cooking, a little bit of saffron goes a long way, which is just as well when you consider the price of it! If you are buying this herb, always buy whole strands rather than ground saffron. Unfortunately, ground saffron is often mixed with turmeric or safflower to reduce the cost, meaning you are buying an inferior product.

Before cooking with saffron, you usually prepare it first. Most commonly, a pinch of saffron is soaked in a cup of warm water for between 20 minutes and 12 hours. The saffron expands in the water and releases its flavor. Instead of water, you can use stock, wine or milk.

Alternatively, grind the saffron into a powder with a pestle and mortar, and then add the ground saffron to a dish or steep it first in a liquid. In some dishes, such as 'paella valenciana', toast the saffron, then grind it into a powder before adding it to the paella.

Saffron is a surprisingly versatile herb, though the cost prohibits common use. It is a key ingredient in Spanish paella and used in Italy to make 'risotto alla Milanese'. Saffron is best known for coloring and flavoring rice, being used in Indian biriyani rice dishes.

Brew a pot of coffee together with a pinch of saffron and some cardamom to make a Middle Eastern coffee.

Saffron works very well with ice cream and is used in Iran and India as a flavoring. It also works well in Indian sweets too.

Although you are unlikely to use saffron every day or even be able to grow enough to use it regularly, it is a great herb to grow and is one that people are always interested in. Whenever I show anyone my saffron patch their eyes always widen when I tell them how expensive saffron is! It is easy to grow in the right conditions and is a great herb to try in your kitchen.

Beauty Uses

As well as being prized for its culinary use, saffron also has many beauty and health benefits. Nowadays you can find saffron in certain face packs and skin creams because of its beneficial properties.

Saffron is a good moisturizer for your skin, https://www.ncbi.nlm.nih.gov/pubmed/25362612, where it absorbs UV rays and protects you from sun damage, https://www.ncbi.nlm.nih.gov/pmc/articles/PMC3862060/. It contains active carotenoids which have antioxidant properties that help your skin remain healthy and look young, https://www.ncbi.nlm.nih.gov/pmc/articles/PMC3249922/.

Saffron has anti-inflammatory properties, reducing skin irritation, swelling and rashes, https://www.ncbi.nlm.nih.gov/pmc/articles/PMC3957135/.

It is easy to make your own toners and creams by using dried saffron, either home grown or store bought.

A simple toner is made by soaking a pinch of saffron in rose water for at least 15 minutes before applying the liquid to your skin. A simple cream is made by mixing saffron with honey and massaging it into your skin. This lightens and hydrates your skin, softening it and leaving it glowing.

Despite its yellow color, saffron is a well-known skin lightening agent. Making it into a face pack can help lighten blemishes or a tan. Soak a pinch of saffron in raw milk for an hour, add a squeeze of lemon juice and apply the mixture to your skin, using circular motions and leave for 15 minutes.

Soak basil leaves with a pinch of saffron in some water, then grind into a paste to make a treatment for acne and blemishes. Apply using circular motions and leave for 15 minutes before washing off.

Health Uses

Saffron contains a whole host of antioxidants as well as carotenoids. Crocin and crocetin, responsible for the red color of the saffron pistils, have antidepressant properties, reduce inflammation and appetite, aid weight loss and protect brain cells against progressive damage according to research, https://www.ncbi.nlm.nih.gov/pubmed/26468457.

Safranal is another antioxidant; one that gives saffron is taste and smell. Research, https://www.ncbi.nlm.nih.gov/pubmed/23638289, shows saffron boosts your mood and memory, protects your brains cells from oxidative stress and helps you learn better.

Kaempferol is a compound found in the petals of the saffron flower. This appears to have antidepressant, anticancer and anti-inflammatory properties, https://www.ncbi.nlm.nih.gov/pubmed/23497863.

Due to its ability to lift your mood, saffron earned the nickname, the 'sunshine spice'. In several studies, saffron was more effective than a placebo at treating the symptoms of people suffering from mild to moderate depression, https://www.ncbi.nlm.nih.gov/pubmed/24299602.

Another study, https://www.ncbi.nlm.nih.gov/pubmed/15707766, found that 30mg of saffron taken daily was as effective as the anti-depression tablets Fluoxetine, Citalopram and Imipramine with fewer side effectives. While the flowers petals have no culinary uses, both the petals and the saffron strands are effective in treating depression, https://www.ncbi.nlm.nih.gov/pubmed/16979327.

As with many other herbs, more human studies are required to fully understand the use of saffron in treating depression, but hopefully in the near future, new treatments with fewer side effects will be available.

The high levels of antioxidants found in saffron help neutralize free radicals, which are responsible for cell damage and believed to be linked to diseases such as cancer (https://www.ncbi.nlm.nih.gov/pubmed/19149749). Test-tube studies show saffron kills or suppresses the growth of colon cancer cells without harming normal cells, https://www.ncbi.nlm.nih.gov/pubmed/18004240. Another study, https://www.ncbi.nlm.nih.gov/pubmed/24761112, showed the effectiveness of saffron in treating other cancer cells, including prostate, lung, cervix, breast and bone marrow. In a separate study, https://www.ncbi.nlm.nih.gov/pubmed/26798587, crocin made cancer cells more sensitive to chemotherapy drugs.

Saffron also appears very helpful for women suffering with PMS. Taking 30mg of saffron every day was more effective at treating the symptoms of PMS than a placebo in woman aged 20-45, https://www.ncbi.nlm.nih.gov/pubmed/24701496. In another study, just sniffing saffron for 20 minutes reduced some symptoms of PMS, including anxiety, and reduced the levels of cortisol, the stress hormone, in the body https://www.ncbi.nlm.nih.gov/pubmed/21242071. -

Several studies have shown that saffron improves libido and erectile function (https://www.ncbi.nlm.nih.gov/pubmed/29881706 and https://www.ncbi.nlm.nih.gov/pubmed/22552758, being particularly effective in men who were suffering with libido problems due to antidepressants.

Similarly, in women taken antidepressants who were struggling with a low sex drive, saffron (taken 30mg a day for four weeks) increased sexual desire and lubrication, https://www.ncbi.nlm.nih.gov/pubmed/23280545.

Saffron supplements help you to feel less hungry and fuller, meaning you felt less of an urge to snack so aiding weight loss, https://www.ncbi.nlm.nih.gov/pubmed/20579522. Although scientists do not understand exactly how this works, studies do show that saffron is effective at reducing appetite and aiding weight loss.

Researchers have found many other health benefits from saffron, though these have not had sufficient study yet, including:

- Lowering cholesterol and prevent arteries from clogging - https://www.ncbi.nlm.nih.gov/pubmed/12648816/
- Reducing blood sugar levels and raising insulin sensitivity - https://www.ncbi.nlm.nih.gov/pubmed/28460761
- Improving eyesight and reducing age related macular degeneration

(AMD) - https://www.ncbi.nlm.nih.gov/pubmed/28289690
- Improving memory in sufferers of Alzheimer's disease - https://www.ncbi.nlm.nih.gov/pubmed/27792130

Saffron appears to be a very beneficial herb and 30mg a day is enough for you to reap the health benefits. Avoid ground saffron unless you can verify its content, as it is often adulterated with other, cheaper spices. If you are buying saffron and it appears cheap, best avoid it as it is probably not pure saffron. Doses of over 5g a day can have toxic effects and pregnant women must avoid high doses as it can cause miscarriage.

Pests, Problems & Diseases

One of the main issues facing saffron is that several rodents are rather fond of the corms and will eat them throughout the year. Rabbits in particular will eat both the leaves and flowers, decimating your crop. A secure fence, dug down at least a foot into the ground, will keep rabbits off. Regularly monitor your saffron crop to make sure they are not being dug up and eaten.

Three main fungal infections affect saffron:

- *Rhizoctonia crocorum* – causes damping-off and brown ulceration
- *Fusarium* – attacks the corm
- Violet root rot – highly contagious, known as 'mort du safran' or 'saffron's death', produces damp rot

Unfortunately, these diseases resist most fungicides and do not usually appear until the third or fourth year of growth. If your plants are affected, dig them up and replant them elsewhere and do not plant any corms in the infected area for ten years.

Recommended Varieties

Iran, Spain and Kashmir in India are the main growers of saffron. People consider Kashmiri saffron the best in the world due to the perfect climate and soil conditions. Kashmiri saffron also contain the highest levels of crocin. The quality of the saffron is believed to depend on the color, so the deeper the color, the better the saffron and the more expensive it is.

There are three main saffron cultivars grown around the world:

- 'Mongra' or 'Lacha' Saffron – grown in Kashmir, this cultivar has very dark crimson threads that are the darkest of all cultivars. This is the best saffron in the world, with a strong flavor and smell, being an excellent coloring agent. This cultivar is very expensive and rarely found outside of India.

- 'Aquillia' Saffron – an Iranian saffron, commonly grown in Italy. The plants are smaller than Kasmiri saffron and the threads are shorter and a lighter red. This is a high quality saffron, but cheaper than Kashmiri saffron. It is easy to find around the world.
- 'Spanish Superior' and 'Crème' Saffron - the lowest quality saffron, but commonly found in the USA and Europe. The threads are much more yellow in this variety, meaning it is much cheaper to buy.

Recipes

Saffron Ice Cream

This is a very tasty ice cream, though may be a bit unusual initially to the Western palate, more used to stronger, sweeter tastes. Serve this brightly colored ice cream with dark cakes or desserts of berries for a dramatic color contrast, or just eat it by yourself! This recipe makes enough for between 6 and 8 people and takes about 4½ hours to make.

Ingredients:

- 7fl oz/200ml milk
- 5fl oz/150ml whipping cream
- 2oz/55g white (granulated) sugar
- 3 egg yolks
- ¼g saffron strands
- Few drops of vanilla essence

Method:

1. Put the milk and the saffron into a saucepan and slowly bring to the boil, stirring regularly
2. Remove from the heat
3. Stir in the vanilla essence and cream, then leave to cool for 10 minutes
4. In a separate bowl, beat the sugar and egg yolks together until light and frothy
5. Slowly pour the milk mixture into the egg yolks, stirring as you do
6. Return this to your saucepan and heat on a low heat, stirring constantly, until the mixture thickens
7. Use an ice cream maker to finish off or transfer to a freezer proof container and freeze

Valenciana Paella

Paella is the best-known dish from Spain, though it originated in Eastern Spain in the Valencia district. Made from whatever you have to hand, feel free to adjust the ingredients as you see fit. This serves 4-6 people and talks about 1¾ hours to make.

Ingredients:

- 24 mussels (cleaned)
- 12 prawns (raw or cooked, shelled and deveined)
- 1 onion (chopped)
- 1 red bell pepper (chopped)
- 1 garlic clove (crushed)
- 1 bay leaf
- 18fl oz/510ml chicken or fish stock
- 12oz/350g squid (cleaned and cut into rings)
- 12oz/350g monkfish (skinned and cut into pieces)
- 10oz/285g short-grain rice
- 8fl oz/225ml tinned chopped tomatoes
- 7oz/200g frozen peas
- 4 fl oz/115ml dry white wine
- 4 tablespoons extra-virgin olive oil
- ½ teaspoon saffron strands
- ¼ teaspoon grated lemon zest
- Salt and black pepper

Method:

1. Heat the olive oil in a very large frying pan
2. Add the rice, stir well to ensure it is coated with oil
3. Cook for 3-5 minutes on a medium heat until it changes color
4. Add the pepper and onion, cook for a further 4 minutes, stirring often
5. Add the squid, cook for a further 7-8 minutes until the squid starts to color
6. Add the stock, garlic, saffron and white wine, stir well and bring to the boil
7. Add the bay leaf, tomatoes and lemon zest
8. Stir well, reduce the heat, cover and simmer for 15 minutes until most of the liquid is absorbed
9. Add the monkfish, prawns, unopened mussels and peas
10. Cover the pan and cook until the prawns are pink and the mussels opened

11. Season to taste and serve

Risotto alla Milanese

A traditional Italian dish that does not usually contain any meat or fish. Feel free to add some mushrooms, chicken or other vegetarian alternative to bulk this dish out. Do not leave this dish when cooking and do not reheat it, always serve immediately. This recipe serves four people and takes about 50 minutes to make.

Ingredients:

- 1 pint/570ml vegetable stock
- 1lb 2oz/500g Arborio (risotto) rice
- 4½oz/125g butter
- 2oz/55g Parmesan cheese (grated)
- 5fl oz/140ml white wine
- 1 onion (chopped)
- 1 teaspoon saffron threads
- Salt and black pepper

Method:

1. Heat half the butter in a deep frying pan or wok
2. Add the onion and any meat/vegetarian meat/mushrooms and cook on a medium heat for around 10 minutes until the onions have softened
3. Add the rice and stir well so the grains are coated in butter
4. Cook for 5 minutes, stirring often to make sure the rice does not stick
5. Heat the stock until it is at boiling point in a separate pan
6. Add the stock gradually to the rice, stirring regularly and only adding more when the rice has absorbed the liquid
7. Add the crumbled saffron and the white wine, then season to taste
8. Stir well, reduce the heat and leave to cook for around 20-25 minutes until the rice is soft but firm and the risotto creamy in texture
9. Remove from the heat
10. Stir in the cheese and remaining butter, mix well and serve immediately

Sandalwood Saffron Face Pack

An excellent face pack for rejuvenating and cleansing your skin, leaving it feeling smooth and looking great. Use this up to three time a week.

Ingredients:

- 1 tablespoon sandalwood powder
- 2-3 saffron strands
- 2 teaspoons milk (use rose water if you are sensitive to dairy products)

Method:

1. Mix all the ingredients together in a small bowl
2. Apply to your (washed) face, spreading evenly
3. Massage in circular motions for a couple of minutes, then leave to dry for 20 minutes
4. Splash water on your face to rinse in off, then pat your skin dry

Acne Busting Face Mask

An excellent face mask for anyone who suffers from acne or spots. The saffron helps improve your complexion and fight the acne, while the milk exfoliates your skin and acts as an astringent. Use this three or four times a week.

Ingredients:

- ¼ cup milk
- 3-4 saffron strands

Method:

1. Steep the saffron in the milk for 2-3 hours
2. Apply the mixture to your face and neck
3. Leave for 15 minutes, then wash off

Dark Circle Wash

Use this face wash every morning to get rid of dark circles under your ryes or any dark patches on your face. Saffron brightens your complexion and improves you skin tone.

Ingredients:

- 2-3 saffron strands
- 2 tablespoons water

Method:

1. Soak the saffron in the water overnight until they have completely dissolved
2. Apply to dark patches on your skin or to the dark circles under your eyes
3. Leave for 20 minutes
4. Rinse off with warm water and pat dry

Skin Brightening Face Pack

A simple face mark for brightening your skin. The Bengal gram absorbs the grease and dirt from your face while exfoliating your skin.

Ingredients:

- 2 tablespoons milk
- 1 tablespoon Bengal gram
- 7-8 saffron strands

Method:

1. Soak the Bengal gram overnight in the milk
2. Add the saffron strands and grind into a paste
3. Apply to your face, leave for 15-20 minutes then wash it off

Sage

Common sage, *Salvia officinalis*, is popular herb with many cultivars grown for ornamental, culinary and even ceremonial purposes! Perhaps best known for its role with onion in the famous 'sage and onion stuffing', this herb has a multitude of uses and is surprisingly easy to grow.

At a Glance Facts

~~Annual~~ / ~~Biennial~~ / **Perennial**	
Position:	Full sun to partial shade
Soil:	Moist, well-drained
Hardiness	Yes to 14F/-10C to 5F/-15C
USDA Zones:	4-8
Sow:	March to May
Harvest:	May to October

Sage holds great importance in the Native American traditions as a ceremonial plant. White sage (*Salvia apiana*) is a purifying herb, used as an incense, particularly with sweetgrass as a smudge stick for cleansing spaces.

White Sage

Greeks and Romans used sage to preserve meat, believing it to enhance memory too. The name Salvia comes from the Latin '*salvus*' meaning both healthy and saved. Over the years, herbalists used sage to treat a wide variety of complaints from snakebite to intestinal worms and epilepsy!

In the 10th century, Arabian herbalists believed sage extended life, making the consumer virtually immortal. After the crusades when the knights brought sage back home to Europe a saying appeared, 'Why should a man die who grows sage in his garden?". Even Charlemagne grew sage in his garden, believing it to be a powerful herb.

Originating in the Mediterranean area, this herb has spread all over the world. Popular as a tea or in a meal, sage is an easy plant to grow and worth having in your garden.

Growing Instructions

Although sage does grow from both seeds and cuttings, most people buy ready-grown plants as it is quicker to harvest.

Sow seeds in small pots in spring, covering with a thin layer of perlite. Place in a warm position where they will germinate in 2 to 3 weeks. Apply the same principles if planting outside, though note germination will not occur if the soil temperature is below 65F/18C.

Plant out after the risk of frost has passes in a sheltered spot, out of the wind and in full sun. Dig in plenty of good quality compost or well-rotted manure first and remove all weeds. The quality of the leaf improves when it gets a lot of sun, so ensure it gets as much as possible.

Sage grows well in containers, though use 12" pots filled with a good quality compost.

Plant Care

Water sage regularly, particularly when it is dry, though be careful not to overwater as sage does not appreciate having wet roots.

Prune once flowering is complete to encourage new growth and maintain the shape.

Lift containers off the ground in winter on pot feet to allow moisture to drain away. Fleece in winter to protect the leaves, allowing you to harvest all year round. A glut of leaves can be dried or frozen to preserve them. Store the fresh herb in the salad crisper in your refrigerator for up to two weeks in a ziplock bag.

Culinary Uses

Salvia officinalis is a popular herb in cooking, with the gray form having the best flavor. The golden, purple and tricolor sages have culinary uses, though their flavors are not so good. Pineapple sage (*Salvia elegans*) and other flavored cultivars are used fresh as they lose their flavor when dried; when fresh their flavor is very fruity! Clary sage (*Salvia sclarea*) has a very strong aroma, making it unsuitable for the kitchen, though it is popular as an essential oil.

Sage leaves are best dried whole, then crushed just before use for maximum flavor. Rub them between your hands to crush them as you put them in a dish. The flowers can also be eaten and have a much more delicate flavor than the leaves.

Use sage carefully as with such a strong flavor, it can overwhelm a dish and mask other flavors. Like rosemary, thyme, oregano and savory, sage can be added to a dish at the start of cooking as it retains its flavor well.

Sage acts as a digestive aid and so works well with fatty foods such as sausages and pork, hence its use as a stuffing for meat. Mediterranean and European cuisine makes extensive use of this herb in everything from focaccia bread to pizza to gnocchi and to grilled cheese sandwiches!

Try adding sage to scones, biscuits or corn bread to give them an interesting taste. Cover a pork roast with sage leaves before roasting. Bean soups benefit from a little sage and it also works well with apple dishes such as applesauce, apple pie (use 2-3 tablespoons of minces leaves for a 9" pie) and baked apples.

Sage compliments many vegetables from winter squashes to mushrooms to eggplant and pumpkins.

This is a very versatile herb in the kitchen, with uses in many sweet and savory dishes. It has a very pleasant flavor, though be careful it does not overpower the other flavors in a dish as it has a strong taste.

Beauty Uses

As well as its culinary uses, sage as many beauty uses too. Use the oil or fresh leaf, though much of the modern research has been done with sage oil rather than the leaves.

Sage leaf oil improves circulation and stimulates the renewal of cells, being rich in vitamin A and calcium. With high levels of antioxidants, sage fights the signs of ageing such as fine lines or wrinkles. Mix the oil with a face cream or make face masks from the leaves to benefit from this effect.

As sage promotes healthy blood circulation, it is very good at removing cellulite. Rubbing sage leaf oil into cellulite affected areas or using a sage leaf poultice will help reduce the appearance of cellulite.

Sage oil is very good for your scalp too. Massaging the oil into your scalp helps promote blood flow, which reduces hair loss and improves the formation of hair follicles. Make a tea from sage leaves and rinse your hair with it to give your hair a shine. Add rosemary to this tea to naturally cover gray hair.

Sage has antifungal, antiseptic and antibacterial properties that are very beneficial to your skin. Use sage tea as a skin toner after washing your face to reduce inflammation and combat acne.

Health Uses

With high levels of antioxidants, you know sage will have a whole host of health benefits as it neutralizes harmful free radicals that are linked to chronic diseases.

Over 160 different polyphenols are found in sage, all of which act as antioxidants on your body. Of these, caffeic acid, rosmarinic acid, rutin, ellagic acid and chlorogenic acid are all linked with reducing the risk of cancer and improving memory and brain function - https://www.ncbi.nlm.nih.gov/pubmed/29034191. According to research, https://www.ncbi.nlm.nih.gov/pubmed/19865527, one cup of sage tea drank twice a day increases your body's antioxidant defences significantly. Researchers also discovered this lowered bad cholesterol (LDL) and raised good cholesterol (HDL).

As an antimicrobial, sage can also neutralize the microbes that cause dental plaque. A study, https://www.ncbi.nlm.nih.gov/pubmed/26668706, showed a sage based mouthwash effectively kills the bacteria *Streptococcus mutans* that causes dental cavities. In another study, https://www.ncbi.nlm.nih.gov/pubmed/23646301, sage essential oil killed *Candida albicans*, a fungus linked to dental cavities, and stopped it from spreading.

Herbalists traditionally prescribed common sage to reduce menopause symptoms, https://www.ncbi.nlm.nih.gov/pubmed/23670626 including hot flushes, excessive sweating and irritability. According to research, sage contains compounds with similar properties to estrogen, which bind to receptors in your brain to treat these symptoms and improve your memory, https://www.ncbi.nlm.nih.gov/pubmed/29403626. In one study, patients taking sage daily experienced significantly fewer and less intense hot flushes over two months, https://www.ncbi.nlm.nih.gov/pubmed/21630133.

Another traditional use of sage is to treat diabetes. Modern research indicates this traditional use has a basis in science. In a study on rats with type 1 diabetes, https://www.ncbi.nlm.nih.gov/pubmed/20696231, sage extract reduced blood glucose levels by clearing fatty acids from the blood and improving insulin sensitivity.

In a separate study, researchers discovered sage tea to have a similar effect to metformin, a drug used to manage blood sugar in diabetics, https://www.ncbi.nlm.nih.gov/pubmed/16923227. In a study run on humans, sage leaf extract lowered blood sugar and improved insulin sensitive to a similar level as the anti-diabetes drug, rosiglitazone - https://www.ncbi.nlm.nih.gov/pubmed/29333341.

With high levels of antioxidants, sage has a beneficial effect on your brain and helps to improve its general health and prevent decline due to age. In a human based study of patients with mild to moderate Alzheimer's disease, researchers studied the effect of 2ml of sage extract versus a placebo over a four month period, https://www.ncbi.nlm.nih.gov/pubmed/12605619. At the end of the trial, those who had taken the sage leaf extract performed better in memory, reasoning and problem-solving tests than those who had taken the placebo.

In low doses, sage improves the memory of any adult, with higher doses working to improve your mood, boost alertness and make you feel calmer and more content, https://www.ncbi.nlm.nih.gov/pubmed/15639154. Studies show that sage has a very positive effect on brain health, including memory function - https://www.ncbi.nlm.nih.gov/pubmed/12895685.

Sage also lowers the levels of bad (LDL) cholesterol in your body. In one study, patients drank sage tea twice a day, https://www.ncbi.nlm.nih.gov/pubmed/19865527. In just two weeks, their bad cholesterol levels had dropped while their good cholesterol levels had increased.

Researchers recommend drinking no more than 3 to 6 cups of sage tea per day, https://www.ncbi.nlm.nih.gov/pubmed/21777420, as there are some concerns about the compound thujone contained in sage. Although research discovered this compound to be toxic to animals in high levels, https://www.ncbi.nlm.nih.gov/pubmed/21777420, no evidence has been found that it is toxic to humans, https://www.ncbi.nlm.nih.gov/pubmed/23201408. If you are concerned about thujone, use Spanish sage to make tea as it does not contain this compound.

Pests, Problems & Diseases

Sages can suffer from a few different diseases, with some cultivars being more susceptible than others. Powdery mildew is a particular problem; minimize the risk by keeping the soil moist, watering at the base of the plant, and ensuring there is adequate air circulation between the plants. Verticillium wilt plus foot and root rots can also be an issue with most of the sage family.

Sage is susceptible to damage from slugs and capsid bugs, which are pale green insects that suck the sap out of plants, causing leaf damage. The leaves are distorted with small, brown edged holes in them. In small amounts, these bugs are not a problem, but in larger infestations they can cause a lot of damage. Regularly check your plants and remove infected plant material by hand. If required, use sprays to treat these bugs.

Recommended Varieties

There are close to a thousand different varieties of Salvia, with more bred all the time, mainly for ornamental purposes. There are around 500 species from Central and South America, around 250 from the Mediterranean and central Asia and a further 90 species found in eastern Asia. The Salvia family has had many name changes over the years, with *Salvia officinalis* having six different scientific names since 1940!

These are some of the most commonly cultivated culinary Salvia varieties:

1. Clary Sage (*Salvia sclarea*) – mainly used for medicinal purposes, people have used this herb for thousands of years. It uses include as an eyewash, a replacement for hops in beer to make you more drunk but give you a worse hangover, as an astringent and more. It stimulates estrogen production in women and nowadays is mostly used as an essential oil.
2. White Sage (*Salvia apiana*) – highly valued by the Native Americans, white sage is burned ceremonially to cleanse an environment or person. The leaves are white to light green when young and as the plant matures, turn very white. The leaves have a sweet aroma and are partially dried, then tied into bundles for use over winter.
3. Golden Leaf Sage (*Salvia officinalis* 'Icterine') – an attractive plant that is also very tasty, growing up to two feet tall and wide with variegated golden yellow and pale green leaves. Hardy in USDA zones 6 to 10, this cultivar has good drought tolerance when established. Use this cultivar in cooking as you would common sage.
4. Purple Sage (*Salvia officinalis* 'Purpurascens') – another ornamental cultivar that also tastes great, this variety has purple and silver/green leaves and looks great in the garden. It is hardy in USDA zones 6 to 9 and grows to about two feet tall. It pairs well with lavender and purple sage for a striking display in your garden.
5. *Salvia officinalis* 'Tricolor' – used like common sage, this is a smaller cultivar, growing up to 18 inches tall and is hardy in USDA zones 6 to 9. This variety has very attractive leaves that are purple and green with a white outline. It is great in the kitchen, but also a very attractive ornamental plant.
6. Pineapple Sage (*Salvia elegans*) – with bright scarlet flowers and pineapple-scented leaves, this late summer bloomer is only hardy in USDA zones 8 to 10. It grows up to four feet tall and is excellent in the kitchen, particularly in iced tea! The unique flavor of this herb makes it well worth growing and using.

The following cultivars are popular ornamental plants and have little or no use in the kitchen:

- Scarlet Sage (*Salvia splendens*) – a very common cultivar often found in stores. Hardy in USDA zones 8 to 10, this is grown as an annual elsewhere. This profuse bloomer is available in a wide range of colors now including pink, orange, lavender and white, plus the standard red. This cultivar pairs well with grasses and daylilies and is traditionally grown with zinnias or marigolds.
- *Salvia guarantica* 'Black and Blue' – with stunning, cobolt blue flowers, this cultivar is a great addition to your garden. Growing up to 5 feet tall and hardy to USDA zones 8 to 10, the 12 inch long flower spikes are very attractive to hummingbirds. This cultivar pairs well with oriental lilies and daylilies.
- Mexican Bush Sage (*Salvia leucantha*) - blooming in late summer, this cultivar has lavender colored flowers and velvety, gray leaves. It grows up to three feet tall and is hardy in USDA zones 8 to 10. After several years in the ground, this cultivar starts to look like a small shrub. This variety pairs very well with ornamental grasses.
- *Salvia microphylla* 'Hot Lips' – a stunning plant with very unusual bi-color flowers looking like a white salvia kissed by someone wearing bright scarlet lipstick. It is popular in the garden with hummingbirds and bugs, plus humans will always stop to look at it. Hardy in USDA zones 8 to 10 and growing up to three feet tall, this cultivar pairs very well with peony and flowering daylilies.
- *Salvia x sylvestris* 'May Night' – growing to just 18" tall and hardy in USDA zones 4 to 9, this cultivar produces an attractive show of blue flowers in spring and then, with some deadheading, repeatedly flowers throughout the summer. This cultivar tolerates clay soils, blooms very early in the year and pairs well with ornamental alliums.
- *Salvia nemerose* 'Sensation Rose' – hardy in USDA zones 4 to 8, this pink flowering cultivar grows to just 12" tall. This plant will also flower repeatedly during the summer months when deadheaded.
- *Salvia nemerose* 'Marcus' – hardy in USDA zones 4 to 8 and growing up to 10" tall, this deep violet flowered cultivar is excellent at the front of a flower bed.

Recipes

Smudge Stick

Used traditionally for cleansing and purifying a space or a person, these originate with the Native American tribes. Light the tip of the smudge stick and, once the flame is steady, blow it out so the stick is smouldering and producing smoke. Hold the stick above a fireproof bowl (many people use an abalone shell) and fan the smoke with a feather or your hand over the person or yourself or around the space you are purifying.

Ingredients:

- Large handful of 7-10" lengths of sage or white sage
- Length of cord four times the length of the cut branches

Method:

1. Leave the freshly cut branches overnight to wilt before continuing
2. Form a two inch thick bundle of the sage branches
3. Point the tip of the bundle down and wrap the cord tightly around the base of the bundle
4. Holding the sage tightly together, wrap the cord around the bundle until you get to the tip
5. Then work back towards the base, continuing to wrap the cord around the tightly held sage bundle
6. Tie the two ends of the cord together
7. Trim the cord or sage if you want to make it look neater
8. Leave to dry for 7 to 14 days before use, depending on conditions

Cheesy Sage Wafers

These delicious wafers combine the flavor of sage with cheese and it works very well! This recipe makes around 36 crackers.

Ingredients:

- 1 cup/4oz sharp (mature) cheddar cheese (shredded)
- ¾ cup flour
- ¼ cup pecans or walnuts (chopped)
- ¼ teaspoon rubbed sage
- ¼ teaspoon salt
- ⅛ teaspoon ground red pepper
- ⅓ cup butter (cut into small pieces)

Method:

1. Process everything except the butter for 10 seconds in your food processor
2. With the processor running, add the butter a piece at a time until the mixture turns into a ball
3. Roll out on a lightly floured surface to ¼" thick
4. Cut using a 1½" round cookie cutter (alternatively, shape the dough into a roll, refrigerate and then cut)
5. Bake at 350F/175C for 12-14 minutes until the edge turn golden brown

Sage and Onion Stuffing

This is a traditional recipe for British sage and onion stuffing that takes around 55 minutes to make. Make this in advance and freeze it, or prepare it on the day as it tastes best when served immediately. This recipe takes 55 minutes to make and serves 6 people.

Ingredients:

- 3½oz/100g breadcrumbs
- 1¾oz/50g butter
- 1 tablespoon fresh sage (chopped)
- 1 tablespoon oil
- 1 large onion (chopped)

Method:

1. Heat the butter and oil in a pan, then cook the onion until it has softened
2. Add the breadcrumbs and sage, then season to taste
3. Transfer to a baking dish and pat down so the surface is even
4. Preheat your oven to 350F/180C
5. Bake the stuffing for 40 minutes
6. Remove from the oven and serve immediately with gravy

Thanksgiving Stuffing

This is a classic Thanksgiving stuffing flavored with a mixture of sage, thyme and parsley. This makes approximately 16 servings and works very well with your Thanksgiving turkey.

Ingredients:

- 1lb unflavored croutons or 1kg crusty Italian/French bread, cut into ½" cubes, dried and toasted into croutons
- 2 onions (diced)
- 2 celery stalks (diced)
- 2 large eggs
- 2 cups chicken/vegetable broth
- ½ butter (cubed)
- ¼ cup fresh parsley leaves (minced)
- 1 teaspoon dried thyme leaves
- 1 teaspoon dried sage (rubbed)
- ¾ teaspoon salt
- ½ teaspoon ground black pepper

Method:

1. Spread the bread cubes in a single layer on one or two cookie sheets. Leave to dry overnight
2. Adjust the racks in your oven to the lower and upper middle positions
3. Heat the oven to 400F/200C
4. Bake the bread for 12-15 minutes until golden and remove from the oven
5. Reduce the oven temperature to 350F/180C
6. Heat the butter in a large skillet on a medium to high heat
7. Cook the onions and celery for 8-10 minutes until soft
8. In a large bowl, mix everything together
9. Transfer to a 3-quart baking dish
10. Cover with foil and cook for 30 minutes, until steamy
11. Remove the foil and bake for a further 10 minutes until crusty

Sage Body Scrub

This body scrub leaves your body feeling soft and moisturized. Sage promotes cell renewal and improve circulation, which also reduces the appearance of cellulite. This scrub is based on salt that may be too harsh for people with sensitive or irritated skin. If this is the case, then replace the salt with brown sugar. Store in a glass container in your refrigerator between uses, where it will last for about two weeks.

Ingredients:

- 2 cups fine sea salt (or brown sugar)
- 1 cup extra-virgin olive oil
- ½ cup date sugar
- 1 grapefruit (white or red)
- 4-6 large sage leaves

Method:

1. Puree the oil and sage in a blender on a high speed for 1 minute
2. Add the salt and date sugar, mixing well
3. Remove the zest from the grapefruit and add the zest into this mixture
4. Use 1-2 tablespoons of the scrub, applied to your body in circular motions, leave for 1-2 minutes, then rinse with warm water

Summer/ Winter Savory

Summer savory, *Satureja hortensis*, and winter savory, *Satureja montana*, are two herbs from the same family. Winter savory is a semi-evergreen perennial while summer savory is a half hardy annual. The former has a slightly stronger taste and is harvested throughout the year.

At a Glance Facts

~~Annual~~ / ~~Biennial~~ / **Perennial**	
Position:	Full sun
Soil:	Well-drained
Hardiness	Half hardy/semi-evergreen
USDA Zones:	Summer – 6-8 Winter – 4-10
Sow:	Spring
Harvest:	Summer months

The strong flavor of this herb makes it ideal for meat or bean dishes, sausages or as an addition to stuffings. Savory is a key flavor in salami, for example.

There are around thirty different types of savory, but only the summer and winter are used in the kitchen. While popular in the past, this herb is less popular today and not commonly used.

Summer Savory

Originating in the Mediterranean region and southern Europe, savory has spread to northern Europe and North America. The Romans introduced savory into Britain, where it was one of the few spicy herbs available until the spice routes opened up many centuries later.

The Romans, Greeks and Egyptians considered summer savory an aphrodisiac, and its Latin name originates from its association with lusty satyrs and the god Pan. Druids used savory to celebrate fertility in the summer and in the Middle Ages, monasteries banned this herb to avoid tempting the monks into breaking their vows of chastity.

Growing Instructions

Summer savory requires planting every year as it is an annual. Plant the seeds direct to the soil after the last frost. Leave 3-5" between seeds and push them down just below the surface. Let the plants grow to at least 6" before you start harvesting the tender growth for use in the kitchen. At the end of the growing season, harvest the entire plant and hang to dry, storing the leaves to use over winter.

Winter Savory

Winter savory is perennial and sown direct after the last frost or started indoors between two and six weeks before the last frost date. Leave one to two feet between plants and push down so they are just under the surface. These plants will grow very big. Again, use the tender leaves for cooking and harvest the leaves later in the growing season for drying and storing.

Although a member of the mint family, these herbs are not invasive. Savory likes a rich, well-drained soil with plenty of organic material dug into it. It grows best in full sun. However, it will tolerate most soil types but will not survive in very wet, heavy clay soils. Summery savory is relatively drought tolerant and does not require any fertilizer provided you dug in compost before planting.

Plant Care

Start harvesting summer savory when the plants reach six inches tall. Pinch the stems off about half way down, just above a leaf node and then remove the leaves from the stalk. This harvesting method encourages bushy growth, preventing the plants from becoming weak and leggy.

Although the leaves can be harvested throughout the summer, the flavor is most intense and sweetest just before the plant starts to flower. Fresh leaves have the most flavor, but they can be dried or frozen to store throughout winter.

Summer savory will reseed itself if the plants are left in place, but this is not a very reliable method of propagation. You can leave some plants in place to harvest the seeds in the fall.

Culinary Uses

Winter savory is a versatile herb in the kitchen, blending with a variety of other herbs such as basil, thyme and oregano. It works well in almost any fish, meat or poultry dish and is ideal in a herb cheese. Although the flavor is intense when fresh, it quickly loses its flavor when cooked, so is best added towards the end of cooking.

Summer savory is almost as versatile and often used interchangeably with thyme, being a key ingredient in the French 'herbs de Provence'. Summer savory works well with beans, pork, lamb, stuffing, sauces and most vegetables. Italian, German, Romanian and Bulgarian cuisines make frequent use of this herb.

Beauty Uses

Both winter and summer savory are rarely used for beauty applications.

Health Uses

Savories contain a lot of flavonoids and polyphenols that give it strong antimicrobial, antioxidant, antitumor, antidiabetic and anti-inflammatory properties. However, researchers have discovered that the actual content of this herb varies significantly depending on environmental conditions and the maturity of the plant, https://www.ncbi.nlm.nih.gov/pmc/articles/PMC4142450/. This makes it very difficult to use the herb reliably for health purposes.

The leaves and tender shoots of summer savory have strong antioxidant properties and are high in dietary fiber, so help to reduce bad cholesterol levels and raise good cholesterol levels. The leaves are high in oils such as thymol (a strong antiseptic and antifungal) and carvacrol (an antibacterial).

Savory is high in many vitamins and minerals including B vitamins, vitamins A and C as well as niacin and thiamine. It also contains zinc, magnesium, iron, potassium, calcium and selenium too, all of which are important in the healthy functioning of your body.

Drink winter savory as a tea, taking one cup a day. This infusion treats wind, gas, indigestion and nausea as well as being gargled to treat a sore throat.

Pests, Problems & Diseases

Both savory varieties have no pest and disease problems, though can occasionally be infected by aphids on new growth.

Recommended Varieties

Of the many varieties of savory, only winter and summer savory are grown commercially. Other varieties exist, though these are usually grown for their ornamental value. Some of these cultivars have culinary uses but are not popular outside of their native area. These include:

- Lemon Savory (*Satureja biflora*) – a warm season annual or very tender perennial usually found in USDA zones 11+. Native to East Africa, this plant likes warm conditions and grows best in a rich, well-drained soil in full sun. It has a strong, lemony flavor and most gardeners will have to grow this indoors (keep the soil relatively dry if growing inside). When dried, the leaves retain their lemon scent and taste.
- Creeping Savory (*Satureja spicigera*) – a perennial, hardy in USDA zones 7-9 and originally native to the Caucuses and West Asia. It likes a well-drained, alkaline soil, ideally rocky and not a heavy clay in full sun. This plant tolerates hot, dry conditions and has a strong, peppery taste when fresh. Harvest in the summer and dry for winter use.
- Indian Mint (*Satureja douglasii*) – a perennial, hardy in USDA zones 7-10 and native to the West Coast of America and eastwards towards Montana and Idaho. It likes a shady position in a moist, but well-drained soil. This plant is very tolerant of soil conditions, growing in both sandy and clay soils. When grown in dense shade, such as under a tree, it acts as evergreen groundcover. It will grow up to two feet tall and six feet across, and works well in hanging baskets where it will trail nicely. It is drought tolerant, but does need watering in the summer months. The leaves make a tea similar to mint and have been used to treat colds, toothache, indigestion, insomnia and

arthritic pain.

- Jamaican Mint Bush (*Satureja viminea*) – a perennial, native to the Caribbean and hardy in USDA zones higher than 10. It likes a well-drained soil and grows in full sun or partial shade. In the Caribbean, this plant grows as a large shrub or small tree. If growing in a cooler area, grow in a reasonable sized container and bring indoors when it gets cold. Be careful not to overwater it though. The leaves have an aroma that is a cross between mint and the normal savory smell and a piquant taste.
- Pink Savory/Thyme Leaved Savory (*Satureja thymbra*) – a perennial herb, hardy in USDA zones 7-10 and originating in the Mediterranean regions. It likes a well-draining, alkaline soil that is ideally a little rocky, in full sun or a little shade. The flavor of this plant is similar to winter savory, but with a definite hint of thyme and oregano. The flowers appear in the middle of summer, are edible and attract plenty of bees.
- Pygmy Savory/Create Mountain Savory (*Satureja spinose*) – a perennial hardy down to temperatures of -10F/-23C, this plant is native to the southern Aegean Sea around Greece. It likes a full sun position in a well-draining, alkaline soil. Originally growing high up in mountains, from 4,000 to 7,000 feet high, it is very hardy and an ideal addition to an Alpine garden as it only grows to about 6" tall.
- Limestone Savory/Arkansas Mint (*Satureja arkansana*) – a perennial, hardy to -10F/-23C, this plant likes moisture in well-draining soil and full sun. Native to North America, this species is common in the Ozark mountains in Missouri. It prefers shady, moist areas but does well in sunny spots so long as the soil is good and moist. This is a low growing plant and is usually smelt before it is seen. The leaves turn red in the fall and it has purple/pink flowers from spring to fall.

Recipes

Savory and Apple Stuffing

This stuffing is excellent for vegetables such as marrow or squashes, but works well with meat too, particularly port.

Ingredients:

- 1 onion (chopped)
- 1 celery stick (chopped)
- 1 small cooking apples (peeled, cored and chopped)
- 2oz/50g fresh white breadcrumbs
- 2oz/50g hazelnuts (roughly chopped)
- 1oz/25g butter
- ½ tablespoon parsley (chopped)
- ½ tablespoon winter savory leaves (chopped)
- Salt and pepper to taste

Method:

1. Heat the butter in a large frying pan
2. Cook the onion for 5-7 minutes until softened
3. Add the hazelnuts and cook, stirring continuously, for 20-30 seconds to toast them
4. Add the apple, celery, breadcrumbs and herbs, stir well
5. Season to taste and stir, adding more butter to bind if required

Tuscan Bean Soup

A delicious soup that is dry easy to cook. The beans are used for the liquid in the soup too, meaning no meat stock is required. The recipe serves six.

Ingredients:

- 12oz/350g dried cannelloni beans (soaked overnight)
- 11oz/300g black kale or dark green kale
- 4 ripe tomatoes (peeled, de-seeded and chopped)
- 2 celery sticks (finely chopped)
- 2 carrots (finely chopped)
- 2 leeks (finely chopped)
- 2 garlic cloves (finely chopped)
- 2 sprigs fresh thyme
- Handful of winter savory leaves
- 6-8 tablespoons olive oil
- Salt and pepper to taste

To Serve:

- 6 slices of 2-3 day old, stale country bread
- 7oz/200g Savoy cabbage (finely chopped)
- 1-2 red onions (sliced)
- Extra-virgin olive oil

Method:

1. Drain the beans, put in a large saucepan and cover with water until the beans are 2" under the surface
2. Bring to the boil and boil hard for 10 minutes
3. Drain and cover again with fresh water
4. Add the winter savory and bring to the boil again
5. Reduce the heat and simmer for 90 minutes until the beans are whole but tender
6. Drain the beans and set aside one quarter of them
7. Pass the rest of the beans through a sieve into a bowl, together with 2 pints of water
8. Heat the oil in the saucepan and cook all of the vegetables until soft
9. Add the tomatoes, thyme and garlic
10. Cook for 5 minutes, then add the kale and season to taste
11. Cook for 10 more minutes, then add the bean puree
12. Cook for 60 minutes, adding more water if the soup becomes too thick
13. 5 minutes before the end of cooking, stir in the whole beans
14. Cook the Savoy cabbage in a little oil
15. Serve the soup over a slice of bread, topped with the cooked cabbage with olive oil and red onions on the side

Savory Marinade

This marinade is great for meat or game and incorporates fresh ingredients from your garden. There are some variations on the ingredients, depending on what meat you are marinating.

Ingredients:

- 2½ cups red wine (replace with white wine for chicken)
- ¾ cup red wine vinegar (replace with white wine vinegar for chicken)
- 2 carrots (diced)
- 2 garlic cloves (sliced)
- 2 bay leaves (broken into pieces)
- 1 celery stalk (chopped)
- 1 small onion (chopped)

- 2 teaspoons each of oregano and fresh thyme (for meat or game)
- 2 teaspoons each rosemary, French tarragon and lemon thyme (for chicken)
- 2 teaspoons fresh mint (only for pork)
- Salt to taste
- Handful winter savory leaves (coarsely chopped)

Method:

1. Mix the ingredients together in a large bowl
2. Marinate the meat for 12 hours or overnight

Savory Chicken Salad
This is a simple chicken salad that has a bit of a punch to it. Use a stronger curry powder to give it more of a kick.

Ingredients:

- 2½ cups diced chicken (cooked)
- 2 cups cooked pasta (cooled)
- 1½ cups celery (diced)
- 1 cup frozen peas
- ¾ cup mayonnaise
- ¼ cup chicken broth
- ¼ cup pecans (chopped)
- ¼ cup stuffed olives (sliced)
- 1 teaspoon winter savory leaves (finely minced)
- ¾ teaspoon salt
- Dash of curry powder

Method:

1. Gradually add the broth to the mayonnaise, blending well
2. Add a dash of curry powder and the winter savory, stir well
3. In a separate bowl, toss together the pasta, peas, olives, pecans, celery and chicken, then season to taste
4. Add the dressing and mix well
5. Serve immediately with chopped lettuce and tomatoes

Winter Savory Stuffing

This is another stuffing recipe that is delicious, working very well with chicken. This makes enough stuffing for a 10-12lb turkey. Baste the turkey in butter and Burgundy wine.

Ingredients:

- 12 slices of bread (cubed)
- 2 eggs
- 1 medium onion (chopped)
- ¼lb butter (melted)
- 2 cups raisins
- 1½ cups Burgundy wine
- 1 tablespoon winter savory (dried)
- Salt and pepper

Method:

1. Put the bread cubes into a large bowl and add the wine
2. Mix well and leave for 5-10 minutes for the bread to absorb the wine
3. Add the rest of the ingredients and stir well until thoroughly combined
4. Use the mixture to stuff the turkey

Herbes de Provence Blend

This is the famous French herb blend popular in their cuisine. It is very quick to make using dried herbs and is stored in an airtight container.

Ingredients:

- 2 tablespoons marjoram
- 2 tablespoons savory
- 2 tablespoons thyme
- 2 tablespoons lavender flowers
- 1 tablespoon rosemary

Method:

1. Put all the ingredients into your blender and mix on a low speed for 10-15 seconds until the lavender flowers have broken up into small pieces
2. Store in an airtight container until required

Sorrel

Common sorrel, *Rumex acetosa*, is a perennial herb known for its lemony leaves that work well with eggs, salads and in sauces.

At a Glance Facts

~~Annual~~ / ~~Biennial~~ / **Perennial**	
Position:	Full sun
Soil:	Well-drained
Hardiness	Fully hardy
USDA Zones:	3-9
Sow:	February to July
Harvest:	June to September

Sorrel grows to about two feet (60cm) tall with deep taproots and edible, arrow shaped leaves with a slightly sour taste due to high levels of oxalic acid. The flowers appear early in the summer and transform from red/green to a purple color. Growing in the wild, sorrel is found at the side of roads, on the edge of wooded areas and in grasslands.

Wood Sorrel

Growing Instructions

Grow sorrel from seed, sown any time from February through to July. Either start in pots, sowing the seeds ½" deep and putting them somewhere light to germinate, or sow direct in their final location. When seedlings are large enough to handle, repot into individual pots and then repot again when they are larger into a 12"/30cm container. Seedlings can be planted out in late spring.

Plant Care

Although these plants have a deep taproot, they still require regular watering, particularly during hot, dry weather. Remove the flowers to prevent the plants going to seed and spreading.

The foliage dies back in the fall. Container grown plants need their containers lifting up on pot feet to allow moisture to drain to prevent root rot.

Every couple of years, divide established plants in the spring or in fall to keep them productive. Sorrel will become congested if left alone and dividing helps to rejuvenate the plant.

Red Veined Sorrel

Pick fresh leaves from spring through to early fall. The younger leaves from the ends of the shoots have a better taste than the larger leaves.

Culinary Uses

Sorrel has a taste very reminiscent of lemons, with a bright but tart flavor. This can make it hard to work with as the lemony flavor is offset with a green, grassy flavor. It is both a leafy green and a herb, so can be chopped up for use in soups, dressings and marinades or eaten raw in salads.

The tartness of sorrel makes it ideal for dishes made from eggs, whole grains or potatoes. It works extremely well with oily or smoked fish such as mackerel or salmon and is often paired with sour cream or yogurt. Add sorrel to cooked greens such as kale, chard or spinach to give it a more interesting flavor.

Store sorrel for a couple of days in your refrigerator loosely wrapped in plastic. To store for 7-10 days, rinse, pat dry and roll in paper towels before putting in plastic and refrigerating. Cook fresh leaves in butter until they wilt and then freeze for later use in soups or stews.

As well as eating the leaves, the flowers can be used as a garnish on a salad or cooked. Dry and ground the roots or seeds for a flour substitute. The seeds are also eaten raw or cooked.

Beauty Uses

Sorrel leaves are rich in vitamins A, B and C, making it ideal for your hair. Use a sorrel infusion as a rinse for your hair to help stop hair loss, treat baldness and leave your hair looking lustrous.

Health Uses

With high levels of vitamins and flavonoids plus plenty of iron, sodium, potassium, calcium and phosphorus, sorrel has many health benefits.

The leaves are good for your eyes due to their levels of vitamin A. Research, http://archive.unu.edu/unupress/food2/UIN07E/UIN07E0C.HTM, indicates that sorrel leaves can help reduce night blindness and improve eyesight.

Sorrel tea is very helpful when you are detoxing. It is both a diuretic and purgative, plus the leaves contain protocatechuic acid, which is known to help with a detox diet. Sorrel tea is also good at relieving bloating, http://www.ncbi.nlm.nih.gov/pmc/articles/PMC3157304/.

Oxalic acid, found in abundance in sorrel leaves, acts to prevent cancer. The other vitamins and minerals found in the leaves plus their high levels of carotenoids and chlorophyll have been shown to be useful in treating breast cancer, http://www.ncbi.nlm.nih.gov/pubmed/17212569.

The antioxidants found in the leaves help to reduce inflammation and lower bad cholesterol levels while also lowering blood pressure levels.

In general, the leaves are good for you, but should not be consumed in excess. They are packed full of beneficial vitamins and minerals which do a lot of good for your body.

Pests, Problems & Diseases

Sorrel is generally diseases free, but slugs and aphids often attack it.

Caterpillars of certainly species of butterfly will eat sorrel, notably the blood-vein moth.

Recommended Varieties

There are several varieties of sorrel, with the following three being the most commonly grown apart from common sorrel.

- French Sorrel (*Rumex scutatus*) – often cultivated and sometimes found at farmer's markets. The leaves are smaller and more rounded than common sorrel and have a milder flavor.
- Red-Veined Sorrel (*Rumex sanguineus*) – has deep red veins running through the leaves with a very mild flavor that lacks the normal tartness found in sorrel. It is often used in salads where it looks great.
- Sheep's Sorrel (*Rumex acetosella*) – growing wild in the United States, this variety is rarely cultivated, usually being foraged instead. It tastes very similar to common sorrel, but the leaves are smaller.

Recipes

Sorrel Tea

A great tea, sweetened to taste to offset the tartness of the leaves. This can be refrigerated and turned into an iced tea if you prefer.

Ingredients:

- 2-3 cloves
- 1 cup hot water
- 1 cinnamon stick
- Handful of sorrel leaves
- Sweetener to taste (sugar, honey, etc.)

Method:

1. Put the spices and sorrel leaves into a cup
2. Boil the water and pour into the cup
3. Steep for 5 minutes, then drain and sweeten to taste before serving

Caribbean Sorrel Drink

This is a refreshing twist on sorrel tea and makes for a fascinating drink that is full of flavor. This dish is best served chilled.

Ingredients:

- 2 cups sorrel leaves (dried)
- 1 cup white (granulated) sugar
- 8 allspice berries
- 6 cloves
- 1 tablespoon white rice (uncooked)
- 1 tablespoon orange juice
- 1 teaspoon grated ginger
- Pinch of ground cinnamon

Method:

1. Mix everything except the sorrel leaves together in a saucepan
2. Bring to the boil
3. Remove from the heat, add the sorrel leaves, cover and leave for a day to infuse
4. Strain, refrigerate and drink

Sorrel Soup

Sorrel makes for an excellent soup which contains over half of your recommended daily allowance of vitamin C.

Ingredients:

- 3 cups sorrel leaves (washed and dried)
- 2 cups vegetable broth
- 6 small potatoes (cubed)
- ½ sweet onion (chopped)
- 1 egg (lightly beaten)
- 2 tablespoons butter
- Salt and pepper

Method:

1. Cut the sorrel leaves into ribbons and put to one side
2. Heat the butter in a large saucepan on a medium heat
3. Add the onion and cook, stirring often, until browned
4. Add the potatoes and sorrel together with enough broth to cover them
5. Bring to the boil, reduce the heat and cook for a further 15 minutes

until the potatoes are soft

6. Puree half the mixture until smooth and return it to the pan (puree more for a smoother soup)
7. Put the egg into a jug together with a ladle full of soup and mix well
8. Add this back to the main soup mixture and cook until the soup has thickened
9. Season to taste and serve with the garnish of your choice or a crusty white loaf of bread

St. John's Wort

St John's Wort, *Hypericum perforatum*, is a popular herb with distinctive, star shaped yellow flowers. Considered an invasive weed in some parts of the United States, this herb is highly adaptable and grows anywhere from prairies and pastures to woodlands and ditches.

At a Glance Facts

~~Annual~~ / ~~Biennial~~ / **Perennial**	
Position:	Full sun to partial shade
Soil:	Moist, well-drained
Hardiness	Yes, down to -4F/-20C
USDA Zones:	5-10
Sow:	Indoors, 6-9 weeks before last frost
Harvest:	Summer to fall

Native to Northern Africa, Europe and western Asia, including the Himalayan Mountains, settlers transported St. John's Wort to America in the late 1600s. Being such a tolerant and adaptable plant, it quickly made itself at home and spread across the country to the extent that some states class it as a noxious weed.

Traditionally, St. John's Wort flowers in June on St. John the Baptist's day (24th), hence its name. This is an important commercial crop, used in many products from oils to tinctures to the dried herb. Commercial growers harvest just before or during flowering, using all of the plant above the surface or, in some cases, just the flowering tops.

The Latin name, *Hypericum perforatum*, comes from Ancient Greek, translating roughly as "over an apparition", which relates to the belief that St. John's Wort was so offensive to evil spirits that the slightest hint of it would scare them of. Folklore claims that on the anniversary of John the Baptist's beheading, red spots appear on the leaves, symbolizing his blood.

In medieval times, St. John's Wort was placed under the pillow on St. John's Eve. This summoned St. John to that persons dreams where the saint would bless them and prevent them dying in the coming year.

St. John's Wort has been used medicinally for over 2,000 years, with the first references coming from the Greeks. Historically, this herb has been used to treat everything from depression and anxiety through to viral infections, wounds and lung ailments.

Growing Instructions

Grow St. John's Wort either in full sun or partial shade. If you live in a hot climate, grow this plant in a position that gets shade in the afternoon. Too much sun can cause leaf scorch, but too little reduces the number of flowers. If you can find a location that gets lots of sun in the morning but some shade in the afternoon when it is hottest, then this plant will thrive.

This herb thrives in moist, well-drained soil, though does not tolerate salty or very alkaline environments. It will tolerate dry soil and even occasional flooding, plus is quite drought tolerant too. There needs to be 24-36" between plants. Avoid siting the plant anywhere that people will brush past the foliage such as by a path as the leaves give off an unpleasant smell when brushed or bruised.

Before planting, dig in some well rotten compost or manure to at least eight inches deep. St. John's Wort grow up to three feet tall and has a spread of between 1½ and 2 feet, so need space between plants. Water slowly and deeply after transplanting, until the plants are well established.

Hypericum seeds can be difficult to germinate. Soaking them in water on paper towels overnight can help improve the germination rate. Surface sow the seed indoors between 6 and 8 weeks before the last frost as the seeds can easily be lost when grown outside. St. John's Wort seeds need sunlight to grow so do not germinate well outdoors where they quickly get buried under the soil.

The seeds will take between 10 and 20 days to germinate, but need the soil to be kept consistently moist for reliable germination.

Plant Care

St. John's Wort needs the flowers removing before the seeds form to stop it spreading. It is a prolific self-seeder so needs to be controlled before it takes over your garden.

Prune early in spring, removing damaged, dead or crossing stems and shaping the plant according to your preferences. Disinfect your pruning shears both before and after pruning to avoid the risk of infection.

Harvest early morning or late afternoon, when the plants are dry and free from dew. Cut the stems to an inch above the woody base and dry the leaves and flowers before use.

The most potent part of the plant are the flower buds. Cut off flower clusters with unopened flowers and hang upside down to increase their potency.

Culinary Uses

There are no modern culinary uses for St. John's Wort. Previously, the tea was given to disturbed people to banish evil spirits, but that practice has ended now.

Beauty Uses

As a fresh herb, St John's Wort is not a popular beauty treatment as it can be an irritant to some people. The essential oil is added to creams where it helps to firm and tighten skin, as well as kill harmful bacteria.

Health Uses

If you are taking any mood regulating medications, do not use St. John's Wort. It interacts with many commercial medicines, causing them to be less effective. If you are on any medication at all, consult your doctor before starting taking St. John's Wort as this herb interacts with a lot of different medication. The oils in this plant can cause photo dermatitis and rashes in some people.

This herb is best known for its ability to lift the mood without the side effects often found in ant-depressant drugs. Research, https://nccih.nih.gov/health/stjohnswort/sjw-and-depression.htm, indicates this is a great alternative to prescription drugs for mild to moderate cases of depression. With its lack of side effects, it has become a popular treatment across the world. If you have acute depression, please ensure you speak to a medical professional rather that self-prescribe. Early research indicates that St. John's Wort can help reduce anxiety in people.

OCD or obsessive compulsive disorder is a serious problem for many people yet this herb is showing promise as a treatment for OCD, reducing its symptoms: https://www.ncbi.nlm.nih.gov/pubmed/10982200. Research also indicates that St. John's Wort is helpful in smoking cessation too, https://www.ncbi.nlm.nih.gov/pmc/articles/PMC3110810.

With its ability to affect moods, St. John's Wort works well to control mood swings caused when a woman goes through the menopause, https://www.ncbi.nlm.nih.gov/pmc/articles/PMC1764641/).

When growing your own St. John's Wort for medicinal use, air dry the plant in a warm, well-ventilated area. This can be used to make a tea.

A tincture can be made by crushing the leaves and flowers and then soaking them for several weeks, shaking occasionally, in a high-alcohol vodka. Strain the mixture and then store the tincture in a light resistant dropper bottle.

Make an oil for topical use by crushing the leaves and flowers and leaving them to soak for two or three weeks. At the end of this time, strain the mixture and use the oil for healing or disinfecting wounds.

Pests, Problems & Diseases

St John's Wort suffers from no serious disease or pest problems.

Recommended Varieties

There are many St. John's Wort cultivars available, most of which are grown for their ornamental value. The different cultivars usually have some variation in the leaves, flowers or berries so you can pick a cultivar that suits the color scheme of your garden. These are generally available from specialist suppliers.

- *Hypericum x moserianum* 'Tricolor' – a cultivar with variegated foliage in shades of red, cream, green and pink.
- *Hypericum frondosum* 'Sunburst' – hardy to zone 5, this cultivar grows in a bushy mound of up to two feet wide.
- *Hypericum calycinum* 'Brigadoon' – smaller flowers, but chartreuse foliage that turns a golden orange color when exposed to bright sun.
- *Hypericum androsaemum* 'Albury Purple' – a deciduous shrub with purple/green leaves up to four inches long and star-shaped or cupped yellow flowers. In the fall, round, red fruit appears on the plant.

Recipes

St. John's Wort Tea

This is a very easy tea to make that allows you to benefit from this healing herb. Drink three cups of this tea during the day for relief from a hangover. This tea also helps with alcoholism and two cups should be drunk daily for 4 to 6 weeks.

Ingredients:

- 1 cup water
- 1 tablespoon St. John's Wort (dried)
- 1 teaspoon sweetener (honey, sugar, or alternative)

Method:

1. Heat the water to a boil
2. Add the St. John's Wort, reduce the heat and simmer for 5 minutes
3. Strain the tea
4. Add the sweetener, stir well and drink

St. John's Wort Oil

This is great for bumps or bruises as a topical healing agent.

Ingredients:

- Olive oil
- St. John's Wort Flowers
- Kilner Jar or other jar with sealable lid
- Cheese Cloth
- Light proof (brown) bottle for storage

Method:

1. Spread the flowers on a cookie sheet and leave for a day to dry and for excess moisture to evaporate
2. Fill a jar with the flowers
3. Cover with olive oil and seal before leaving in a warm, dark place
4. Regularly check to ensure the flowers remain fully submerged. Remove the lid every few days and wipe off any condensation
5. Leave for 4 weeks, then strain the flowers out using cheese cloth
6. Pour the oil into a light proof bottle and store in a cool, dark place

St. John's Wort Tincture

An easy to make tincture. Take 15-20 drops three times a day.

Ingredients:

- St. John's Wort flowers
- High proof vodka
- Kilner jar or equivalent
- Cheese cloth
- Light proof dropper bottle

Method:

1. Put the flowers in a jar, pack down and cover with vodka
2. Leave in a dark place
3. Shake every day for four weeks
4. Strain out the flowers and pour the tincture into light proof dropper bottles

Tansy

Tansy, *Tanacetum vulgare*, is also known by the Latin name, *Chrysanthemum vulgare*. It is a decorative yet pungent perennial plant that once had an important place in the herbal medicine cabinet, yet is now rarely used except as an insect repelling ingredient in pot-pourri.

At a Glance Facts

~~Annual~~ / ~~Biennial~~ / **Perennial**	
Position:	Full sun to partial shade
Soil:	Moist well-drained
Hardiness	Fully hardy to -40F/-40C
USDA Zones:	3-9
Sow:	February to May or August to October
Harvest:	June to September

Many of the cultivars, particularly the variegated or curled forms, are very attractive in the garden, with the variegated varieties preferring light shade. This plant is easy to grow and is considered invasive as it spreads so quickly. It has been banned in several states, including Colorado, Wyoming and Montana, as well as being prohibited in the provinces of Alberta and British Columbia in Canada.

As a powerful insect repellent, it is sometimes planted near fruit trees or hung by windows and doors, or kept in the kitchen. The flowers not only repel flies, but also fleas, ants, moths and mice. When boiled, the flowers produce a good quality, golden yellow dye. When composted, this herb boosts the potassium levels of the finished compost.

Tansy is native to the Mediterranean regions of Europe and was brought to America by settlers as an important medicinal and culinary herb. Over the years, this plant has steadily fallen out of favor and now is rarely used except as an ornamental plant.

The name tansy derives from the Greek word 'athanatos' which means immortality as tansy was used during the embalming process. In Greek Mythology, Zeus gave Ganymede immortality by giving him tansy. The ancient Greeks recognized the insect repelling qualities of tansy as they wrapped corpses in tansy leaves to preserve the body until burial.

Before refrigerators were used, tansy was used to preserve meat by covering each layer of meat with tansy leaves to prevent insects from coming near it.

In medieval Europe, tansy was strewn on the floor of homes to keep away insects. The leaves were also commonly used as bookmarks in Bibles, hence one of its names 'Bible leaf'. When the Bible was opened, the leaves would give off a mint like scent.

According to superstition, a tansy flower in your shoe ensured a safe journey. The flower was also known as the fairy button as people believed fairies lived in the flowers.

Growing Instructions

Sow seeds under glass early spring or sow directly during warmer weather. When growing in seed trays, cover the seed with a light sprinkling of compost and keep watered, but not wet. Pot on when the seedlings are large enough to handle and then harden off before planting out at 12"/30cm intervals in late spring or early summer.

As an insect repellent, tansy makes for a good companion plant for the brassica family, particularly cabbages as it keeps away many of the pests that affect these vegetables.

Plant Care

Tansy is a prolific self-seeder, so needs to be controlled. Either remove the flowers before the plant goes to seed or remove unwanted seedlings in the spring.

The leaves can be picked as and when you need them, with the flowers appearing later in the summer. In late summer, cut the plants back to ground level to allow for fresh growth.

Be aware that tansy leaves are poisonous to some animals and can cause dermatitis in some people due to its oils. These oils break down in the liver and produce toxic metabolites, which is why this herb is no longer used in the kitchen.

Culinary Uses

Tansy leaves are very bitter, and although eaten in the past, are no longer used as they produce toxic compounds. They were used in Easter dishes, particularly in a dish called Tansy Pudding, served in England during Lent.

Official advice is to not use tansy as a culinary herb.

Beauty Uses

As tansy causes dermatitis in some people, it does not have any beauty uses.

Note that blue tansy oil is from a different plant, *Tanacetum annuum* or Moroccan Chamomile. This is not the same as tansy oil and is sold and used as a beauty treatment. Blue tansy oil is safe to use.

Health Uses

Tansy must not be used by pregnant women, nursing mothers or women trying to conceive. Tansy can cause miscarriage.

Tansy tea was used in the 12th century to expel worms from the body, but now it is not recommended to be used at all as is harmful and considered dangerous. Tansy oil contains thujone which is considered toxic. This herb also contains tannic acids, which are fatal in large doses.

Do not grow this plant if you have small children or animals because it is very toxic if eaten.

Pests, Problems & Diseases

Tansy is generally disease and pest free.

Recommended Varieties

There are about 160 different species in the *Tanacetum* genus. Many of these species are grown purely for ornamental purposes.

Recipes

No recipes are provided as it is not recommended to consume this herb any more.

Tarragon

Tarragon, *Artemisia dracunculus*, is an upright perennial with narrow leaves and small, pale yellow flower appearing late in summer.

At a Glance Facts

~~Annual~~ / ~~Biennial~~ / **Perennial**	
Position:	Full sun
Soil:	Well-drained, but not clay
Hardiness	Yes, down to -4F/-20C
USDA Zones:	4-10
Sow:	Late summer
Harvest:	May to September

Tarragon has a strong aniseed scent and flavor, working very well with fish, egg and chicken dishes. It is used in béarnaise sauce and often infused with white wine vinegar to use in dishes.

There are two main types of tarragon:

1. French tarragon – the tarragon of choice for the kitchen with a pleasant, strong flavor
2. Russian tarragon – used in the kitchen, but has an inferior flavor

Tarragon is thought to be native to Mongolia and Siberia, having spread to Europe by invading Mongols who brought it to Italy. They used tarragon to aid sleep and to freshen breath. The Latin name '*dracunculus*' means 'little dragon' and the genus (Artemisia) comes from the Greek goddess of the moon, Artemis. The Roman goddess, Diana, gave tarragon to a centaur. The references to dragons come from the serpentine shape of the roots.

How tarragon left Italy and spread further afield is not entirely clear. It is believed that Saint Catherine brought tarragon back to France after her 14th century visit to Pope Clement VI, though as she was only five years old when Clement VI died, it seems unlikely. If St. Catherine was responsible for importing tarragon to France, then it is more likely after she met Pope Gregory VI in 1376. Other historians claim tarragon arrived in France in the 16th century.

Once the French adopted tarragon, its popularity rose. Now it is grown across Europe and America and is popular in many European cuisines.

Growing Instructions

French tarragon cannot be grown from seed. Either buy young plants in spring or transplant established plants in the spring or fall. Young plants need large containers filled with a gritty compost or to be planted in a sunny but sheltered spot in well-drained soil.

Leave two or three feet between plants to give them plenty of space as they grow about 12" wide and up to three feet tall.

Keep young plants well-watered until they have established themselves, then they require more infrequent watering.

Plant Care

Water frequently after planting and less often in winter. Fertilize well with a balanced fertilizer in early spring. Mulch the plants in winter as the plant dies back and remains dormant until spring.

To ensure a regular supply of leaves, pinch off flowers from May until September. Use a sharp pair of secateurs to cut the shoot tips off, then strip the leaves with your fingers. Tarragon is best used fresh, but can be dried and stored, though they do lose their flavor if stored too long. Tarragon can be frozen, which keeps the flavor better.

Harvest regularly throughout the growing season and prune to keep the plant to about two feet tall otherwise it can fall over.

Tarragon plants, although perennial, tend to run out of steam after two or four years and need to be replaced with fresh plants. Divide the root clump into new plants in spring or fall. New plants can also be grown from root or stem cuttings.

Culinary Uses

Although tarragon is an excellent herb in the kitchen, most people are not very aware of it and do not think to use it unless a recipe specifically asks for it. However, it is a very versatile herb with use in dishes from fish to meat to sauces and more.

Tarragon is popular in French cuisine, being part of the 'fine herbes' blend and used in béarnaise sauce. The leaves compliment fish very well and are frequently used in many different fish dishes.

As the leaves are tender, they are often used in a salad or as a garnish, similar to how you would use parsley. The anise flavor of the leaves works very well in tomato based dishes such as soups and pasta salads.

Beauty Uses

Tarragon does not have any beauty uses.

Health Uses

Tarragon has been used medicinally since before the Mongols brought it to Europe, used for everything from malaria to liver diseases. It is commonly used as an essential oil which has a wide variety of uses from antiseptic to anti-inflammatory.

The essential oil contains a wide variety of beneficial compounds such as flavonoids, phenolic acid and more. The oil content of tarragon is highest in early spring when the flower buds form and later in the year as the flowers start to open. The climate and location of the plants has an impact on the oil content.

Plenty of research is underway into tarragon and it appears to help diabetics by improving insulin sensitivity and how your body uses glucose. In a seven day animal study, researchers discovered that tarragon extract lowered blood glucose concentrations by around 20%, https://www.ncbi.nlm.nih.gov/pubmed/16920509.

In a 90 day, randomized, double-blind study of 24 people, researchers found that 1,000mg of tarragon twice a day decreased total insulin secretion which kept blood sugar levels better balanced throughout the day, https://www.ncbi.nlm.nih.gov/pubmed/27097076.

The Mongols used tarragon as a sleep aid, and modern research backs up this claim. In one study, https://www.ncbi.nlm.nih.gov/pubmed/26119953, tarragon had a sedative effect and regulated sleep patterns.

Traditionally, tarragon has been used for pain relief. In a 12 week study, taking a drug containing tarragon extract had a positive effect on reducing pain compared to a placebo, https://www.ncbi.nlm.nih.gov/pubmed/26631103. Another study found that the *Artemisia* plants were helpful in treating pain and could be used instead of traditional pain management, https://www.ncbi.nlm.nih.gov/pubmed/24074293.

Pests, Problems & Diseases

Tarragon is generally pest and disease free, though can suffer from powdery mildew if there is insufficient air circulation between plants.

In some areas, tarragon can be affected by rust, which causes yellow, black or orange spots or blisters on the leaves, which then results in leaf fall and in worst cases, plant death. Dig up and dispose of infected plants and carefully check any plants you buy for signs of infection before introducing them to your garden.

Recommended Varieties

There are a number of tarragon varieties available, though the three most common are French, Russian and Mexican. When you buy tarragon from a seed catalog, it will be Russian tarragon as French tarragon does not reliably grow from seed.

- Russian Tarragon (*Artemisia dracunuloides Pursch*) – grows from seed with thinner, spikier and lighter green leaves, growing up to four feet tall. The taste of this cultivar is considered inferior to French tarragon.

- Mexican Tarragon (*Tagetes lucida*) – also known as winter tarragon, Mexican marigold or Spanish tarragon, this tastes very similar to French tarragon but has a slightly stronger anise flavor.

Recipes

Tarragon and Watermelon Fizz

This refreshingly cool drink works well with the sweetness of the watermelon and the anise flavor of the tarragon.

Ingredients:

- 2oz watermelon puree
- 2oz gin (a flowery one works best)
- ½oz tarragon syrup
- ¼oz Pastis

Method:

1. Make the syrup by mixing a cup of water, a cup of sugar and ½ cup of tarragon leaves and simmering for 10 minutes in saucepan. Strain, cool and bottle
2. Put all of the ingredients together in a cocktail shaker together with some crushed ice
3. Shake well and serve in a highball glass with a tarragon leaf garnish

Pea & Leak Soup

This seasonal soup takes the flavor of leeks and peas and brightens it up with a selection of fresh herbs. Serve with crème fraiche and some delicious crusty bread. This recipe makes enough for four servings.

Ingredients:

- 4 cups peas (fresh or frozen)
- 2 leeks (halved and thinly sliced – use both white and light green parts)
- 2 garlic cloves (minced)
- 5 cups chicken or vegetable stock
- ⅓ cup dry white wine
- 4 tablespoons olive oil (divided)
- 3 tablespoons fresh tarragon leaves (chopped)
- 1 teaspoon fresh thyme leaves
- Salt and pepper

Method:

1. Preheat your oven to 400F/200C
2. If you are using fresh peas, boil them in a pot of salted water for 3-5 minutes until tender and then drain and cool
3. Put the peas into a bowl and toss with two tablespoons of olive oil, then season to taste
4. Spread the peas in a single layer on a baking sheet and roast until lightly browned, about 15 minutes
5. Heat the remaining 2 tablespoons of olive oil in a large pot on a medium heat
6. Add the leeks and cook, stirring regularly, for around 6 minutes until softened
7. Add the tarragon, garlic and thyme, season to taste and cook for a further two minutes
8. Add the wine and cook until it is almost reduced
9. Add the stock, stir well and bring to the boil
10. Reduce the heat to a simmer
11. Add the peas, stir well and cook for a further 2 minutes
12. Blend the soup, season to taste and serve

Barley Salad

This is a particularly tasty salad with a lovely tarragon dressing. The barley can be made in advance and the salad can be prepared several hours in advance, covered and refrigerated. Remove an hour before serving and drizzle with olive oil to refresh. This recipe makes enough to serve 4 people.

Barley Ingredients:

- 2 cups water
- ¾ cup pearl barley
- 2x1" strip of lemon zest
- 3 peppercorns
- Pinch of sea salt

Salad Ingredients:

- 2 celery stalks (halved lengthwise and cut into ¼" slices)
- ½ cup green onions (finely chopped)
- ½ cup tangy apple (chopped)
- ¼ cup dried figs (chopped)
- 2 tablespoons lemon juice
- 2 tablespoons extra-virgin olive oil
- 2 tablespoons flat leaf parsley (finely chopped)

- 2 tablespoons fresh tarragon (finely chopped)
- 2-3 teaspoons honey
- 2 teaspoons lemon zest
- ¼ teaspoon fine sea salt
- ¼ teaspoon freshly ground black pepper

Method:

1. Put all of the barley ingredients into a saucepan and bring to the boil
2. Reduce the heat, cover and simmer for 30-40 minutes until the barley is tender, but slightly chewy
3. Remove from the heat and leave covered for 5-10 minutes
4. Drain and discard the liquid, transferring the barley to a bowl to cool
5. Remove the peppercorns and lemon zest
6. Put the figs into a small bowl and stir in 1 tablespoon of lemon juice, then put to one side
7. Put the green onions, apple and celery into your serving bowl and stir to combine
8. In a small bowl, mix together the tablespoon of lemon juice, the lemon zest and 2 teaspoons of honey
9. Season to taste, adding more seasoning or honey as required
10. Stir in 1 tablespoon each of tarragon and parsley
11. Add the barley and figs (together with the juices) to the serving bowl and stir well
12. Drizzle on the dressing and toss
13. Stand at room temperature for 15-20 minutes
14. Toss once more then sprinkle with 1 tablespoon each of parsley and tarragon before serving

Thyme

Common thyme, *Thymus vulgaris*, is a small, bushy shrub originating in Greece, on the edge of the Mediterranean Sea. It has a distinctive scent, attracts butterflies, bees and other insects, plus the leaves are popular in cooking being a key ingredient in bouquet garni and herbes de Provence.

At a Glance Facts

~~Annual~~ / ~~Biennial~~ / **Perennial**	
Position:	Full sun
Soil:	Well-drained
Hardiness	Yes, to 23F/-5F to 14F/-10C
USDA Zones:	2-10
Sow:	March to April
Harvest:	June to September

The name thyme, pronounced the same as the word 'time's, is thought to originate from the Greek word 'thumos' which means smoke. After this, the history and origins of this plant become somewhat muddled. It is thought its name derives from its use during sacrifices, for fumigation or from its fragrance. Thyme was used to perfume Greek temples, which may also indicate the origin to the name.

An alternate meaning of thumos is courage, and the Ancient Greeks believed thyme to be a symbol of bravery. In days of yore, when ladies gave knights favors, they often embroidered a bee above a sprig of thyme on the scarves they gave to the knights.

Thyme has a whole host of folklore and myths surrounding it. It features in the Bible as one of the herbs in the manger where Mary gave birth to Jesus, along with woodroof and groundsel. The Danes and Germans believe wild thyme is a good place to find fairies and thyme oil was part of a concoction that allowed the user to see fairies.

Thyme has been used for centuries for bees. The plants have plenty of flowers that attract bees and the resulting honey has a particularly pleasant flavor. The Romans were known to grow thyme purely for bees.

Growing Instructions

Thyme is easy to grow from seed, though many people buy ready-grown plants purely because they can harvest the leaves faster and get a larger plant quicker.

Seeds are sown in early spring, with a few seeds scattered on the surface of a small pot. Cover the seeds with a thin layer of sieved compost or vermiculite and water carefully. Leave in a warm place or propagator to germinate. Once the seedlings are big enough to handle safely, they can be transferred to individual pots.

Once the weather has warmed, plant out into a sunny spot in well-drained soil. If the ground is too wet during winter, the plants will rot. Thyme will grow to maturity in a 6"/15cm pot if your soil is too heavy.

Thyme can be challenging to start from seed. Most people propagate thyme from cuttings or layering. Cut three inches off the end of a shoot, dip the end in rooting hormone and then plant into sand or vermiculite until roots form in about six weeks. Then transfer to a pot with compost and the root ball will fully form at which point you can transplant it out or to a larger container.

Layering is slightly different. A long thyme stem is pinned to the soil using wire, leaving four inches above the soil. The pinned part must be touching the soil for this to work. After about a month, roots will start to form on the stem and then you can cut the new plant away and transplant it.

Thyme will happily grow in a container with rosemary as they have similar environmental and watering needs. In your garden, thyme is an excellent plant as it attracts pollinating insects. It is a good companion plant to cabbages, eggplant, broccoli, tomatoes, Brussels sprouts and strawberries.

Plant Care

Thyme is quite drought tolerant and does not like too much water. However, if you are growing in containers, do not allow the plants to dry out completely during hot weather.

Once the plant has flowered, it can be pruned into your desired shape to maintain a manageable herb. In fall, keep the plant free from fallen leaves to prevent the herb from rotting.

Thyme benefits from a collar of grit or gravel around the plants to protect the leaves from resting on the soil.

In winter, raise pots up on pot feet to prevent the plants from rotting. This is a common problem in winter months and the main reason many people grow this herb in containers rather than the soil.

Thyme is best harvested just before it flowers to get the most flavor. The taste is pretty much the same whether the herb is fresh or dried; it does not lose its flavor when dried unlike some herbs. Thyme is an evergreen, so the leaves can be picked throughout the year.

Culinary Uses

Thyme is popular in a wide variety of cuisines from European to American to Caribbean to Mediterranean to Latin America. Individual leaves are used or sprigs of thyme are used for flavoring and then removed before eating.

Although dried thyme has the same flavor as fresh thyme, it does benefit from being rehydrated before use. When using dried thyme, use a third more than you would if you were using fresh thyme.

When cooked, thyme leaves release more flavor the longer they are cooked. The woody stems do not break down in cooking, so need removing, but the leaves can stay in the dish and be eaten.

Fresh thyme can be wrapped in damp kitchen paper, sealed in a plastic bag and refrigerated for up to two weeks. If the leaves start to turn brown, then discard the thyme. Leaves removed from the stem and sealed in a plastic container will stay fresh when refrigerated for around three days. Store dried thyme in an airtight container where it will retain its flavor for up to three years.

Thyme works particularly well with vegetables and seafood as it has a slightly sour flavor. It is used in stuffing and with meat or poultry, though when cooked overly long, can lose its flavor.

In soups, add thyme just before you serve the dish to retain maximum flavor. Add the herb, remove the soup from the heat and cover until you are ready to serve to get a wonderful aroma from the soup. Likewise, with stews, add right at the end of cooking to get maximum taste from the thyme.

Thyme really brings out the flavor in poultry and works very well with chicken and turkey. Mix some lemon juice with thyme and then baste the chicken with this mixture for a delicious flavor.

As red meat has a much stronger taste, thyme is not usually used with meats as its flavor is drowned out. However, is used as a marinade to give them flavor.

Thyme leaves work well in salad to give the vegetables a pleasant kick. Adding a pinch or two of dried thyme to flour will make for a tasty, herb bread. Add fresh, crushed thyme leaves to the butter for garlic bread to really bring out the flavors.

Pasta dishes benefit from dried thyme being added to it. The thyme really enhances the flavor of the pasta.

Thyme is a popular herb in the kitchen and has a multitude of uses. It works well in many dishes and is a staple of many cuisines.

Beauty Uses

Thyme has strong antifungal and antibacterial properties, meaning it can help to protect your skin from infections. Thyme oil works well against acne, scars, cuts and sores, even relieving burns and skin rashes. Combine thyme oil with witch hazel for an excellent anti-acne wash! Thyme is also high in antioxidants, which are essential in slowing the aging process and making your skin look good.

Mix thyme with lavender oil and apply it to your hair and it may well promote hair growth. A study, https://www.ncbi.nlm.nih.gov/pubmed/9828867, showed that participants had positive results after seven months of use.

Health Uses

Thyme has a significant positive effect on heart health. A study, https://www.ncbi.nlm.nih.gov/pubmed/28534268, showed thyme reduced cholesterol levels and reduced the heart rate in rats suffering with high blood pressure. Researchers recommend replacing salt in your diet with thyme to reduce your blood pressure and benefit your heart.

Research also indicates that thyme helps treat atherosclerosis, a form of cardiovascular disease, https://www.ncbi.nlm.nih.gov/pmc/articles/PMC3345235.

A study in Portugal, https://www.ncbi.nlm.nih.gov/pubmed/23285814, showed that thyme is particularly good at treating cancers and specifically, colon cancer. Researchers determined this was down to various constituents in thyme including ursolic acid, lutein, beta-sitosterol and oleanolic acid.

As well as this, research shows thyme to benefit breast cancer by increasing cancer cell death and that carvacrol, found in thyme essential oil, is effective at preventing the migration and proliferation of cancer cell lines, https://www.ncbi.nlm.nih.gov/pubmed/26214321.

Carvacrol is of particularly interest to researchers as it is an anti-inflammatory and appears to work in a similar manner to resveratrol, a compound found in red wine that is very beneficial to your health.

Thymol is another anti-inflammatory found in thyme and has been shown to ease the pain associated with gout and arthritis, https://www.ncbi.nlm.nih.gov/pmc/articles/PMC3418667/.

With high levels of vitamin C and its ability to support the creation of white blood cells, https://www.baylor.edu/content/services/document.php/156373.pdf, thyme is very good for boosting the immune system. A steam inhalation of thyme is excellent for combatting colds and flu.

Thyme is a carminative, reducing gas in your intestines, https://www.ncbi.nlm.nih.gov/pmc/articles/PMC4893422/. It also is an antispasmodic, so can relieve intestinal cramps too.

With high levels of vitamin A, thyme is beneficial for your eyes and vision, which is supported by research – https://www.ncbi.nlm.nih.gov/pmc/articles/PMC5087098/). Low levels of vitamin A are linked to night blindness and macular degeneration.

Thyme oil is an effective treatment against bacteria that is resistant to antibiotics, https://www.ncbi.nlm.nih.gov/pubmed/22313307, particularly in your mouth. Use thyme oil as a mouthwash by adding a drop to a cup of lukewarm water and rinsing your mouth. This helps everything from gingivitis to plaque to bad breath and more, https://www.ncbi.nlm.nih.gov/pmc/articles/PMC4054083/.

Pests, Problems & Diseases

Thyme is generally pest and disease free. Occasionally you will find mealybugs attacking thyme. These hide in leaf joints or under loose bark where they suck sap and secrete a honeydew which then causes black sooty mold to develop on the leaves. Treat these using biological controls and encourage their predators, ladybugs, into your garden to prevent the population growing out of hand.

Recommended Varieties

There are many varieties of thyme available. These are some of the more commonly grown cultivars.

- Common Thyme (*Thymus vulgaris*) – used in cooking, available with yellow, green or variegated foliage.
- Lemon Thyme (*Thymus x citriodorus*) – an upright plant with both golden and silver, variegated foliage with a strong lemon smell.
- Wooly Thyme (*Thymus pseudolanuginosus*) – grey stems and leaves, ideal for a rock garden due to its low form.
- Creeping Thyme (*Thymus praecox*) – known as mother-of-thyme, this cultivar only grows a couple of inches tall, producing white, crimson or mauve flowers depending on the variety.
- Wild Thyme (*Thymus serpyllum*) – available in upright or prostrate forms with flower colors from red to purple and leaves that can be green, variegated or gold, depending on the cultivar.
- Elfin Thyme (*Thymus serpyllum* 'Elfin') – a creeping variety growing no more than two inches tall. It has very fragrant leaves and pink or purple flowers. Ideal for rock gardens.
- *Thymus citriodorus* 'Archers Gold' – a mat forming, golden leafed variety with a lemon scent.
- *Thymus citriodorus* 'Variegata' – a variegated variety of lemon thyme with pink flowers in the summer months
- *Thymus nititdus* 'Peter Davis' – a mat forming thyme with strong smelling, grey/green leaves and pink flowers.

Recipes

Honey Mustard Salmon

This is an unusual way to serve salmon, but the glaze and thyme works very well with the fish. Try making this with lemon thyme for an interesting taste as the lemon really compliments the flavor of the salmon.

Ingredients:

- 4 x 6oz salmon fillets (skin removed)
- ¼ cup honey
- ¼ cup Dijon mustard
- ¼ cup whole-grain mustard
- 1 garlic clove (minced)

- 2 tablespoons soy sauce
- 1½ tablespoons thyme (chopped)
- Salt and pepper
- Canola oil

Method:

1. Mix the honey, mustards, garlic, thyme and soy sauce together in a medium sized bowl
2. Preheat an oiled grill pan
3. Brush the salmon fillets with oil and season to taste
4. Grill the salmon fillets on a medium heat for 3 minutes, turn and grill for a further 3 minutes
5. Generously brush both sides of the salmon with the honey mustard mixture
6. Grill for another minute on each side before serving

Chicken Thyme Salad

This is a lovely salad, great for any time of the year. Use common thyme or lemon thyme, which compliments the chicken very well. Serve with a nice, crusty bread.

Ingredients:

- 4 skinless and boneless chicken breasts (cut into strips)
- 1 garlic clove (crushed)
- Zest and juice of 1 lemon
- 1 small red onion (halved and thinly sliced)
- 5oz/150g mixed salad leaves
- 3 tablespoons oil
- Several sprigs of fresh thyme (leaves removed from stalks)
- Handful of black olives (pitted and halved)
- Salt and pepper

Method:

1. Add the chicken, thyme and lemon zest to a bowl, season well and mix thoroughly
2. Heat a tablespoons of oil in a pan and fry the chicken for 10 minutes, until evenly cooked
3. Spread the onion and salad on a serving platter
4. Add the olives and garlic to the pan and cook for a further minute
5. Remove from the heat
6. Add the remaining oil and lemon juice, stirring well

7. Arrange the chicken and dressing over the salad leaves and serve

Herby Roast Potatoes

These are a delicious take on the roast potato which is ideal for any holiday meal or family gathering. This takes about 40 minutes to make and will serve 8 to 10 people.

Ingredients:

- 4lb baby Yukon Gold (or similar) potatoes (halved)
- 3 tablespoons canola oil
- 1 tablespoon fresh thyme leaves (chipped)
- 2 teaspoons salt
- ½ teaspoon ground black pepper
- ½ teaspoon grated nutmeg (fresh is best)

Method:

1. Position your oven racks in the upper and lower thirds of the oven
2. Preheat the oven to 450F/230C
3. Rinse the potatoes
4. Place in a large bowl with the nutmeg, oil, thyme, salt and pepper and toss well
5. Arrange on rimmed baking sheets with the cut side down
6. Roast for 25 minutes, rotating the baking sheets front to back and top to bottom halfway through
7. When crispy and golden, serve

Raspberry and Thyme Hot Toddy

A wonderful, warming punch served warm after a meal or to welcome people to your home in cold weather. This certainly packs a punch, but is very warming. This recipe makes enough for 8 to 10 servings and takes about 20 minutes to make.

Ingredients:

- 4 English Breakfast tea bags
- 1 orange (thinly sliced)
- 1 lemon (thinly sliced)
- 1½ cups raspberry liqueur (e.g. Chambord)
- 1½ cups whiskey (rye is ideal)
- ¼ cup sugar
- ¼ cup fresh lemon juice
- 12 sprigs of time plus extra for serving

- 1 tablespoon cloves

Method:

1. Boil 10 cups of water in a large pan, reduce the heat and simmer
2. Add the lemon and orange slices, the teabags, cloves, thyme sprigs and cover
3. Simmer for 10 minutes
4. Remove from the heat and discard the tea bags
5. Stir in the raspberry liqueur, lemon juice and whiskey
6. Divide between mugs, garnish with thyme sprigs and serve

Buttered Sautéed Mushrooms

These are delicious and a great way to serve mushrooms. Use whichever mushrooms you prefer; this is a great opportunity to experiment with some of the more exotic mushrooms. This recipe serves four people and takes 15-20 minutes to make.

Ingredients:

- 16oz mushrooms (washed and sliced)
- ¼ cup shallots (finely chopped)
- ⅓ cup dry white wine
- 1 tablespoon butter
- 1 tablespoon canola oil
- 4 teaspoons fresh thyme (chopped)
- ¼ teaspoon salt

Method:

1. Melt the butter in a large pan on a medium to high heat
2. Add the oil and cook the shallots until tender, around 1-2 minutes
3. Add the salt and mushrooms and cook for 10-15 minutes until the mushrooms are brown and the liquid has evaporated
4. Add the wine and cook for another 2 minutes until the liquid has almost completely evaporated
5. Add the thyme, stir well and cook for another 30 seconds before serving

Turmeric

Turmeric, *Curcuma longa*, is a popular plant attributed with many health properties. Known as the 'Golden Goddess' to the Indians, the roots of this herb has been used in Ayurvedic medicine for thousands of years and is a key ingredient in Indian cuisine.

At a Glance Facts

~~Annual~~ / ~~Biennial~~ / **Perennial**	
Position:	Light shade
Soil:	Well-drained
Hardiness	No
USDA Zones:	8-11
Sow:	Spring
Harvest:	Late fall to early winter

Turmeric is relatively easy to grow, though does not tolerate cold weather. In a sunny spot it grows like crazy and has very attractive tropical foliage.

Turmeric is in the same family as ginger but has large green leaves, growing to over three feet tall. When mature, the plant sends up a spike of green/white or even pink flowers. This herb comes from a tropical environment and likes warm, humid conditions with a well-drained soil.

The roots are either used fresh or boiled in water for 30-45 minutes, then dried in ovens before being ground into the powder we see stocked in our supermarkets. It is popular in curries and is frequently used as a dye.

The precise origin of turmeric is not known, though it is believed to have started out somewhere in Southeast Asia. Nowadays, it is strongly associated with India which hosts 40-45 different species. Thailand, by comparison, is home to just 30-40 different species of turmeric.

Hindu monks dyed their robes yellow using turmeric, which is associated with the sun due to its yellow color. There are many traditions associated with turmeric as it has been used for thousands of years in Ayurvedic medicine.

Growing Instructions

Turmeric is grown from pieces of root, or rhizomes. Each 6-8 inch piece of root requires its own 14-18" container, though often they are started off in smaller containers and transplanted once they have some leaves. You can grow turmeric direct in the ground, but you need to live in an area with tropical weather. For most of us, it will be grown in containers indoors or in a greenhouse, only being placed outside on the hottest days.

The rhizome can be cut into smaller sections, so long as each part has two or three buds on it. Start the rhizomes off in 3" pots. Fill the pot two thirds of the way with a good quality soil, then lay the rhizome on its side flat before covering it with soil. Water the pot well, then put a plastic bag around the pot to act as a mini-greenhouse.

Place the pot in a warm location (86-95F/30-35C) to germinate. If the temperature is not warm enough, the turmeric will be slow to germinate or the rhizomes will rot.

Once the rhizome has germinated, remove the plastic bag, and move the pot to a warm, light location. Move the plant to a bigger pot once the plant is 6-8" tall. Keep the plant well watered and do not allow the soil to dry out as this will reduce your harvest.

Plant Care

When the plant has been transplanted, you can move them to a cooler location. Over a few weeks, the heat can be reduced to 70F/21C. Do not reduce the heat too rapidly otherwise it will shock the plant and stop it from growing. Turmeric will continue to grow so long as the temperature remains above 68F/20C.

When there is no risk of frost, turmeric can be moved outside, though do not leave it outside if the temperature is likely to drop too much at night. Position the containers in partial shade for a few days to prevent the leaves from getting scorched.

Feed turmeric every couple of weeks during the growing season using a root crop or potato fertilizer. If you make your own compost tea, this is ideal for turmeric.

When the stems and leaves start to turn brown, the roots are ready to harvest. This will be anywhere from seven to ten months after planting. Empty the plants out of the container, shake the soil from the rhizomes and cut the stems off about an inch above the rhizome mass. Wash the roots thoroughly before using or storing.

The rhizomes will remain fresh for up to six months when stored in an airtight bag or container in your refrigerator. The roots can also be frozen. Remember to keep some of the larger rhizomes to replant the following year.

Culinary Uses

Turmeric is extensively used in Eastern and Middle Eastern cuisine both for its taste and as a dye. In India, it is used to color many sweet dishes. In Moroccan cuisines, it is used to flavor meat, notably lamb, and vegetables, but it is best known for its use in curries, providing the yellow color curry powder is known for. It is common in fish curries as turmeric masks the smell of fish.

Turmeric is known as 'Indian Saffron' and is commonly used in place of saffron as the taste and color are very similar.

Fresh turmeric has a spicy, peppery and zesty flavor with a hint of ginger. When dried, the flavor is much milder.

It is easy to make your own turmeric powder. Boil clean rhizomes in water and simmer for as long as it takes for them to become soft enough that you can easily pierce them with a fork. Drain the liquid away and rub the skin off using your hands, though wait for them to cool a little first.

Dry them in the sun, on a low heat in an oven or in a food dehydrator set at 140F/60C until they are brittle and snap when you bend them. Then grind them into a powder. Note that it is worth wearing gloves throughout this process as the turmeric will dye your hands yellow!

Beauty Uses

Turmeric has several beauty uses as it is high in antioxidants and has anti-inflammatory properties.

Consuming turmeric helps to control psoriasis and reduces acne scarring or breakouts. You can use a turmeric face mask, which is very good for your skin, but can end up with your face looking a little yellow! Mixing turmeric with Greek yogurt and honey makes for an excellent face mask.

Before using turmeric on your skin, patch test it to make sure you are not allergic to it as it can irritate some people. As it can temporarily stain your skin, many people are not keen on using it on their face. While it has some positive beauty qualities, its ability to dye your skin means it is not commonly used.

Health Uses

Turmeric has been hailed as a superfood that can cure everything and everyone should be eating it. Science is heavily divided on this herb as, while some people claim it is a miracle plant, other researchers are finding that for it to have a positive effect, large amounts must be consumed.

Turmeric contains many beneficial compounds known as curcuminoids which are beneficial to your health. It also contains many other substances that has a positive effect on your wellbeing.

Curcumin is a compound found in turmeric that is a known anti-inflammatory. According to the Arthritis Foundation, turmeric helps with arthritis treatment by reducing and preventing joint inflammation, http://www.arthritis.org/living-with-arthritis/treatments/natural/supplements-herbs/guide/turmeric.php.

According to research, https://www.ncbi.nlm.nih.gov/pubmed/19594223, turmeric is as effective at reducing inflammation in arthritis sufferers as some of the drugs they are given. Research is also underway, https://www.ncbi.nlm.nih.gov/pubmed/17569207, to use these anti-inflammatory properties in the treatment of cancer.

As a strong antioxidant, turmeric has a variety of other benefits for the body. In a study performed on rats, https://www.ncbi.nlm.nih.gov/pubmed/18049430, turmeric prevented diabetes induced oxidative stress. These antioxidant properties also helps to improve memory and inhibits cell death, https://www.ncbi.nlm.nih.gov/pmc/articles/PMC4439456.

Turmeric provides protection for your brain and helps prevent beta-amyloids accumulating. These are destructive agents present in the brains of people suffering with Alzheimer's disease. According to research, turmeric can provide some help, http://articles.mercola.com/sites/articles/archive/2014/10/13/turmeric-curcumin.aspx.

Heavy metal poisoning is a major concern in today's society. Turmeric prevents neurotoxicity which comes from a build-up of metals such as lead or cadmium in your brain, https://www.ncbi.nlm.nih.gov/pmc/articles/PMC2781139/. Other studies show turmeric to be promising in reversing some Alzheimer's symptoms and reducing the risk of the consumer suffering from neurodegenerative diseases, http://firescholars.seu.edu/honors/23/.

In ancient Chinese and Indian medicine, turmeric was used to treat chest pain, usually caused by heart problems. Turmeric reduces bad cholesterol levels while increasing good cholesterol levels, https://www.ncbi.nlm.nih.gov/pubmed/19233493. It can also help prevent myocardial infarctions, https://www.ncbi.nlm.nih.gov/pmc/articles/PMC3083808/.

Cancer levels in countries that regularly consume turmeric have been found to be much lower. Early research shows turmeric has some anti-cancer properties, http://www.cancerresearchuk.org/about-cancer/cancer-in-general/treatment/complementary-alternative-therapies/individual-therapies/turmeric, and could become a promising future treatment. It appears turmeric can slow cancer growth and improve the effectiveness of chemotherapy while protecting health cells from radiation damage, http://www.mayoclinic.org/diseases-conditions/cancer/expert-answers/curcumin/faq-20057858.

The antibacterial and anti-inflammatory properties of turmeric make it a good treatment for acne and pimples. Mix a teaspoon of turmeric with three tablespoons of milk, two tablespoons of flour and a drizzle of honey to make a face mask that really helps improve your skin quality and reduce acne. The same mixture is also very effective in treating dry skin. This mixture is also good for burns, stretch marks and to reduce scarring as it heals the skin.

Pests, Problems & Diseases

The main problem with turmeric is rhizome rot that typically occurs in monsoon season between June and September. If you are growing turmeric in containers in a non-tropical area, you probably do not have to worry about monsoons, but do need to be careful the roots do not rot when germinating them.

A Turmeric Flower

Leaf spot is a soil-borne disease that manifests between July and October as brown spots on the top of young leaves. The spots will usually have white or gray centers. This is not likely to be a problem outside of turmeric's native habitat. Keep the ground around your plants free from plant debris and this should reduce any incidences of this disease.

Most of the diseases that turmeric suffers from are only going to be encountered when it is grown in its native environment. As the majority of people will be growing turmeric in containers outside of its normal, tropical habitat, these diseases are very unlikely to be encountered.

Recommended Varieties

There are a number of varieties of turmeric grown in India as commercial crops, usually bred to grow in certain conditions or to provide high yields. Outside of India, *Curcuma longa*, is the main variety grown by the home gardener, though you may occasionally find other varieties in specialist shops. You can usually plant turmeric root bought in shops and it will sprout. Specialist Asian shops may stock some of the more unusual varieties of turmeric

Recipes

Indian Golden Milk (Halda Ka Doodh)

Golden Milk is an Indian healing remedy dating back hundreds of years. It can be made with fresh root or dried powder, depending on what you have to hand.

Ingredients:

- 1 cup milk
- 4 black peppercorns
- 2 cloves
- Seeds from 2 cardamom pods
- ½" piece of fresh turmeric
- ¼" piece of fresh ginger
- Honey to taste

Method:

1. Crush the cloves, cardamom seeds and peppercorns using a mortar and pestle
2. Peel and finely chop both the ginger and turmeric root
3. Heat the milk in a small pan together with all the spices for 2-3 minutes
4. Allow to cool until warm, then strain into a cup
5. Sweeten to taste and then drink

Chicken Marinade

This is a simple marinade that is good for around 1lb/450g of chicken. Increase the quantities as required if you have more chicken to marinate.

Ingredients:

- 1 cup natural yogurt
- ¼ cup extra-virgin olive oil
- 1 garlic clove (minced)
- Juice of 1 lemon
- 1 teaspoon ground cumin
- 1 teaspoon salt
- 1 teaspoon turmeric root (grated)
- 1 teaspoon ginger root (grated)
- ½ teaspoon cayenne pepper

Method:

1. Mix all the ingredients together in a bowl until thoroughly combined
2. Add the chicken, rubbing the spices into the meat until it is evenly coated
3. Seal with plastic wrap or a lid and refrigerate for a minimum of 2 hours before cooking the chicken as normal

Bombay Potatoes

There are many regional variations of this dish, but the basic idea is frying potatoes in yogurt and spices, then cooking in your oven and serving as a dish. This recipe makes enough to serve four people and takes an hour and half to prepare and cook.

Ingredients:

- 1½lb/710g waxy potatoes (washed and peeled)
- ½ pint/285ml natural yogurt
- 2 tablespoons tomato puree
- 2 tablespoons vegetable ghee
- 3 teaspoons ground turmeric
- 1 teaspoon panch poran spice mix (or curry power)
- Chopped coriander
- Salt

Method:

1. Boil the potatoes in a pan of salted water for 10-15 minutes until they are just cooked, then drain and cool until you can handle them comfortably
2. In a separate saucepan, heat the ghee
3. Add the tomato puree, yogurt, turmeric and panch poran, then season to taste with salt
4. Gently simmer for 5 minutes, stirring regularly
5. Preheat your oven to 350F/180C
6. Quarter the potatoes
7. Add the potatoes to the pan with the yogurt and cook for a further 2-3 minutes
8. Transfer the mixture to an ovenproof casserole dish and cover using the lid
9. Cook in your oven for 35-45 minutes until the sauce has thickened and the potatoes are soft all the way through
10. Serve garnished with the chopped coriander

Vegetable Bhajis

These are a delicious take on the onion bhaji, but with other vegetables. The wide range of spices used to flavor this dish is common in Indian cooking. Ideally, cook these in a deep-fat fryer, but a large saucepan or deep frying pan will be okay. This produces enough for four people and takes around 55 minutes to prepare.

Ingredients:

- 6oz/170g gram flour
- 3½oz/100g cauliflower florets (lightly cooked)
- 1 small onion (halved and sliced)
- 1 small leek (sliced)
- 10-12 tablespoons cold water
- 2 tablespoons fresh cilantro (chopped)
- 2 teaspoons ground cilantro (coriander)
- 1½ teaspoons chilli powder
- 1½ teaspoons turmeric powder
- 1 teaspoon baking soda (bicarbonate of soda)
- 1 teaspoon garam masala
- Salt and pepper
- Vegetable oil for frying

Method:

1. Sift the baking soda and gram flour into a large bowl
2. Add the spices and cilantro, and add salt to taste, then mix very well
3. Divide the mixture into three different bowls
4. Add the onion to one bowl and mix
5. Add the leek to a second bowl, and mix
6. Add the cauliflower to the third bowl, and mix
7. Add 3-4 tablespoons of water to each bowl and mix until the flour becomes a paste
8. Heat the oil to 350F/175C
9. Shape the mixture in each bowl into small balls
10. Fry for 3-4 minutes until browned then drain on kitchen paper
11. Keep warm until they are all fried
12. Serve on the side or with a salad

Turmeric Smoothie

Turmeric is very popular at the moment as a superfood, and this smoothie makes a great way to get your daily intake of this spice.

Ingredients:

- 2 cups of carrots
- 1½ cups water
- 1 cup fresh pineapple
- 1 cup almond milk (unsweetened)
- ½ cup carrot juice
- 1 large ripe banana (peeled and sliced)
- 1 tablespoon lemon juice
- ½ tablespoon fresh ginger (peeled)
- ¼ teaspoon ground turmeric

Method:

1. Make the carrot juice by blending the carrots and water together to make a smooth mixture (add more water if necessary)
2. Strain the juice through cheese cloth
3. Add all the ingredients to your blender and blend until smooth
4. Add more carrot juice or almond milk as required and drink

Valerian

Common valerian, *Valeriana officinalis*, is a popular herb, commonly found in wild planting schemes, known for its ability to help with sleep. In early summer, it produces clusters of white to blue/pink flowers that are a great source of nectar for bees and pollinating insects.

At a Glance Facts

~~Annual~~ / ~~Biennial~~ / **Perennial**	
Position:	Full sun to partial shade
Soil:	Moist, well-drained
Hardiness	Yes, to 23F/-5C to 14F/-10C
USDA Zones:	4-9
Sow:	January to March
Harvest:	June to December

Native to Europe and Asia, valerian has been used medicinally since the ancient Greeks and Romans, if not before that. Hippocrates is known to have described the medicinal properties of valerian and the Roman, Galen, also prescribed valerian as a treatment for insomnia.

In the Middle Ages in England, the dried root of valerian was used in broths and stews because it benefited the health of the peasants. Valerian root was made into a tea and drank to protect against the plague and it proved useful in treating coughs, particularly when mixed with aniseed or liquorice.

Valerian is most commonly used today to combat sleep problems. Although it does grow in the wild across Europe, Asia and the USA, it is not commonly grown in the garden except for ornamental purposes.

Growing Instructions

Seeds can be started indoors or ready grown plants can be bought. Seedlings are planted out two to four weeks before the last frost in your area. Leave 3 feet/90cm between plants, with the same distance between rows as valerian will grow into an 18"/45cm wide clump after just a couple of years.

Valerian is great for attracting bees and butterflies, producing large clusters of flowers every year. It is good grown against a fence or wall at the back of a herb patch.

Plant in a sunny location as valerian likes at least six hours of sun per day in a nitrogen rich, well-drained but moist soil.

Plant Care

Valerian will self-seed and spread everywhere given half a chance. Remove the spent flowers to stop the plant producing seeds.

The roots are harvested in fall of the first year or early spring in the second year. Dig them up and dry outdoors as they give off a rather unpleasant smell while drying. Wash well before drying. Once dry, store in an airtight container. Be aware that cats and dogs are very fond of this root.

Valerian Root

Store the roots whole, roughly chopped or ground into a powder, depending on how you are planning on using the root.

Culinary Uses

Valerian is not used in the kitchen.

Beauty Uses

Valerian is not used for beauty purposes.

Health Uses

Valerian root is mainly used to treat sleep problems. It reduces the amount of time it takes to fall asleep and improves the quality of your sleep. Lots of research has been performed on valerian root and how it helps sleep, https://ods.od.nih.gov/factsheets/showterm.aspx?tID=177. One of the biggest advantages of this herb is that it does not have the addictiveness and withdrawal issues found with modern day sleeping tablets.

The research shows that valerian does take several weeks before it is truly effective, but benefits are felt within the first few days. Its effectiveness is shown that many people prefer to use it to traditional sleeping pills because valerian calms rather than sedates. This means that when you wake up the next morning you do not have the grogginess so often encountered from sleeping tablets. This feeling of being refreshed and properly rested is hugely beneficial to many people.

Researchers recommend that no more than 750mg should be taken before sleep as doses over this can cause drowsiness similar to those caused by prescription sleeping tablets.

Although research indicates valerian is beneficial for sleep, the opinion on valerian is still divided. More research is underway to learn more about the effectiveness of valerian in helping people sleep.

With its calming effect on the nervous system, valerian also has some antispasmodic benefits, helping to reduce abdominal cramps, particularly when caused by being nervous. As valerian acts like a mild tranquiliser, it is helpful in treating exhaustion and emotional stress. It has been used to wean patients off anti-depressants, though it is not recommended to attempt to do this without medical supervision.

Valerian has become very popular with women who are going through the menopause. Studies are showing that valerian reduces the frequency and severity of hot flushes by as much as 30% after 4 weeks and 50% after 8 weeks.

Although you can take supplements, many people prefer taking valerian as a tincture or tea, though the aroma of these has been likened to old socks so is not palatable to everyone.

Valerian is best taken an hour before bed, and it can take up to four weeks of daily supplements before the full effect are experienced. Expert advice is to take valerian in cycles so that the body does not get used to it and its affects are reduced. Every 10-12 weeks, stop talking valerian for about two weeks.

There are no major side effects reported for valerian, though there have been some reports of minor side effects such as headaches, dizziness, an upset stomach and itchiness. It is best not to take valerian if you are taking any tranquillizers or medication for depression. If you are on any prescription drugs, talk to your medical professional before starting to take valerian.

Pests, Problems & Diseases

Valerian does not suffer in particular from any pests, problems or diseases.

Recommended Varieties

There are over 150 species in the genus *Valeriana*, many of which are ornamental plants grown for their flowers. *Valeriana radix*, *Valeriana sambucifolia*, *Valeriana procurrens*, *Valeriana collina* and *Valeriana exalta* are used to prepare valerian supplements to aid sleep. *Valeriana wallichii* (from India and Pakistan) and *Valeriana edulis* (from Mexico) are used as daytime sedatives.

Recipes

Valerian Tea

This is a simple tea that you can use to help you sleep. Use a sweetener of choice with this.

Ingredients:

- 16oz boiling water
- 1 teaspoon dried valerian root

Method:

1. Steep the valerian for 3-4 minutes, then remove, sweeten to taste and drink

Sleepy Time Tea

This tea combines several herbs to make a tea that is very beneficial for sleep. Again, sweeten to taste using your preferred sweetener.

Ingredients:

- 2 teaspoons Kava-Kava
- 2 teaspoons catnip
- 1½ teaspoons ground valerian root
- 1⅓ teaspoons French tarragon
- 1 teaspoon parsley
- 1 teaspoon chamomile
- 1 teaspoon lavender
- ½ teaspoon dried hibiscus petals
- 4 cups of water

Method:

1. Pour boiling water over the herbs, steep for 3-4 minutes
2. Remove the herbs, sweeten to taste and serve

Witch Hazel

Witch hazel, *Hamamelis*, is a winter flowering shrub known for its spicy aroma and spidery yellow, orange and red flowers. It is a perfect addition to any garden for some winter color.

At a Glance Facts

~~Annual~~ / ~~Biennial~~ / **Perennial**	
Position:	Full sun to partial shade
Soil:	Moist, well-drained
Hardiness	Hardy, flowers are frost resistant
USDA Zones:	3-8
Sow:	Fall to winter
Harvest:	Spring to fall

The Latin name, *Hamamelis* comes from Greek, indicating the resemblance between witch hazel and an apple tree. In the USA, witch hazel bears nuts, but in the UK the tree does not bear seeds. When ripe, the seeds are violently ejected from the pods, giving this plant its nickname 'Snapping Hazel'.

'Witch' is from the old English word 'wych' which means this shrub has pliable branches, and had 'hazel' added as the leaves look similar to those of the hazel tree.

Growing Instructions

Witch hazel likes an open, sunny position, though will tolerate partial shade. In too much shade, the plants will become straggly. Do not plant in an exposed or windy location as the plant will not like it.

When young, witch hazel is susceptible to frost damage, so avoid frost pockets or protect your plants with fleece in their first few years.

The soil needs to be free-draining, but moist with plenty of organic matter. Witch hazel can be planted in heavy or clay soils, though dig in plenty of organic matter and improve the drainage first.

Most witch hazel trees are store bought as it can be tricky to propagate this plant at home. Commercial cultivars are usually budded or grafted on to a *Hamamelis virginiana* root stock, which is typically raised from seed.

Softwood cuttings are taken in spring and planted in a free draining compost, but are usually difficult to root and keep alive. Provide bottom heat of 68F/20C and cover the cutting with a clear polythene tent and the plant will root, if at all, in eight to ten weeks. Keep them indoors in the cutting compost until the following spring and then plant into potting compost. Layering can work with witch hazel for some extra plants.

Plant Care

When young and still establishing itself, witch hazel needs a lot of watering. It can get too dry in both winter and summer, which causes the flowers to fall. A good mulch applied in later winter or early spring will help retain moisture at the roots.

Top dress with a balanced fertilizer in late winter or early spring. Apart from this, feeding should not be necessary.

Little pruning is required unless you are restricting the growth of the plants or training them into a shape. If left to grow naturally, you can leave them to it and only prune out dead or damaged wood or crossed, weak or congested shoots.

Once the leaves have fallen, remove any suckers coming from below the graft point. Cut these flush with the main trunk as these will not be the variety you have planted, but from the rootstock, which is usually *Hamamelis virginiana*.

When the flowers have died back, prune back last year's growth, if required, to two leaf buds. Leaf buds are long and narrow while flower buds are more rounded. Try to avoid removing flower buds. Pruning like this encourages more growth and for flower buds to form at the base of these new shoots. A witch hazel tree can be fan trained if necessary.

The plant is harvested either in fall or in spring, it is up to you as to which is most convenient. Avoid harvesting more than 20% of a single tree in any one year to ensure the tree has enough energy to survive and regrow. Cut smaller branches off close to the base of the branch. If you can, leave a raised ridge or branch collar where you make the cut to help the tree heal faster.

Remove leaves and flowers from the harvested branches and cut the twigs into 2" long sections. Finally, strip the bark, including the under layer (which is moist), then discard the woody core.

Harvested bark can be used immediately or dried for use later in the year. Dry by spreading in a single layer on cardboard or screens in a dry, airy place. Once fully dry, store in airtight containers in a dry, dark place.

Culinary Uses

Witch hazel is not used in the kitchen in modern times. The Native Americans did eat the nutty seeds, but this is no longer very popular.

Beauty Uses

Witch hazel is popular in beauty products because it has strong antibacterial action and is an astringent, used instead of acetone. It is an excellent facial toner and the oil can be used directly on cotton balls for acne, spots of blemishes to dry them up. Witch hazel has the same effect when applied directly to cold sores, plus it speeds up their healing.

Witch hazel is very good for treating scalp irritation and for reducing inflammation and pain with haemorrhoids. Apply cotton pads soaked in witch hazel to the area under your eyes to reduce dark circles and bags. Witch hazel compresses reduce pain from bruises and speeds healing.

Mix aloe vera gel with witch hazel to treat sunburn. Alternatively, add two cups of witch hazel of bath water to sooth swelling and pain from sunburn.

Health Uses

Although inflammation is part of your normal immune response to protect your body against injury, chronic inflammation is believed to be a key component in the development of some diseases. Witch hazel contain anti-inflammatory compounds including gallic acid and tannins, as well as antioxidants. This makes witch hazel ideal for treating a wide variety of inflammatory issues including acne, psoriasis and eczema.

Studies show that witch hazel supresses erythema, which is the reddening of the skin from irritation or injury by almost a third, https://www.ncbi.nlm.nih.gov/pubmed/9621139. Using a 10% solution of witch hazel and skin lotion was found to reduce inflammation and erythema, https://www.ncbi.nlm.nih.gov/pubmed/11867970/).

Its use in treating haemorrhoids has been researched, https://www.ncbi.nlm.nih.gov/books/NBK279466/), with initial results proving it to be beneficial in reducing swelling and inflammation. Witch hazel also has hemostatic properties, so can help stop bleeding from hemmorrhoids, https://www.ncbi.nlm.nih.gov/pubmed/11302778. Research is still underway; though early indicators are promising.

Witch hazel helps in reducing scalp irritation. In one study of 1373 people, witch hazel extract was proved effective, https://www.ncbi.nlm.nih.gov/pmc/articles/PMC4158622/. As it reduces inflammation, it is helpful in reducing scalp sensitivity from conditions such as eczema and psoriasis.

Witch hazel contains high levels of tannins, which makes it a strong, natural antioxidant. The extract acts as a barrier on your skin, preventing substances that cause inflammation from getting into your skin, https://www.ncbi.nlm.nih.gov/pubmed/29211928. A test-tube study showed that witch hazel also stopped skin cancer cells from spreading, https://www.ncbi.nlm.nih.gov/pubmed/18311930. An animal study showed witch hazel slowed skin tumor growth too, https://www.ncbi.nlm.nih.gov/pubmed/10965522. Few human studies have been performed at the time of writing, but more research is required to understand these potentially exciting properties of witch hazel.

Pests, Problems & Diseases

Rabbit and deer are a common problem in rural areas, so you will have to protect your plants from these creatures. When grown in containers, vine weevil larvae are sometimes a problem.

Although you may occasionally experience powdery mildew on the leaves, root diseases such as honey fungus and *Phytophothora* root rot are the most common issues for *Hamamelis* plants.

Recommended Varieties

There are a number of varieties of witch hazel, with the main difference being the color of the flowers and leaves. These are some of the most common varieties:

- Virginian Witch Hazel (*Hamamelis virginiana*) – usually grows to 16 feet/5m high, but has been known to grow up to 32 feet/10m tall in some situations. The oval, nearly round leaves, grow up to 6"/15cm long, opening as a light green and turning darker green as the season progresses. The flowers appear from mid to late fall and are slightly twisted with pale yellow petals. This cultivar can be grown from seed, but may take two years to germinate. This is the species that medicinal witch hazel extract is made from.
- Chinese Witch Hazel (*Hamamelis mollis*) – a large, deciduous shrub producing a show of yellow leaves in winter and strong smelling, bright gold colored flowers in late winter. Propagate by seed, by grafting in late winter or you can use chip budding towards the end of summer.
- *Hamamemlis x intermedia* 'Jelena' – a cultivar with copper-orange flowers towards the end of winter and a red/yellow leaf display in fall.
- *Hamamelis x intermedia* 'Pallida' – has yellow leaves in fall and bright sulfur yellow flowers with a subtle scent in late winter.
- *Hamamelis x intermedia* 'Orange Beauty' – a vigorous plant with young leaves that are yellowy/green with a maroon flush, turning dark green in summer and then yellow and orange in fall. The strongly scented flowers appear mid to late winter and have dark purple/red calyces with a yellow orange petals and a reddish-purple tint at the base.

- *Hamamelis* × *intermedia* 'Diane' – lovely, light scented red flowers from mid to late winter, growing up to 8 feet/2.5m tall.

Recipes

Witch Hazel Water

This is an easy way to make the astringent found in pharmacies. The final product is stored in your refrigerator unless you add alcohol, in which case it can be stored at room temperature. You can make this in your slow cooker if you prefer, rather than having your cooker on for a long time.

Ingredients:

- ½lb dried witch hazel bark or 1lb fresh bark
- Distilled water
- Vodka (optional)

Method:

1. Place the bark in a large stainless steel saucepan or jam pot
2. Cover with distilled water and boil
3. Reduce the heat and simmer for 8 hours, checking every hour and adding more water as required to keep the bark covered
4. Turn the heat off and leave to cool
5. Strain through cheesecloth, keeping the water and discarding the bark
6. Add vodka (or other similar alcohol) to make the liquid shelf-stable. Add 1 third as much vodka as you have witch hazel water, i.e. if you have 3 cups of water, add 1 cup of vodka
7. Store in sealed glass jars or bottles

Make Up Remover

This is a simple make up remover that looks after your skin while removing your makeup.

Ingredients:

- ½ tablespoon witch hazel
- ¼ teaspoon olive or coconut oil

Method:

1. Mix ingredients together in a small glass jar
2. Shake well before use as the oil will rise
3. Apply using cotton wool

Air Freshener
This spicy air freshener will cut through bad smells, even those as strong as freshly cut onions!

Ingredients:

- 1 cup witch hazel water
- ½ cup bay leaves (crushed)
- ¼ cup dried sage

Method:

1. Mix the ingredients together well in a large jar
2. Cover and leave at room temperature for 3 days
3. Strain the herbs out of the liquid
4. Pour into a spray bottle and use as required

Witch Hazel Lotion
This can be used as an astringent or as a cold compress if you are running a temperature. It will keep for up to 5 days if tightly covered and kept in your refrigerator.

Ingredients:

- 2 cups water
- ½ cup rubbing alcohol
- ¼ cup fresh witch hazel leaves

Method:

1. Rinse the leaves well and chop coarsely
2. Boil the water in an enamel or glass saucepan
3. Add the leaves and simmer for 15 minutes
4. Remove from the heat and steep until cool
5. Strain, discard the leaves and stir the alcohol into the water

Dandruff Hair Rinse
This simple rinse will relieve itching and stop a flaky scalp. When not in use, store in a sealed jar in your refrigerator.

Ingredients:

- 1 cup witch hazel water
- 1 tablespoon dried lavender
- 1 tablespoon dried rosemary
- 1 tablespoon comfrey root (dried)

Method:

1. Mix all the ingredients together in a bowl
2. Cover and steep for 2 days
3. Strain off the herbs and discard them
4. Massage the remaining liquid into your scalp, leave to dry and then shampoo your hair

Witch Hazel General Purpose Cleaner

This simple cleaning solution is great for any cleaning around your home. Try adding a few drops of lemon or orange essential oil to give this an even better smell.

Ingredients:

- ½ cup baking soda
- 4oz dishwashing liquid
- 2oz water
- 2oz witch hazel water
- 1 teaspoon tea tree extract

Method:

1. Put all the ingredients into a spray bottle and shake well
2. Spray on surfaces, then wipe with a damp cleaning rag

Yarrow

Common yarrow, *Achillea millefolium*, or milfoil as it is sometimes known, is native to the UK, USA, Asia and Europe where it grows in the wild almost anywhere.

At a Glance Facts

~~Annual~~ / ~~Biennial~~ / **Perennial**	
Position:	Full sun
Soil:	Moist, well-drained
Hardiness	Fully Hardy
USDA Zones:	3-9
Sow:	Spring
Harvest:	Summer to fall

The wild plant bears white flowers, though sometimes there is a hint of pink. Domestic cultivars are available in a wide variety of colors from red to pink and yellow to white.

Yarrow is very attractive to butterflies and the flowers are often cut and dried. It is both pest and drought resistant, plus it is an aromatic herb with centuries of use as a healing herb.

One of its best known uses is with the Chinese divination system known as the I-Ching. Bundles of 64 yarrow sticks are used to tell the future. This herb has been popular with herbalists for a long time, mainly for its ability to slow and stop blood flow, hence its old name of woundwort.

Humans have been using yarrow for thousands of years. Archeologists discovered fossilized yarrow pollen in caves in Iraq inhabited by Neanderthal man over 60,000 years ago!

More recently, yarrow has roots in Ancient Greece. According to Greek mythology, the hero Achilles was dipped in yarrow tea by his mother to make him invincible. She held him by his ankle to dip him, and as everyone knows, Achilles was killed in the Troyan war when an arrow hit that part of his ankle. Since then, yarrow has been used on the battlefield to staunch wounds.

Growing Instructions

Plant yarrow in average to poor, but well-drained soil in the spring. This herb thrives in hot and dry conditions, disliking wet soil. When grown in rich soil, yarrow can get a bit overenthusiastic and will require staking to stop it falling over.

Plants are spaced one to two feet apart and will grow anywhere from two to four feet tall, depending on the cultivar. Yarrow will establish itself very quickly and spread. Be aware that some cultivars are very aggressive growers and will take over the area they are planted in, crowding out other plants. It is considered a weed in many places and grows freely in the wild.

Start yarrow from seed indoors between six and eight weeks before the last frost in your area. Sow the seeds in normal potting compost and cover lightly with soil. Keep the soil moist and place in a warm, sunny area. The seeds will germinate in anywhere from 14 to 21 days. Germination can be improved by covering the pots with plastic wrap and then removing it when the seeds have sprouted.

Plant out in full sun after the last frost date.

Plant Care

Each spring, mulch your plants to a depth of around 2" and give them a feed with something like pelleted chicken manure. They are not greedy plants and grow wild in scrubland, meadows and disused areas.

Yarrow is relatively drought tolerant, but will require watering if the weather is unusually hot.

Yarrow clumps need dividing every three to five years in fall or early spring. Lift the clumps, remove any dead growth and divide the clump as required. Replant each division in an appropriate location.

Harvest yarrow on a sunny day, when the essential oils are at their peak. The stems are tough and best cut with scissors. Remove the flowers tops and leaves, dry in a cool dark place then store for up to a year in an airtight container.

Culinary Uses

Today, yarrow has virtually no culinary uses, yet in the 1600s, it was a popular vegetable, with the leaves being cooked and eaten like spinach. Yarrow is similar in flavor to tarragon and can be used as a substitute if you run out of tarragon.

The flavor of yarrow is destroyed by prolonged or high heating, so it is best used in cold preparations such as salads, marinades or vinaigrettes mixed with parsley.

Beauty Uses

Yarrow is a very strong astringent, shrinking the skin and promoting healing. It is very useful for anyone who suffers with oily skin, scarring or acne as it will control the production of sebum. It is very good at tightening the skin to prevent sagging and for reducing visible fine lines.

The oils in yarrow have strong anti-inflammatory properties, so is ideal for treating swollen spots or reddened skin. It is good for anyone who suffers from eczema, rosacea or acne.

Yarrow also has antiseptic and antifungal properties, meaning it will protect wounds from infection. It will balance the pH levels of your skin and help reduce rashes and pimples. Used in a body lotion or oil, yarrow will soften and soothe your skin, nourishing it so it looks fantastic.

Your hair will also benefit from a yarrow treatment as it promotes hair growth and keeps your scalp healthy. It is also very beneficial for anyone that suffers with oily hair.

Health Uses

Traditionally, herbalists used yarrow for treating wounds. Yarrow powder was sprinkled onto wounds to relieve pain and stop bleeding, http://www.ncbi.nlm.nih.gov/pmc/articles/PMC2077876. It is a natural antiseptic and helps to protect wounds from infection. If you look closely at the ingredients of many commercial healing ointments, they will contain some yarrow.

Researchers discovered that yarrow has a similar effect to diazepam (Valium) for treating anxiety issues. The study proved yarrow was effective even in the short-term http://www.ncbi.nlm.nih.gov/pubmed/?term=yarrow%2C+insomnia.

As an anti-inflammatory, yarrow is used to treat the breast infection mastitis. Leaf poultices are particularly effect at provided virtually instant pain relief and for healing sore or cracked nipples, http://www.storknet.com/cubbies/breast/naturalremediespt2.htm.

Yarrow has a place in Indian and Chinese medicine where it has been used for centuries to treat inflammation, particularly of the female reproductive system and intestines, http://www.ncbi.nlm.nih.gov/pmc/articles/PMC3834722.

With antispasmodic properties, yarrow is helpful for treating issues such as cramping, flatulence and diarrhea by reducing muscle spasms, http://www.ncbi.nlm.nih.gov/pmc/articles/PMC3608287.

In 2013, a study showed that yarrow could improve breathing, relax blood vessels and reduce high blood pressure. It was also shown to be effective in treating asthma, http://www.ncbi.nlm.nih.gov/pubmed/20857434.

Pregnant women should avoid yarrow as it can stimulate the uterus. Taking too much of the herb internally has been known to cause headaches. Some people will experience skin irritation from prolonged external use.

Pests, Problems & Diseases

Yarrow is susceptible to a few diseases and pests, namely aphids, spittlebugs, powdery mildew and botrytis mold, the last two are both treated with fungicides.

Recommended Varieties

There are a number of cultivars available as ornamental plants if you want something more interesting than common yarrow including:

- Coronation Gold – has silvery gray leaves and mustard yellow flowers
- The Beacon – produces deep red flowers that have yellow middles
- Cerise Queen – produces bright pink flowers

Recipes

Yarrow Tea

A simple way to drink and benefit from this powerful herb.

Ingredients:

- 1 heaped tablespoon yarrow
- 1 cup boiling water
- Sweetener of choice

Method:

1. Put the yarrow in a tea ball and place in a large cup
2. Fill with hot water, cover and steep for 10-15 minutes
3. Sweeten to taste and drink

Endnote

Herbs have a whole host of uses in your garden from attracting pollinating insects, to culinary, health and beauty uses and let's not forget, a lot of them look fantastic!

In general, herbs are easy to grow and for those that are hard to germinate, you can usually buy the part-grown plants from a local nursery or plant store. Many supermarkets now stock living herbs very cheaply and these can usually be planted outdoors after they have been hardened off and adjusted to sunlight.

Every gardener should be growing some herbs. Fresh herbs are great in the kitchen and as you start to experiment with the healing and beauty properties of herbs, you realize how incredibly useful these plants are. With the rising cost of medical care and the risk of side effects and adverse reactions to modern medicine, there is a resurgence of interest in the healing properties of herbs. Today, a lot of the traditional uses of herbs have been backed up by scientific research, showing that they are effective treatments for many conditions. Of course, for any serious complaints you should not self-medicate and must seek professional medical advice.

If you are on any prescribed medication, then be careful taking herbs as many of them can interact with these medicines and change their effect or render them useless. If you have been prescribed any medication, no matter what it is, then talk to your doctor before taking herbs medicinally as they could negatively interact with your medication. Some herbs boost estrogen production and can stop the birth control pill working, whereas others stop anti-depressants working or allow drugs like lithium to build up in your system to potentially harmful levels.

Growing herbs is incredibly rewarding. I love having fresh herbs on my windowsill and at my kitchen door for use in meals. It is great to be able to make a herbal poultice for an injury or drink fresh herbal tea.

You have learned a lot about herbs in this book, from what they are to how to use them and now you can start planning out your herb garden. Think about the herbs that you regularly buy from the supermarket to use in your kitchen and start by planting them. As you gain more experience, start growing new herbs to use in your cooking. Then try making some into tea as a change from coffee or black tea. Many herbal teas have a delicious flavor and you can combine different herbs to make a tea specifically for you.

I keep all my dried herbs separate and then combine them to make a tea based on what I want it to do for me. This allows you to benefit from the herbs and keep yourself feeling fantastic.

Remember when planting herbs together to ensure they have the right soil conditions. The biggest problem people have when growing herbs is planting herbs with very different environmental requirements together. Planting a herb that loves a dry soil in the same container with one that likes a moist soil is a recipe for disaster as one of the herbs, if not both, will die off. This is by far the most common complaint I hear from people trying to grow their own herbs.

Whether you grow herbs indoors or outdoors, in large quantities or small, is entirely up to you. Herbs are wonderful plants and you have had an introduction into some of the most popular and commonly used culinary and healing herbs. There are many more herbs out there plus many of those listed here have a wide variety of cultivars that may not have healing properties or be edible, but look fantastic! There is no reason that a herb garden should be drab and boring. In fact, many herb gardens are alive with insects and abundant in color from the purple flowers of chives to the blue of borage and the orange of calendula.

Your herbs can be frozen or dried to store, so you can enjoy your herbs all year round. Literally nothing needs go to waste.

Growing your own herbs is very beneficial for you because you are reducing your environmental footprint by not buying herbs that have been transported to supermarkets. You recycle glass jars for storage, reducing the garbage from your home. Your home-grown herbs will also be free from pesticides and chemicals and you will know exactly what has gone onto the herbs.

I strongly recommend growing your own herbs at home, even if it is just a few like basil, parsley, chives and cilantro; popular herbs, regularly used in the kitchen. You have learned everything you need to know about growing your own herbs and now is the time to go out and start growing! Whether you grow in containers or in the ground is up to you, but enjoy growing and using your own herbs.

Please share pictures of your herb garden with me on Instagram or Twitter as @Allotmentowner. If you have enjoyed this book, then please leave a review on Amazon as I appreciate the feedback and love to hear from my readers. You can contact me through me website, www.gardeningwithjason.com.

Glossary

Annual
A plant that completes its entire lifecycle, i.e. from germination to flowering to producing seeds and to dying in a single growing season.

Bareroot
Plants that have been grown in a nursery by a supplier and are provided in a dormant state with no soil on the roots, e.g. roses, currant or raspberry bushes.

Biennial
A plant that completes its entire lifecycle over two years. In the first year, it grows and in the second it produces flowers, then seeds and dies, e.g. foxglove.

Bolting
To flower and go to seed prematurely.

Broadcast sowing
Scattering seeds, usually by hand, over the soil rather than planting in drills or rows; usually done with wildflower or grass seed.

Calyces
The sepals of a flower, usually green and forms a whorl enclosing the petals and provides protection to a flower in bud.

Cloche
A structure, usually glass or plastic, but can be made from horticultural fleece. These are placed over plants or seeds to protect the plant from frost and keep the soil warm.

Cold Frame
An unheated glass or plastic frame, sometimes half made from bricks, that is used to start seeds off and to harden off outdoor plants.

Cordon
A plant trained to grow as a single main stem, though occasionally refers to plants with two or three main stems such as apple trees or tomato plants. Usually you have to prune the side shoots.

Corm
Similar to a bulb, this consists of a stem base, usually with a fibrous outer layer such as begonias and saffron.

Crown
The growing point where new shoots emerge, either at or just below the soil level, e.g. asparagus.

Cultivar
A variety of a plant specifically grown for its unique flowers, foliage color, disease/pest resistance, growing habit and so on. It has different characteristics from the original species.

Deciduous
A plant that sheds its leaves at the end of the growing season and renews them at the start of the next.

Direct Sow
To sow seeds in the position where you want them to flower or crop outdoors, i.e. in their final positions.

Drill
A straight, narrow furrow in the soil in which you sow seeds or plant seedlings.

Evergreen
Plants that keep the majority of their leaves all year round.

Ericaceous
Describes plants that do not like alkaline soils and need an acidic soil to grow, e.g. blueberries.

F1 Hybrid
The first generation plant bred from two distinct pure-bred lines. Usually they are uniform and vigorous plants, often with a degree of disease resistance and good for exhibiting. F1 seeds are not true to their parents so are not worth saving.

Foliage
Refers to the leaves of a plant.

Genus
A taxonomic category used in plant and animal naming. Always capitalized and ranks above species and below family.

Germination
The act of a seed turning from a seed into a plant.

Grafting
Artificially joining the rootstock of one plant with a piece of wood from another to create a single plant with the rooting properties of the rootstock and the fruiting properties of the other piece of wood. Commonly done with fruit trees to create dwarf cultivars.

Half-Hardy Annual
A plant that completes its life cycle from germination to seeding and death in a single growing season. It can be grown outside but does not tolerate temperatures below 32F/0C and requires protection from frosts.

Half-Hardy Biennial
Tolerates cold in the same way as the above, but as it is a biennial, it grows in the first season and reproduces and dies in the second, providing the winter does not kill it.

Half-Hardy Bulb/Corm/Rhizome/Tuber
Grows like a normal bulb/corm/rhizome or tuber, usually supplied dormant with no top growth. These can be grown outside, but will require protection during winter from temperatures below 32F/0C and from frosts.

Half-Hardy Perennial
A perennial plant that requires protection during winter from temperatures below 32F/0C and from frosts.

Harden Off
Acclimatizing young plants that have been grown indoors or under glass to being outside. Achieved by moving plants outside during the day and then bringing them back under cover at night.

Hardy Annual
An annual plant that can tolerate outdoor winter temperatures as low as 5F/-15C.

Hardy Biennial
A biennial plant that can tolerate outdoor winter temperatures as low as 5F/-15C.

Hardy Perennial
A perennial plant that can tolerate outdoor winter temperatures as low as 5F/-15C.

Herbaceous Plant
A non-woody perennial, usually dies back in winter to become dormant. Grows back from a woody base or underground rootstock in spring.

Lime
A calcium compound applied to the soil to make it more alkaline (i.e. lower the pH level). Useful to prevent brassicas from contracting club root diseases.

Medium
A growing material for plants.

Mulch
A layer of compost, gravel, well-rotted manure or plastic sheeting, placed on top of the soil around the base of plants. This helps to improve the soil, feed the plants (in the case of compost and manure), suppress weeds and help the soil retain moisture.

Organic Matter
Plant or animal matter such as leaf mold, manure or compost, that is dug into the soil to feed the plants and improve the soil.

Perennial
A plant that lives for three or more years, e.g. asparagus

Pinching Out
Removing the growing tips of a plant to encourage side shoots and bushier growth. This results in more flowering stems and ultimately, more fruit.

Pollination
Transferring pollen between flowers. Usually performed by insects, animals or the wind (e.g. sweetcorn), it is performed by hand when breeding plants or sometimes when growing in a greenhouse if there is a lack of pollinating insects near the plant.

Pot On
Removing a plant from one pot, usually because it has outgrown the pot, and moving it to a large container so it can continue to grow.

Pot Up
To put cuttings or seedlings into a container to allow them to grow on.

Prick Out
To remove seedlings from a seed tray and transfer them to modules or pots so they have more space to grow. Done to prevent overcrowding and stunted growth.

Propagate
To grow more of one plant, either from saving and planting seeds or through cuttings or grafting.

Raceme
A flower cluster that has separate flowers attached for short stalks of equal length at equal distances on a central stem. Typically, the flowers at the base of the central stem are the first to develop.

Rhizome
A mass of roots such as those found in ginger and turmeric. Can usually be divided and new plants grown from the rhizomes.

Rootball
The roots and soil around the roots when a plant is lifted from the ground or removed from its container.

Rosette
A cluster of leaves, usually at ground level, radiating out from roughly the same point

Rootstock
The roots of a plant. In grafting, the scion (plant) is grafted on to a rootstock, which is the roots and a length of main trunk.

Self-Fertile
Refers to a plant that does not require pollination from another plant.

Semi-Evergreen
A plant that keeps all or some of its leaves all year round.

Semi-ripe Cutting
Where the cutting has not reached seasonal maturity, but is too mature to be used as a softwood cutting. The base of the cutting will be turning woody (lignifying) and the tip will still be soft.

Senescence
The period of a plants life where it has passed maturity but before it dies off. The plant has lower levels of chlorophyll, which means carbohydrate production reduces. In annual plants, this takes place within a year and in biennials, it takes place in the second year. This often results in fewer flowers and fruits, but some plants increase production to ensure survival of the species. Senescence is not reversible. This can be triggered by temperature, day length, water supply and more.

Standard
A tree or shrub, such as bay or roses, that has been trained to certain height with a long, bare stem and the foliage at the top.

Tender Annual
An annual plant that cannot tolerate temperatures below 41F/5C.
Tender Biennial
A biennial plant that cannot tolerate temperatures below 41F/5C.

Tender Perennial
A perennial plant that cannot tolerate temperatures below 41F/5C.

Thin
Refers to the act of removing seedlings, shoots, flowers, fruit or buds to improve the viability, growth and quality of those you leave. For example, you thin your carrots which are difficult to sow with sufficient space between them, eat the thinnings and then the remaining carrots have the space to grow to maturity.

ABOUT JASON

Jason has been a keen gardener for over twenty years, having taken on numerous weed infested patches and turned them into productive vegetable gardens.

One of his first gardening experiences was digging over a 400 square foot garden in its entirety and turning it into a vegetable garden, much to the delight of his neighbors who all got free vegetables! It was through this experience that he discovered his love of gardening and started to learn more and more about the subject.

His first encounter with a greenhouse resulted in a tomato infested greenhouse but he soon learnt how to make the most of a greenhouse and now grows a wide variety of plants from grapes to squashes to tomatoes and more. Of course, his wife is delighted with his greenhouse as it means the windowsills in the house are no longer filled with seed trays every spring.

He is passionate about helping people learn to grow their own fresh produce and enjoy the many benefits that come with it, from the exercise of gardening to the nutrition of freshly picked produce. He often says that when you've tasted a freshly picked tomato you'll never want to buy another one from a store again!

Jason is also very active in the personal development community, having written books on self-help, including subjects such as motivation and confidence. He has also recorded over 80 hypnosis programs, being a fully qualified clinical hypnotist which he sells from his website www.MusicForChange.com.

He hopes that this book has been a pleasure for you to read and that you have learned a lot about the subject and welcomes your feedback either directly or through an Amazon review. This feedback is used to improve his books and provide better quality information for his readers.

Jason also loves to grow giant and unusual vegetables and is still planning on breaking the 400lb barrier with a giant pumpkin. He hopes that with his new allotment plot he'll be able to grow even more exciting vegetables to share with his readers.

Other Books By Jason

Please check out my other gardening books on Amazon, available on Kindle and paperback.

Canning and Preserving at Home – A Complete Guide to Canning, Preserving and Storing Your Produce
A complete guide to storing your home-grown fruits and vegetables. Learn everything from how to freeze your produce to canning, making jams, jellies, and chutneys to dehydrating and more. Everything you need to know about storing your fresh produce, including some unusual methods of storage, some of which will encourage children to eat fresh fruit!

Container Gardening - Growing Vegetables, Herbs & Flowers in Containers
A step by step guide showing you how to create your very own container garden. Whether you have no garden, little space or you want to grow specific plants, this book guides you through everything you need to know about planting a container garden from the different types of pots, to which plants thrive in containers to handy tips helping you avoid the common mistakes people make with containers.

Greenhouse Gardening - A Beginners Guide To Growing Fruit and Vegetables All Year Round
A complete, step by step guide to owning your own greenhouse. Learn everything you need to know from sourcing greenhouses to building foundations to ensuring it survives high winds. This handy guide will teach you everything you need to know to grow a wide range of plants in your greenhouse, including tomatoes, chilies, squashes, zucchini and much more. Find out how you can benefit from a greenhouse today, they are more fun and less work than you might think!

Growing Fruit: The Complete Guide to Growing Fruit At Home
This is a complete guide to growing fruit from apricots to walnuts and everything in between. You will learn how to choose fruit plants, how to grow and care for them, how to store and preserve the fruit and much more. With recipes, advice and tips this is the perfect book for anyone who wants to learn more about growing fruit at home, whether beginner or experienced gardener.

Growing Garlic – A Complete Guide to Growing, Harvesting & Using Garlic
Everything you need to know to grow this popular plant. Whether you are growing normal garlic or elephant garlic for cooking or for health, you will find this book contains all the information you need. Traditionally a difficult crop to grow with a long growing season, you'll learn the exact conditions garlic needs, how to avoid the common problems people encounter and how to store your garlic for use all year round. A complete, step-by-step guide showing you precisely how to grow garlic at home.

Growing Giant Pumpkins – How to Grow Massive Pumpkins At Home
A complete step by step guide detailing everything you need to know to produce pumpkins weighing hundreds of pounds, if not edging into the thousands! Anyone can grow giant pumpkins at home and this book gives you the insider secrets of the giant pumpkin growers showing you how to avoid the mistakes people commonly make when trying to grow a giant pumpkin. This is a complete guide detailing everything from preparing the soil to getting the right seeds to germinating the seeds and caring for your pumpkins.

Growing Tomatoes: Your Guide to Growing Delicious Tomatoes At Home
This is the definitive guide to growing delicious and fresh tomatoes at home. Teaching you everything from selecting seeds to planting and caring for your tomatoes as well as diagnosing problems this is the ideal book for anyone who wants to grow tomatoes at home. A comprehensive must have guide.

How to Compost – Turn Your Waste into Brown Gold
This is a complete step by step guide to making your own compost at home. Vital to any gardener, this book will explain everything from setting up your compost heap to how to ensure you get fresh compost in just a few weeks. A must have handbook for any gardener who wants their plants to benefit from home-made compost.

How To Grow Potatoes - The Guide To Choosing, Planting and Growing in Containers Or the Ground
Learn everything you need to know about growing potatoes at home. Discover the wide variety of potatoes you can grow, many delicious varieties you will never see in the shops. Find out the best way to grow potatoes at home, how to protect your plants from the many pests and diseases and how to store your harvest so you can enjoy fresh potatoes over winter. A complete step by step guide telling you everything you need to know to successfully grow potatoes at home.

Keeping Chickens For Beginners – Keeping Backyard Chickens from Coops to Feeding to Care and More

Chickens are becoming very popular to keep at home, but it isn't something you should leap into without the right information. This books guides you through everything you need to know to keep chickens from decided what breed to what coop to how to feed them, look after them and keep your chickens healthy and producing eggs. This is your complete guide to owning chickens, with absolutely everything you need to know to get started and successfully keep chickens at home.

Hydroponics: A Beginners Guide to Growing Food without Soil

Hydroponics is growing plants without soil, which is a fantastic idea for indoor gardens. It is surprisingly easy to set up, once you know what you are doing and is significantly more productive and quicker than growing in soil. This book will tell you everything you need to know to get started growing flowers, vegetables and fruit hydroponically at home.

Raised Bed Gardening – A Guide To Growing Vegetables In Raised Beds

Learn why raised beds are such an efficient and effortless way to garden as you discover the benefits of no-dig gardening, denser planting and less bending, ideal for anyone who hates weeding or suffers from back pain. You will learn everything you need to know to build your own raised beds, plant them and ensure they are highly productive.

Straw Bale Gardening – No Dig, No Bending Productive Vegetable Gardens

This book tells you everything you want to know about the innovative method of straw bale gardening. Discover this no dig, no bend, low maintenance form of growing fruits, vegetables and flowers that is gaining a lot of attention. This book will guide you through the whole process from setting up your bales to planting and more. A complete, step by step guide to this innovating gardening method.

Vertical Gardening: Maximum Productivity, Minimum Space

This is exciting form of gardening allows you to grow large amounts of fruit and vegetables in small areas, maximizing your usage of space. Whether you have a large garden, an allotment or just a small balcony, you will be able to grow more delicious fresh produce. Find out how I grew over 70 strawberry plants in just three feet of ground space and more in this detailed guide.

Worm Farming: Creating Compost at Home with Vermiculture

Learn about this amazing way of producing high quality compost at home by recycling your kitchen waste. Worms break it down and produce a sought after, highly nutritious compost that your plants will thrive in. Not matter how big your garden you will be able to create your own worm farm and compost using the techniques in this step-by-step guide. Learn how to start worm farming and producing your own high quality compost at home.

Want More Inspiring Gardening Ideas?

This book is part of the Inspiring Gardening Ideas series. Bringing you the best books anywhere on how to get the most from your garden or allotment.

You can find out about more wonderful books just like this one at: www.OwningAnAllotment.com

Follow me at www.YouTube.com/OwningAnAllotment for my video diary and tips. Join me on Facebook for regular updates and discussions at www.Facebook.com/OwningAnAllotment.

Find me on Instagram and Twitter as @allotmentowner where I post regular updates, offers and gardening news. Follow me today and let's catch up in person!

Thank you for reading!

Printed in Great Britain
by Amazon